THE HOUSES OF CHILDHOOD

THE HOUSES OF CHILDHOOD

Kathleen Beryl Tyler

UNITED WRITERS
Cornwall

UNITED WRITERS PUBLICATIONS LTD
Ailsa, Castle Gate, Penzance, Cornwall.

British Library Cataloguing in Publication Data
A catalogue record for this book is available from the British Library.

ISBN 1 85200 049 X

Printed in Great Britain by
United Writers Publications Ltd
Cornwall

Written for my cousins,
their children and their grandchildren.

CONTENTS

ACKNOWLEDGEMENTS

I wish to thank the following people for their encouragement and help in the collection of details for this book:

My cousin Mrs W.W. Jenkins of Loveland, Colorado, USA.

My cousin Mrs Muriel Collier of Idyllwild, California, USA.

My cousin Mr E. Smith of Coff's Harbour, Australia.

My friend Mrs Joan Timperley of Manchester, England.

THE HOUSES OF CHILDHOOD

These bright and 'far pavilions',
The jousting courts of youth,
Where many a fleeting fancy
Out-winged the course of truth.

These safest of all strongholds;
In tallest towered-keep,
Many a dreaming princess
Was roused from her sleep.

These best-loved of galleries,
Where knights and squires wait
With burnished armour, dazzling
The dragons at the gate.

And should we not recall them,
The race, now almost run,
Like fast retreating rainbows,
They'll melt into the sun!

Kathleen Beryl Tyler

1

5 DEAN AVENUE, NEWTON HEATH, MANCHESTER

"That is where you were born," said my mother, pointing. "There, in that house."

We had been walking, hand in hand, towards Grandma's but had stopped for a moment so that I could peer between the bars of the front gate of the house in question. I must have been about four years old and it was the first time that I can remember ever having become really aware of No. 5 Dean Avenue; but I was far more interested in the facts of my birth, than in the house where I had been born.

"How?" I asked. "How was I born?"

"The fairies brought you."

"How?"

"In a bag," said Mother – which was partially true! "They left you on that window-ledge up there." And she pointed into the sky. I raised my eyes beyond front-door level and became aware that the house and the world went on high above my head. All I could see was a wide window-ledge – quite black. I began to think it was a bit mean of the fairies to have left me so high up, outside the house, and on a filthy piece of stone. I might never have been found.

"Did you know I was coming?" I asked.

"Oh yes, we'd been waiting for you for a long time, but the window cleaner found you on the very day you arrived, and handed you in."

"Was I dirty?"

Mother laughed – "Yes, very, but we soon cleaned you up. Grandma gave you a bath."

Puzzled and full of questions I didn't know how to put into words I walked on. It wasn't until many years later that I learnt the truth of the matter.

At 10 am on the 25th February 1920, my mother, in a highly expectant condition, was scrubbing her scullery floor as if her very life depended upon it. She had been told that if a baby was late in coming, violent and continued exercise would speed it on its way. At that time, she and my father rented a modest 'three up and two down, near the end of a terrace' in Dean Avenue, Newton Heath, Manchester. My father was a teacher – both of Day and Sunday School, and my mother, as was common in those days, had never had a job or been trained for any occupation other than that of housewife and mother. Her father had made a small fortune in the grocery trade and in the two decades previous to my birth, had owned several businesses in and around Manchester, the profits from which had enabled him to send three of his four sons to expensive schools and to 'finish' my mother at a prestigious establishment for young ladies at Buxton in Derbyshire.

Her floor-scrubbing activities achieved the desired effect and by 2.00 pm my mother was tossing in great unease on the large marital bed in the front bedroom of No. 5 Dean Avenue. It was a beautiful day, she told me later. One of those gently sunny afternoons which occasionally punctuate the gloom of winter and are made precious in retrospect by their rarity. As she lay on her bed of pain, she was visited in turn by each of her four brothers – and by the window cleaner who was doing his rounds that week in the purlieus of Dean Avenue. He was a cheerful chap, whistling as he mounted to first floor level. My mother's bedroom window was open – he stuck his head inside – looked first at my mother and then at the large framed photograph on the opposite wall. It showed my mother and father posing on their wedding day in 1914. Arm in arm they stood, in full regalia, outside the entrance to Newton Heath Weslyan Methodist Chapel, and a fine looking young couple they made.

"Ee Mum," said the window cleaner. "Yer not trailing that train today, are yer?"

He withdrew his head, polished the panes and departed. My grandmother arrived and shortly afterwards the midwife. By 4.30 my father came home from school and went out again almost immediately on his bicycle to summon the doctor.

By 8.00 pm I was born, a fortnight late and dragged into the world with forceps. I was red and angry-looking and covered in a caul – up to my neck! I had a shock of spiky black hair, due my mother said, to the number of sour green apples which she had eaten during the early months of her pregnancy. Fortunately the hair fell off soon afterwards and I was left in the usual state of most newborn babies – bald and shiny. I must have been very ugly. When my mother, who was a bonny woman, first set eyes on me, she couldn't believe that I was her child. Had I been born in a hospital, she would probably have insisted that there had been a 'mix-up' in the delivery ward.

Those were not the days in which fathers assisted at the births of their children, so, once the caul had been removed and I had been bathed and swaddled, my grandmother carried me straight downstairs to the kitchen where my father was anxiously waiting. It was a mistake – newborn babies should always be taken *upstairs* first if they are to be successful in later life. Thirty-nine years later when my little goddaughter was born, I took her at once from her parents' flat and carried her to my own attic quarters which were immediately above theirs. It was the right thing to do. She has always prospered. However, my grandmother knew nothing of this as she presented me to my father. He was a warm-hearted, loving and emotional man. I was his first and destined to be his only child. As my grandmother turned back my long flannel nightgown, apparently to show him the perfection of my feet, and as I, feeling for the first time the warmth from the coals in the kitchen grate, uncurled my toes and stretched them towards the blaze, my father wept with joy, and my grandmother named me there and then, 'Grandma's Little Pink', which, much to my embarrassment, she would often use as an endearment in later years.

Upstairs, the doctor and midwife were fighting for my mother's life. She was very ill. Much later, she told me rather ghoulish stories of a whole bottle of brandy being poured down her throat to keep her alive, and of such a severe loss of blood that the bright blue bedroom carpet had subsequently to be removed and dyed bright red! 'Twilight Sleep' was the 'in' thing at that time. My mother had refused to avail herself of it because she had heard that it could injure the unborn child. Whether this were so or not, I couldn't say, but I wish she had not needed to suffer so much pain – and there was worse to come.

My mother stayed where she was for fourteen days, which at that time, was the recognised period for confinements. She began gradually to recover from her ordeal, but during the first week that she was in bed, her milk dried up and she could no longer feed me. I reacted immediately to my first taste of rejection in life by refusing all other forms of sustenance – milk substitutes, patent foods – the lot. My stomach revolted against them all and I began to die of starvation.

After two weeks my mother was allowed to get up for the first time. She sat on the side of the bed and as her feet touched the floor, a crippling pain shot up her right leg and she immediately lay down again. The doctor was called in as the pain became worse. He examined my mother – forbad her to get up – even to sit up. She had 'White Leg'. A blood clot had formed and any movement might dislodge it and cause it to start travelling towards her heart. And there she stayed, flat on her back in bed, for three months.

My father must have been worried sick during those months, but unlike many intellectual men, he was very practical. He seemed to be equally and naturally skilled in whichever direction he turned his mind and/or hands. I can well imagine him taking charge in a hopeful, cheerful way, cooking the meal when he came home at night and doing the cleaning at the weekends. In 1920 there was no question of compassionate leave for such a case as his. He would leave the house at 8.00 am having prepared breakfast and hand-fed my mother, who in the early days, was forbidden to raise her head from the pillow. He attempted to deal with my problems, bathing and changing me and carefully making up the bottle which I continued to reject. He often told me of the occasion when, pushed for time one morning, in his haste as he was trying to feed me, he inadvertently stuck his finger into my eye. He thought he had killed me! I screamed so long and so loudly, that my grandmother who was on her way to 'take over', heard me from the top of the avenue and arrived at a run on our front doorstep. My father had to leave me and my mother, who by this time was in a frantic state of nerves, to be calmed down by Grandma whilst he caught a train to the other side of Manchester where he taught Science and acted as deputy head in a Junior Technical School.

Soon after this a full time daily nurse was found to care for my mother and myself. My mother took to her and she quickly became a much loved and trusted figure in our household. In spite of the family doctor's assurance that all would be well with me, both my parents were convinced that I was on my way out and had little time left. The new nurse, however, thought otherwise and introduced me to a product called 'Glaxo'. It did the trick – I swallowed it without protest and what is more, managed to keep it down. I began to gain weight, I began to lose the embryonic whiteness and the less-than-human look which had hitherto characterised my appearance. Slowly, I started to thrive.

My mother wanted to see me christened and since neither she nor anyone else knew whether she would ever walk again, my father contacted the Methodist minister from the local Weslyan Chapel where my parents and grandparents, uncles and aunts had worshipped faithfully for many years; he agreed to come to No. 5 Dean Avenue and there to hold a christening service in my parents' bedroom. Fortunately, the size of the room restricted the number of would-be guests so severely that eventually only my parents, grandparents, the nurse, the minister and, of course, myself, were present. I say 'fortunately', because I apparently disgraced myself thoroughly and behaved as no lady should. My immediate response to the shock of an unaccustomed dousing on the head with cold water at three o'clock in the afternoon, was to explode at both ends simultaneously! To give the minister his due, he didn't flinch. Someone opened a window and the whole proceeding came to its logical, if somewhat hasty conclusion.

When my mother was allowed up for the first time, over three months after my birth, she told me that she had forgotten how to walk and had to be taught once again to place her feet and to take steps. The first few months were difficult ones. She was weak and I was fractious. The much loved nurse had to leave in order to take on another case. My parents' financial resources had been stretched to their limits but they managed somehow and even scraped together enough to pay a little school leaver to come in as a daily help. Poor child, she was probably only fourteen, if that, and from what I gathered later, not very bright. It seems that through sheer ignorance, she nearly killed me. This may not have been the case at all but my parents always blamed her for my subsequent serious illness.

One morning she took me out in my pram. Soon after we returned I was sick and continued to be sick all day long. No one could understand it, least of all the little maid. By the time my father came home from school, I was beginning to turn blue. He rushed out for the doctor who declared that I had been poisoned and administered antidotes, but I was ill for a long time. That evening my father decided to 'get to the bottom of the matter'. He questioned the little maid. He was one of the kindest men I have ever known, but he could also be one of the sternest. He had piercing blue eyes which, when he chose, he could turn into powerful weapons capable of burning into one's very soul. He possessed 'The Look' – invaluable in the teaching profession. He never had any trouble with discipline at school, he never had to raise his voice, he just used 'The Look' and the most hardened sinners would confess all. He must have used 'The Look' on the little maid who rapidly dissolved into tears, became very scared and admitted that, in an attempt to stop me crying, she had that morning given me a drink from the rubber hot water bottle carried in my pram! Needless to say, she lost her job. I have often wondered whether it was her fault at all or whether I was just having another of my stomach-revolting periods.

My father refused to have me vaccinated. He had a fear of vaccination. His own sister had suffered from asthma after she had been vaccinated and from what his father had told him he suspected dirty needles used a second time, and vaccine being taken from one child and passed on to the next – a procedure which I have never understood. In any case, I suppose standards of hygiene where not high in the eighteen eighties when his sister had been vaccinated. However, whether it were to do with lack of vaccination, or simply because I had had a bad start in life, I don't know, but during my first year, I caught whooping cough, then bronchitis, and finally and disgustingly, I had worms! At least, one worm – it was a big one so I was told. The doctor managed to extract it and took it away in a bottle according to my mother. As a child I always felt put out that it had not been preserved for my inspection – I felt cheated out of my rightful property.

I continued to live at No 5 Dean Avenue until I was three. I left before I was old enough to have formed any lasting memories of my own concerning my life there. However, I came to know the exterior of the house and its location very well and can still visualise it quite clearly today – seventy years later. This is due to the fact that when we moved, we went to live in New Moston, only a couple of miles away and since Grandma and Grandpa continued to live in the big house at the end of Dean Avenue, my mother and I would visit them often, coming almost every day by tram from New Moston. Each time we walked up the Avenue past our former house, my mother would say, "Look, that's where you were born – in that front bedroom up there." The house was near the end of a terrace of six. It always seemed very tall, but this was probably because I was so small. It was black – quite black, the brickwork, the woodwork, the front gate, the flags on the narrow path leading to the front door, the earth in the flower beds and even the grass which struggled to grow on the pocket-handkerchief lawn; they were all black. I took it for granted then, that everything should be that colour (most of Manchester seemed black to me), and it was only many years later that I realised there was a reason for the blackness.

The terrace of six houses which formed Dean Avenue and were the only buildings in it, were on the left as you walked up the avenue towards big double gates at the end, gates wide enough to give access to the tradesmen's horses and carts. I remember those gates clearly. They stood permanently open and finally over the years, rotted into two blackened heaps of timber lying flat, alongside their once imposing pillars. These gates, standing at the far end and looking straight down Dean Avenue, marked the entrance to Grandma and Grandpa's house. There were no houses on the other side of the avenue opposite to the terrace of six – instead, running all the way up to Grandma's gates and beyond, was a wall – a high black wall. From a very early age I was forbidden to go anywhere near that wall. I must always walk on the houses' side of Dean Avenue on my way to Grandma's. I must never touch the wall – it was dirty – and I must never, never attempt to climb it in order to look over. My imagination grew rapidly as a child, far outstripping my reason and understanding. I became terrified of that wall. Loud panting noises, whistles and screams accompanied by clouds of thick white steam would often rise from the hidden depths behind it. Great smuts of black soot would float in the air – panic would seize me. I would break away from my mother's restraining hand and run, run, as fast as I could through the puddles in the middle of the unmade dirt road, up the avenue, through the gates, over Grandpa's lawn, up the steps and in through Grandma's open door! I felt safe there, for never to my knowledge, had the dragon who lived behind the wall been able to get in to Grandma's house.

Dean Avenue was a cul de sac. At its open end (the other end from Grandma's) it ran straight into Dean Lane which crossed it at right angles. Here was another world, a world of noise and heavy traffic, of row upon row of tiny two-up-and-two-down houses whose shallow white-stoned doorsteps opened straight on to the hard grey echoing pavements. Some of the houses didn't even have doorsteps but the owners would then whitestone the pavement flag immediately outside their front doors. Dean Lane was always busy. Over the Manchester setts bumped huge carter's drays, their horses' hooves ringing loudly as they hit each rectangular block of stone set deeply into its base. My father would tell me how strong the setts were – how tough and how they had been laid in the first half of the last century especially to resist the great weight of the carts which carried the cotton bales in and out of Manchester. When I looked at the enormous steel bound wheels and heard them clattering at breakneck speeds over the setts, it seemed to me that no carter, however burly-looking could have complete mastery at all times over those wheels. I was afraid. I didn't need the frequent admonitions of my parents that I was never to try to cross Dean Lane on my own and I would place myself between them, clinging to a hand on either side, until the perilous undertaking had been completed.

Motorised traffic became more frequent as I grew older and great lorries added to the general impression of noisy unrest. Darting in and out between the drays and the lorries were bicycles – always bicycles and always ridden, it seemed to me by workmen, each of whom carried a blue enamel container with tightly fitting rounded lid, slung over his handlebars. My mother used to say that the container was for carrying hot sweet tea to work. You could always tell when it was empty, it swung about in an alarming manner, but the lid never came off.

When we came out of Dean Avenue and into Dean Lane, we always turned left towards the Oldham Road. Just a little way from the corner where we turned left was Dean Lane Railway Station. The line coming from Failsworth ran into a cutting as it approached the station. Looking back now, it seems remarkable to me that I never connected the cutting and the trains with the dragon who lived behind the wall in Dean Avenue. Immediately past the station was the Men's Lavatory. I must never go in there. I never wanted to! The smell was awful and I tried to hold my breath as we went past. Beyond the Men's Lavatory and on the same side, just before we reached the Oldham Road, we would often stop at Mrs Varley's house. Mrs Varley had been my father's landlady before he married my mother. He, together with his friend Jim Giddings, had lodged with her when they had first come to Manchester as raw young teachers, freshly out of training college in London. Mrs Varley had been good to them – made them a 'home from home'. My father never forgot her kindness and would call to see the old lady as often as he could. I can remember very little of Mrs Varley herself, but one thing which I do remember was her horsehair sofa!

Her living-room was tiny, full of furniture and always hot from the coal fire, blazing away, summer and winter in the black-leaded grate beneath the broad mantelpiece which was covered with a tasselled tapestry cloth on which reposed fifteen photographs. Since I could count quite well by the time I was five, I was able to check this number on each visit. It never varied. The sofa faced the fire-grate and was black with a polished wooden rail which ran along its back and curled menacingly over the top of its one arm. There were no cushions or rugs on it. It must have stood quite high, for I can remember being lifted on to it. It was so deep that as I leant back against the rail, my legs stuck out in front of me and my feet just reached to the edge of the seat. The horsehair bristles came through the black shiny covering in their millions. If I ran my hand lightly across its surface, it was like stroking the head of a yard broom. They prickled the bare flesh of my legs unmercifully. Mrs Varley was a great talker, and since it was considered rude to interrupt grown-ups when they were talking, I would have to wait until after each visit to complain about the bristles to my parents, but in spite of this, I always seemed to end up on the sofa the next time. Eventually, I found a solution. I discovered that if you grasped a horsehair firmly and pulled, it would come forth in its entirety, springy and curly and black. It could then be dropped surreptitiously over the back rail of the settee. No one took much notice of me once I had been installed on the sofa. Gradually I cleared a patch where my legs could rest comfortably, and having once achieved this, I found subsequent visits to Mrs Varley's more acceptable and more interesting.

My extractions occupied my time nicely and I continued to clear wider and wider patches. No one ever noticed my activities, but after we had left, Mrs Varley must have wondered, when she did the cleaning, why there were little piles of coarse black hair on the carpet behind the sofa.

Walking on down Dean Lane past Mrs Varley's house, we would come to the Oldham Road. There was even more traffic here than in Dean Lane. In addition to the horses and carts, the lorries and the bicycles, there were the trams. They played such a dominant part in our lives in those days. They were our main means of transport. They took us to the centre of Manchester; they took us to Oldham, and once we had left Dean Avenue for good and were living in New Moston, they took us back to Grandma and Grandpa. Once I was safely aboard and seated downstairs on a wooden seat next to the window, I enjoyed the trams. All the seats were a light yellowy brown with little holes punched in patterns all over them. Their backs were on hinges and could be moved backwards or forwards so that you could sit and face the way you were travelling, or look back along the road you had just passed over. Moreover, they could be arranged so that when the seat in front of you was facing you, you could travel in a cosy group of four – two facing two. The seats were on each side of a central aisle where straps hung down to help keep on their feet those unlucky passengers who, in rush hours, were forced to stand. They would hang on and sway backwards and forwards with each jerking start or grinding halt. Their clothes were often steaming wet and smelt of grease as they pressed against you.

If the tram were full inside, we sometimes had to go upstairs. Getting upstairs was a dangerous undertaking. The stairs were often outside the tram and open to the elements. My mother always made me climb up first in case I fell backwards – when she would be able to catch me – she said. "Hang on to the rail and keep going," was the advice. The steps curved steeply from the platform in a semi-spiral, so difficult for my short legs to manoeuvre, that I would often arrive on the top with bruised knees and fingers covered in filth, especially as the tram would usually start with a jerk when I was only half way up so that I would be thrown forwards to graze my shins against the metal strips which covered the edge of each step. Once I bumped my chin quite badly. And to come downstairs could be even worse. My mother would go first this time and instruct me to wait at the top until the tram had stopped before I attempted to come down. The waiting filled me with panic. I was terrified that my mother, having reached platform level, would alight gaily and leave me on the stairs and that as I clattered down, the tram would start again before I had chance to jump off. In my imagination I saw my mother's figure becoming smaller and smaller as she disappeared into the murk of the Oldham Road, while I, being borne off into the unknown vastness ahead, would be left alone to fend for myself amongst a tramful of strangers. When my father travelled with us, I never minded going upstairs. He, laughing and confident, would carry me, secure in his arms, to the very top.

Getting on to the tram at all was a work of art. The tram lines ran down the centre of Oldham Road. We would stand on the pavement, gazing into the gloomy distance until we saw a great red shape looming towards us out of the rain. "It's coming," the cry would go up and we would make ready to dash out into the middle of the road. As it screeched to a halt, the conductor would lean as far out from the platform as he could, his left leg and foot crooked round the central support, he hung on for dear life, with his outstretched left arm and hand, and facing the approaching vehicles, he extended his right arm and leg to their uttermost length across the line of the oncoming traffic. This was supposed to slow to a standstill whilst we charged in front of champing horses, snorting lorries, hooting cars, and clanging bicycles. Once we were all aboard, the conductor would signal to the driver who would wind a great brass handle which rose up in front of him as he stood in his cab. Sparks of electricity, blue and blinding if you looked at them, would shoot out from the point where a black cable arm joined the tram to the overhead lines, and away we would go, on and on along the Oldham Road.

The Oldham Road – it ran for miles linking Manchester with Oldham. Quite straight it seemed to be, with never a corner to enliven its monotonous, endless row upon row of squalid houses, tacky little shops, shabby theatres and picture palaces, gasometers, factory chimneys and lines of 'Coronation Streets', opening on to the main road and themselves disappearing into the dusty frightening gloom of no-man's-land. Everywhere papers blew about or collected in the gutters. Men in cloth caps, threadbare coats with neck mufflers and women in long black dresses with grey shawls over their heads and clogs on their feet, disgorged from the side roads to board the tram at Failsworth, Hollingwood,

Newton Heath and Miles Platting. Children would be playing on the pavements as we clanked and clattered along. They sat on the kerbstones outside their own front doors. Some of the boys had no shirts, just over-the-knee-length black trousers held up against their bony chests by bits of string which served as braces; some of the girls had no knickers – you could see quite clearly at times and very few of them had shoes. Sometimes, clay-pipe-smoking old women in cloth caps would sit on stools at their front doors, coughing and hawking and spitting out dark brown jets of liquid onto the stone pavements. Poverty was everywhere. My elders talked about 'The Dole Queues'. It meant little to me, but I often saw lines of men, dirty and hungry-looking. They leant against walls or hoardings which were made melancholy by their half detached and flapping adverts. I supposed that these were the 'Dole Queues', but they might just have been waiting for one or other of the many pubs to open. Drunks, rolling about the pavements were quite a common sight at turning-out time in the afternoon.

Even though I can't remember ever having travelled on the tram as far as Oldham itself, I do have faint recollections of alighting at Newton Heath Methodist Chapel which lay a little way down the Oldham Road from Dean Lane. I was taken on a Sunday afternoon by my father, who taught a senior class. I had to join the babies' class, so my father left me in the care of a kind lady who seated me on a minute chair in a circle of some twenty other children. She talked to us about Jesus and then we sang 'Jesus wants me for a sunbeam', we prayed 'Pity my simplicity and suffer me to come to thee'. I didn't understand 'simplicity' but I was old enough to know what 'suffer' meant, and I didn't like the sound of it at all. I can't say that I ever took to religion. As I grew older, visits to Sunday School became rarer. Fortunately, I was never forced to go with my father, but, looking back, I think he must have been pleased when I chose to do so. 'Uncle' Jim Giddings also taught at the Chapel alongside my father, and his youngest daughter Eileen who was my age and became my friend, accompanied her father regularly and faithfully every Sunday. Years later, she said to me, rather sadly, "I used to save a chair for you next to mine,

Sunday after Sunday, but you never came."

Opposite the Chapel, a little further towards Oldham and pointed out to me each time we passed by in the tram, was my grandfather's shop. When I was small, it was his last remaining grocery store. He had owned seventeen of them at one time, but that was in more prosperous days long before I was born. This one was called 'The City Tea Company'. I just knew it simply as 'Grandpa's shop'. It had double fronted windows and a long central passage leading to a mysterious room at the back which I don't recall having entered. Highly polished counters topped with brass rails ran the length of the shop. I think there was sawdust on the floor, for I remember I liked to make little mountains by pushing it sideways with my shoes. Behind the counters shelves rose to ceiling level and standing on them was a remarkable assortment of jars and tins. The tins made a deep impression on me. What they contained I do not know, but they were all oval shaped, tightly lidded and covered in black and gold with red and gold scroll-like patterns. They seemed gigantically tall. Grandpa and my uncle Frank, clad in long white aprons, used to emerge from the mysterious room at the back to preside over this unusual world. Here they wielded the butter pats and turned the handle of the terrifying bacon slicer with great manipulative skill. When the shop cat had kittens, Grandpa gave one of them to me. It was a half grown black and white tom which we very originally christened 'Tiddles'. One evening, after the shop had closed, my mother and father took me to collect it and I can recall my concern when my uncle Frank put it head first into a big white sugar bag. "If it can't see where it's going, it won't be scared," he said consolingly. Tiddles, however, after much frenzied activity on his part, was returned to an upright position and tied into the bag ready for transportation. I can see him now – his head emerging from the sacking, his eyes wild with fright. Held in my father's vice-like grip, he was totally unable to move as finally we managed to get him on to the tram. In spite of my fervent assurances that all would be well with him, he continued to make the most blood curdling cries all the way home.

I have one final memory of Grandpa's shop. It is of

crouching in its darkened window late one night in the company of my parents and grandparents. I was full of excited anticipation. We were all waiting for the 'Illuminated Tram' to pass by on its way to Oldham. Just what it was, or why it was so special, I couldn't say – but I saw it and have retained the memory ever since. To me then, it was what a flying saucer from outer space would be to any child today. It was brilliant; alight inside and out with hundreds of electric light bulbs. It swayed and clanked past in a trice. I saw no one inside – no driver, no conductor. It was a magic tram, or so I was told.

If I cannot remember ever reaching Oldham by tram, I can certainly recollect my trips to Manchester. Almost every Saturday morning, and sometimes during the week as well, my mother would set out in that direction with me in tow. She loved shopping and central Manchester was her Mecca. Away we would go, swaying along the Oldham Road past Miles Platting. (The name used to intrigue me especially when I was learning to plait at school. I would wonder if the place were called after a man named Miles who was renowned amongst plaiters for the excellent quality of his work.) My mother, holding me firmly by the hand would alight at Piccadilly, the tram terminus, and plunge straight into Kendal Milne's or Affleck and Brown's. These were high class shops where the deep-pile carpets, the hushed voices of discreet assistants and obsequious shop-walkers, who would bend from the waist to gush and 'ush in the most delightful way, attracted a rare and genteel clientele. Usually, we only 'looked' in these shops. "I'm only looking," said my mother in reply to polite offers of help. Once we had 'looked' thoroughly, we would be off again across busy roads, heading straight for Lewises.

This was *the* shop of my childhood. Nowhere, anywhere else in the world, could there have been such another. We entered through an arcade in which stood a big toy shop, but I was never allowed much time to gaze into its windows, as my mother was always so anxious to reach her goal. Once through its doors, Lewises enfolded me, reaching out to greet me with its noise, its warmth and its rich scents. Immediately, I became part of it. It was as if I stood at the bottom of a great friendly chasm, for, rising above me, tier upon tier, were low circular galleries, open all the way round to the central well, so that at one and the same time, you could see, hear and smell what was going on at the different floor levels. On the ground floor, exotic scents wafted to me from the perfumery counters, and coffee and pungent spice-like odours came across from the Food Hall. I could actually see ladies trying on fur coats on the second floor, I could hear the clash of crockery coming from the restaurant high above me and catch glimpses of children, mounted on huge toy bears and elephants, having their hair cut in the Children's Hair Dressing Department on the third floor. I even imagined that I could hear the snip, snip of the scissors. It was a wonderful feeling to become so absorbed into this atmosphere, so much a part of its every activity, that I was experiencing a kind of 'one-ness' with Lewises – I had become Lewises and knew everything that was going on there at one and the same time. I didn't ponder on these things, I just knew that they were so, I received them without question, accepted the joy they brought and was momentarily contented.

Even had I wished to ponder, I would not have been given the time, for my mother, always purposeful, made straight for the lifts before whose trellis-work concertina gates we would wait hopefully. I would peer through the diamond-shaped spaces into the dirty and desolate depths. Heavy with grease, on the opposite wall, thick steel cables carried a counter balancing weight, as wide and as tall as the lift itself.

"What would happen if that rope broke?" I asked.

"We would all crash to the bottom!"

I knew by the sound of her voice that my mother was frightened of lifts.

"Couldn't we walk up the stairs?" I enquired, but it seemed that my mother's bad leg and her heart didn't take kindly to this idea. So the lift it had to be, and continued to be. In consequence, I worked out an idea which I kept in the forefront of my mind during the whole time of elevation or descent, and which I apply in similar situations, even today. My idea was this: if on the very moment of impact with the ground, I jumped as high as possible into the air, by the time I landed, the crash would be over.

When the lift arrived, the attendant would push back the concertina door, and in we would surge. There were no seats except a little flap-down one on which the attendant could sit. I can remember feeling disappointed that I was not allowed to use it, it looked just about my size and I longed to try it. Instead, I had to stand – more often than not squashed against a forest of legs. Trouser legs smelling of machine oil, silk-stocking legs, smelling of lavender water, Russian-booted legs smelling of leather, and legs hidden under long rubber mackintoshes. It's a wonder that I didn't develop kinky tendencies at a very early age. Lewises' lifts often came to a sudden standstill as they reached their destination. I dreaded this moment, for my stomach always continued to travel after the lift itself had stopped! However, once they were both fully stationary, I would relax and the attendant's voice would penetrate my anxiety – soothingly he sang – I would listen entranced. The words rolled off his tongue in such a musical way – the alliterative possibilities were endless and later on in bed at night, when I was thinking about Lewises, I would group together the different departments he listed, irrespective of their geographic location in the store, and I would sing quietly to myself:

> "Hosiery, Haberdashery, Hardware and Heating;
> Lingerie, Leatherware, Lampshades and Lighting;
> Furniture, Pharmacy, Foodstore and Fishing;
> Materials, Maternity, Millinery, Menswear;
> Gardening, Groceries, Gowns and Games;
> Kitchens and Cutlery, Crystal-ware, Claims."

Once freed from the lift, my mother, raring to go, would dash from counter to counter, trying on hats, gloves, shoes and sealskin coats, wrapping long furs with tails, glass eyes and mouth-like clasps about her neck, unrolling lengths of dress materials questioning the sales' girls, poking and prying and at sale times, delving into mountains of items marked down to bargain prices, with an energy which took away my breath. Sometimes my father accompanied us on these shopping sprees. He would laugh over my mother's antics, for he loved her dearly.

"Look at your mother – there's no stopping her. Take her for a walk in the country and her bad leg soon makes her give up, but let her loose in Lewises and neither of us can keep up with her." Also, when Father was with us, we often had lunch in the restaurant on the top floor. You could get a very adequate midday dinner there for 9d and a truly wonderful feast for 1/3d.

I so loved Lewises that during the time I lived in the Manchester area, which was the first eleven years of my life, I invented a game about it. I never told anyone, but I played it in my head whenever I was alone or had a boring task to perform like dusting, or cleaning the stairs. I would imagine that I owned Lewises, that it was mine, all mine. I would visit it incessantly, carrying away any of its myriad goods which took my fancy. In this way, I would acquire its best coats, its prettiest party dresses, its most exciting toys. I would roll on its softest carpets, wrap myself in its rolls of dress lengths, furnish my dream house with its most up-to-date beds and sofas, fill my larder with its jellies and fancy cakes and in its restaurant hold parties for all my friends, complete with sherry trifle, lashings of ice cream and orchestral accompaniment. And at Christmas – oh at Christmas, I would spend all the time I wanted in the Fairies' Grotto without being moved on by an impatient queue of parents and children. I would tell Father Christmas of all the toys which I desired, and instead of receiving just one of them, I would be given the lot to take home with me there and then!

Although the house itself, number 5 Dean Avenue, means little to me now, memory-wise, Dean Avenue, Dean Lane and the Oldham Road, so close by, formed the framework of my Manchester childhood. Not only did they lead me to Mrs Varley's house, to Grandpa's shop, to Sunday School, but also, more important than all of these, they led me to the house which stood for eleven years at the centre of my life. They led me to Primrose Bank.

2

PRIMROSE BANK

Beyond the big gates at the end of Dean Avenue lay Grandma and Grandpa Haydock's house. Who had been responsible for naming it 'Primrose Bank', I never discovered. I certainly didn't see any primroses growing there, but perhaps in days long before the trains steamed through the Dean Lane cutting, there was a field of these flowers where the house had been built. I like to think so, for on one side of Primrose Bank ran Cow Lane, through which, my uncle Frank told me, that when he was very young, cows had actually been driven on their way to milking at a nearby farm! When I was small, Cow Lane was part of Grandpa's garden and had nothing in it except an old shed, scrubby trees and tired grass. At one end it entered the street at the back of Primrose Bank through a door in the garden wall and at the other end it came out onto Grandpa's front drive. On the other side of the house there was a 'wood' – a square patch of ground separating the Dean Avenue terrace where I had been born from Primrose Bank. This wood was full of stunted and filthy elderberry bushes. No grass grew between the trees and little foliage covered their blackened branches, but to my Manchester cousins and to me, it was a fine place for Cowboys and Indians and Hide and Seek. You could get your clothes really dirty with no effort at all. I suppose that here and there around Manchester in the 1920s, there still remained patches of ground like Cow Lane and 'the wood', which had escaped industrialisation and development – tiny reminders of the once open countryside, struggling to survive between the endless rows of 'back-to-backs'.

A wide oval drive led in from Dean Avenue. It swept past Grandma's front door – right round it went, with the railway-cutting wall on one side and Primrose Bank on the other. It surrounded Grandpa's lawn – he was so proud of that lawn – it always seemed neat and actually green rather than black. He cut it regularly and I can remember him toiling up and down its length pulling a great heavy roller after him. Grandpa's lawn so impressed me during my childhood, that long before I realised my mother's parents were called Haydock, I would refer to them as 'Grandma and Grandpa Over-the-Green'. A large flower bed, incapable of producing anything but irises, separated the far end of the drive from Cow Lane. In front of the house itself, a wide path ran down from the front steps to join the oval drive. A small lawn lay on each side of the path, surrounded by black-earth flower beds where flourished even more irises, showing blue and yellow between smooth and off-white rockery stones. Two ornamental wrought iron seats overlooked the side lawns, and between the seats rose three wide, shallow and imposing steps leading up to Grandma's front door. They were the sort of steps you might find in a stage set, generous in proportion and each increasing in width towards path level. Their bevelled edges were kept gleaming by the application of whitestone and their flat levels were scrubbed and swept daily. They looked like a gracefully tiered apron-stage, ideal for dramatic exits and entrances and for the accommodation of entire wedding parties. Here in the summer of 1914, my mother and father had posed in the midst of fifty guests. Here, I often held forth; from the top step, alone and unobserved I treated my imaginary audience to many a poetic gem, or I defended Primrose Bank and all who lived in her, from the ravages of a violent and hungry mob.

The front door was square, stout and panelled with a heavy brass knocker which was kept in a gleaming condition by frequent applications of Brasso. Above the door and letting light into the lobby behind it, was a pretty, half-moon shaped window. There were two big bays on each side of the front door and above them rose the house. It was black-looking, of course, and very tall. If you counted the cellars, it was four storeys high.

There was a back garden, square and ordinary. Here Grandpa tried to grow flowers other than irises, but with little success. All the bushes were soot-covered and one's face, hands and knees quickly became black after a short spell on the lawn. Half way down the garden was an exit into Cow Lane – here stood an old stable-shed, and at the bottom of the path, the back gate led into another street parallel with Dean Avenue. A typical Manchester street, it held the usual small terraced houses with smoking chimneys overlooking endless stretches of pavements and cobbled setts.

To Primrose Bank, then, about the turn of the century and at the height of his prosperity, my grandfather, Arthur Haydock, brought his wife Edith and his young family: Lily, my mother, and my uncles Charlie, Tom, Frank and Jimmy. Arthur had come from a large family in Worksop. He had five brothers and one sister and his forefathers had all been cordwainers and saddlemakers to the Dukes of Newcastle. His brothers were all 'in trade' except for one who had trained as a teacher. Arthur had been working in Yorkshire as a young apprentice grocer when he first noticed my grandmother out walking with her mother. She was so beautiful, he said, that people stopped to stare after her as she passed by. It was love at first sight. He determined to marry her, and after making enquiries, found that she came from Slaithwaite near Huddersfield. He began to follow her movements and one evening, through a friend of a friend, he managed to effect an introduction at a concert in Huddersfield where he had tracked her down. Things moved quickly after that. They married and came to Manchester and my Uncle Charlie was born shortly afterwards.

I remember my grandfather Haydock in the twenties as an ebullient, rather bombastic and jolly sort of man. He had a round bald head with a monastic fringe of grey hair. After his business had failed, and he was at home all day, he would often do the dusting, or clean the silver for Grandma, all the while, whistling incessantly through his teeth. You could always tell in which room he was dusting by the low hissing sound coming from it. He was dapper and smart. He made Grandma put fresh creases in his trousers every day and he would always don spats when he went into Manchester. He waxed and twirled the ends of his moustache until they stuck out at right angles from his bright cheeks. The ends could be very sharp which made kissing him rather a spiky business. I liked him. When I was very small, he would call me 'Bella'; bouncing me up and down on his knee, he would recite:

> "There was a little girl,
> And she had a little curl,
> Right in the middle of her forehead,
> When she was good,
> She was very, very good,
> But when she was bad, she was *horrid*."

At this point he would open his knees and with a scream of delight I would fall through them almost to the floor, only to be hauled back to safety in the nick of time! He told my cousins and me wonderful stories and usually managed to keep cheerfully good tempered though we must often have sorely tried his patience as we raced unheedingly through his house, jumping on his furniture and sliding down his bannisters.

I loved my grandmother Haydock without reservation. She and I were kindred spirits. She was naive, she had a gullible nature, and she could be easily teased. My cousin Joan once told me that she always thought of Grandma as a 'whiny sort of woman who was always crying'. It was true that she did cry easily, and I used to hate it when my uncle Jimmy would say unkindly, "Oh Lord, Ma's turning on the water-works again." When I was small she had plenty to cry over – trying to keep house all through the depression years – for three men who were more often out of work than in it, and with hardly any money at all coming in. But if she cried easily, she could also laugh easily and I could always make her double up into silent shaking spasms. She had a big goitre around which she wore a heavy gold chain. When I sat on her knee, I would wind the chain around my own neck, and there we would stay, linked together, whilst she would tell me stories of her own childhood and sing to me; 'Half a pound of tuppenny rice'; 'Wee Willie Winkie'; 'Froggie would a'wooing go, whether his mother would let him or no' – and when we went to Lewises together, it would be a riot, for Grandma would try on any hat which I cared to bring to her. As each one became more and more unsuitable, so our laughter would become more irrepressible until finally, we would be incapable of continuing our search for headgear and would stumble away helplessly under the disapproving eye of the sales assistant.

Uncle Charlie was the eldest son of the family – adored by his parents. According to my mother, he was completely spoilt and could do no wrong in their eyes, but I expect she was jealous. One of the stories which I loved to hear her tell of their childhood together, concerned Uncle Charlie's fear of dentists. Nothing could persuade him to a visit, even though he was in great pain:

"Until one day," said my mother, "I became so fed up with his moaning, that I offered to go with him to have one of my own teeth taken out to show him that it didn't really hurt if you were brave about it."

Apparently this is what happened and Uncle Charlie watched the extraction of my mother's tooth with great interest. Everyone gathered round my mother saying what a brave little girl she was, but when Grandma turned to Uncle Charlie with the words: "Come now Charlie, be as brave as your sister and let the dentist take out your tooth." – Charlie wasn't there, he had bolted and my mother had lost a perfectly sound tooth in vain! I believed that story when I was little, but my guess now is that my mother lost one of her milk teeth which was probably due for extraction anyway.

When I knew Uncle Charlie, he was tall and thin with dark hair and a very strange voice. He had been a cavalry officer in the 1914-18 war and his horse, named 'Polly Turner', had been shot from under him and killed at the battle of Ypres. Later, 'Polly Turner's' hoof was prepared, polished, suitably inscribed and presented to him, and one of my cousins has it in his house today. Uncle Charlie was wounded in the throat. My mother used to say that he had his voice box blown out. He had silver tubes in his throat and spoke ever afterwards with a kind of growl which used to scare me quite a lot. In the spring of 1916 he married Gertrude Louise Hawkins – my Auntie Gertie. She was only twenty then, seven years younger than Uncle Charlie, blonde, slender and lively – quite my favourite aunt. She had an effervescent character and was fun to be with. She was clever – 'talented' – my father called her. She could play the piano wonderfully well, sing, and whistle tunes just like a man. Soon after her marriage she was invited to Blackpool to take part in a series of concerts organised by the Red Cross for the entertainment of wounded troops. This she did happily and enjoyed doing, until someone wrote to my Uncle Charlie who was away at the front and informed him that his young wife was appearing on stage to help the war effort – and Uncle Charlie, being of a jealous nature, as were most of his family, soon put a stop to Aunty Gertie's innocent exploits. She told me years later that she suspected my mother of being the unknown correspondent who put Uncle Charlie 'in the picture'.

After the end of the Great War, Uncle Charlie worked for a while in Grandpa's shop. During this time, my cousins, 'Little' Charlie and his brother Tommy, were born. All of us, arriving within eighteen months of each other, played together, ate together, slept together, whenever we met and stayed with Grandpa and Grandma at Primrose Bank – which was often. Years later, their brother, my cousin John, came to join us, but he was 'Baby John', and I don't know how much he can remember of our grandparents' home.

Uncle Tom was my mother's favourite brother, close to her in age, and the third child of the family. She used to say that when their brother Charlie had been naughty, he was always let off the hook while she and Uncle Tom took the punishment for his misdeeds. I don't suppose for a minute that my mother and Tom were blameless, for she was very strong willed and he, when young, had the reputation of being 'a bit of a lad'. To me, as a child, he appeared handsome and aloof; although he was always laughing and joking with my mother whom he called 'Jane', he took little notice of me. My mother used to tease him about his 'a la' voice and his swanky ways. Like Uncle Charlie during the Great War, he held a commission in the Cavalry, and when Grandpa equipped both of his two eldest sons for battle, Tom used to boast that he had had his officer's uniform made with larger pockets than any other similar uniform in the British Army. Tom's pockets were quite a family joke. He came through the war unscathed, to court and marry Katie Carter. Her curly hair was as dark as Aunty Gertie's was fair, and she was very pretty indeed with a kind of ethereal beauty. I didn't see as much of her as I did of Aunty Gertie since she and Uncle Tom left Manchester after the war to live in Brize Norton where Uncle Tom opened a chicken farm. When we stayed with them, and when later the family came to live at Primrose Bank after the chicken farm venture had failed, I always thought Aunty Katie very kind and very sweet natured. Although no one realised it at the time, she carried the TB germ. These were the days before the antidote had been discovered and she was sadly to die in the early part of World War II. My cousin Joan was born to her and Uncle Tom almost at the same time that my cousin Tommy was born to Uncle Charlie and Aunty Gertie. So now another cousin of our own age sometimes came on visits to join in the fun at Primrose Bank. Her brother Philip was born a few years later. It might have been my imagination, but it always seemed to me that both Joan and Phil, having lived in the country, away from Manchester, were neater and cleaner in appearance than were Charlie and Tommy and I.

Uncle Frank was the fourth of my grandparents' children. His name was something of a problem. He had been christened Francis William, and neither name had proved dominant so that sometimes we called him 'Frank', and sometimes 'Bill'. Joan and Phil solved the problem by calling him Uncle 'Billy-frank'! He was good natured and I never saw him unkind to Grandma. He didn't marry until I was eight years old. He lived at Primrose Bank with his parents and his series of dogs. Two of these I remember well – Micky and Rufus. Micky came first, was my favourite and lasted all through my early years. He had 'speaking eyes', so my mother said, and a stub of a tail which wagged an incredible number of times per minute. Uncle Frank loved Grandma and he loved his dogs, so I loved him. He was the most approachable of my uncles and I never felt ill at ease with him. He had had a hard time as a child. There was something wrong with one of his legs and he was not able to go to school. He had had a governess at home and a little pony and trap all of his own to carry him where he could not walk. Grandpa's riches had paid for specialists and cures so that eventually he walked quite well, with only a slight limp, but whenever he didn't want to play with me and I was being too persistent, he would say, "I can't – I've a bone in my leg."

"Well, so have I," I would reply. "We all have bones in our legs."

"Yes," he would laugh, "but mine is my funny bone."

"That's not in your leg, that's in your elbow."

"Not mine – it's in my leg!" I gave up.

When he married Kathleen Wilkinson at St Chad's church in New Moston, I was a bridesmaid. My cousins Tommy and Charlie were waiting outside the church to throw confetti. Tommy threw his confetti in the correct manner at the newly-weds, but Charlie sneaked up behind me and stuffed the whole of his supply down the neck of my dress, just as on another totally different occasion he put a grass snake down my neck!

Grandpa's shop had been closed down by the time Uncle Frank married Aunty Kathleen so that he had had to find a job other than that of shop assistant. He was lucky and found a position as representative for the firm of Standard Yeast. The company gave him the use of a little van in which he travelled all round the Manchester area. When he left Primrose Bank, he went to live in New Moston with my new Aunty Kathleen, and very soon my cousin Bryan was born – so now there were seven cousins to meet and play with at Primrose Bank.

If I held my uncles Charlie and Tom in awe, I was downright scared of my uncle Jimmy. He was my mother's youngest brother and she used to call him a 'Nowty beggar'. Something always seemed to be making him bad tempered and I was very wary. When he was in work, he went daily to a mysterious place called 'Ferranti's of Hollingwood'. When he was out of work – which seemed to be often – he would stay in bed until the afternoon and when my mother and I would arrive to see Grandma, we would find her complaining that she couldn't 'shift Jimmy'. My mother would stand for no such nonsense, she would mount the stairs, battle would ensue and shortly afterwards Uncle Jimmy would appear looking truly dreadful – depressed as only the unemployed could be depressed in those days when benefits were not easy to come by. He had been educated at Manchester Grammar School and he still had his school cap with a silver owl badge on the front. I think he was really very clever. "Clever but lazy," said my mother. He had lots of books and was a wonderful artist. When I was young, during bouts of unemployment, he started to write a family history of the Haydocks. He and Uncle Tom would do a great deal of research together and Uncle Jimmy would illustrate their findings with neat pen and ink sketches. He completed two enormous books, beautifully hand-written and with drawings and photographs on almost every page. They are a valuable family heirloom, held at the moment in safekeeping by my cousin Bryan for his children and grand-children.

Jimmy's researches led him to believe that we are directly descended from the Haydocks of Cottam, a big Lancastrian family, ardent Catholics all, who fought bravely for the Royalist cause during and after the Civil War. I was glad that we had been Cavaliers rather than Roundheads. They were so much more romantic and wore such beautiful clothes, but I couldn't understand why Grandpa and his brothers all had such round heads. I was convinced that our ancestors, after having succumbed to the attraction of Bonnie Prince Charlie, had later switched sides. Also, if they had been such strong Catholics, how was it that we were all now Weslyan Methodists? They *must* have switched sides.

From Uncle Jimmy's books, years after he had died, I first learnt of one, George Haydock, 'a man in complexions fayre, of countenance mild and in professing his faith passing stoute.' He was convicted of high treason on the 9th February 1594 and executed at the age of twenty-eight. Fortunately, he was dead before his body was cut down, so he escaped the barbaric disembowelling which was the custom in those days. George Haydock was actually beatified by the Church of Rome in 1987. There were many other stories about the

Haydocks of the past, but I was never allowed to browse at leisure and I picked up most of our family history from overhearing the conversations between Uncle Jimmy, Uncle Tom and my father. The latter insisted that Jimmy, in spite of his extensive researches, had never really found the link between our branch of the family and the romantic Catholic Haydocks of the past. Aunty Gertie refused to take Jimmy's work seriously, annoying him with frivolous questions, such as – 'Had he ever come across that Haydock of Cottam who had a whiskery bottom?' and whenever she wrote to Aunty Katie, she would decorate the back flap of the envelope with a drawing which clearly depicted that particular Haydock.

When Uncle Jimmy was dressed for going out he always looked very smart. He would press his own trousers, heating up the flat irons on the gas stove in Grandma's scullery, causing great hissings and clouds of steam to rise up until the kitchen windows were completely steamed over and Grandma would complain about the damp getting on her chest and Uncle Jimmy would shout about 'whiny old women'. He was always secretive about where he went on his outings but I think this was because my mother, with her very curious nature and matchmaking mind, was always trying to marry him off to some good woman who would steady him down! I remember one of his girlfriends particularly well. She was dark and beautiful and called Edith Turner. She always came to Primrose Bank via the back door. I can't ever remember her walking up Grandpa's front drive, and because of this I assumed that she lived in the street at the bottom of the back garden and came to us through the back garden gate, up Cow Lane, past the door of the empty stable and into the backyard. She was very popular with us all, especially with my cousin Little Charlie who really loved her. My Uncle Jimmy courted her for many years. They used to have terrible rows; suddenly, it would be 'all off', and we didn't see Edith for a week or so, until equally suddenly, it was 'all on again'. She gave him up in the end – discouraged, I think, by his laziness and bad temper which didn't quite compensate for the Haydock charm which manifested itself so abundantly in the male members of the family.

My mother must have been a schoolgirl when she first

went to live at Primrose Bank. She once told me how well she remembered sitting on the front steps with Grandma. All Grandma's most treasured possessions lay around them in boxes and bundles which had arrived by the first carter's dray. Grandma and my mother had been there to receive them and to watch over these treasures until Grandpa, complete with the rest of their furniture and the rest of his family, should arrive in the second cart. At that time, Grandpa had the one and only key to the front door, and in any case, he would have insisted on being the first to lead his flock into their new domain. As they sat and waited, Grandma said to my mother, "I shan't ever settle here, Lily, I can't see us staying long – give it a year and we'll be off again!" Then Grandpa and the boys arrived. Grandpa produced the key, knocked dramatically three times on the stoutly panelled door, so that the sound reverberated eerily in the depths of the empty house, then he turned the key – led his wife and children into their new home and there he and Grandma brought up their young family and stayed for nearly forty years.

The house made such a deep impression on me, that even now, seventy years later, I have vivid memories of those who peopled its lofty rooms, of the events which I witnessed there and of other happenings which took place long before I was born and which came alive for me in the nostalgic reminiscences of my elders. At least two of my Haydock cousins share those memories with the same appreciation. It was a house which welcomed and accommodated our growing years. It gave us space in which to develop and it became the focal point of our young lives right up to the day that Grandma and Grandpa were forced to leave it forever.

Immediately behind the front door was a small lobby at the back of which there was another door. This door was quite imposing, half glassed in red, blue and white patterns. On the left and right of the lobby were two full length cupboards. One held golf clubs, trolleys and leather carriers – dusty, forlorn and uninviting. The family's golfing days were over when I was small. At that time, the clubs lay forgotten and I had very little interest in them, but I did enjoy the stories which my father used to tell me of the days when they were very much in use.

Grandpa, it seemed, had once been the president of the local golf club. Both my mother and father were also members, in fact, according to my dad, he and my mother did most of their courting on the links. My mother was then nineteen. She was not allowed a door key of her own and she was expected to be indoors by nine o'clock every evening. Finding this injunction too restricting, Mother thought of a way round it. She enlisted the aid of Florrie, one of Grandma's maids. Grandpa always 'made the back up' regularly at 9.00 pm, irrespective of the whereabouts of the rest of the family. Everyone except Frank and Jimmy, who were too young and my mother who was just a girl, had a key anyway. Many a time, after meeting my father, Mother would return home well after nine o'clock. She would knock quietly on the back door three times and whisper "It's only me, Florrie," and Florrie, on her way to bed, would slide back the bolts and unlock the door. This worked very well for some time, but my mother came back later and later, and one night, Florrie, tired of waiting up, and tired anyway, just went to bed. At 11.00 pm my mother was still knocking and this time, it was Grandpa who heard her.

"I'll give you – 'It's only me, Florrie'," he roared. "It would serve you right if I left you out there all night." But of course, he didn't. However, a very strict watch was subsequently kept upon my mother's leisure time, and the courting suffered as a consequence. It was then that my parents hit upon the idea of meeting early in the morning rather than late in the evening, and of using the excuse of much needed golfing practice, should they be caught and again faced with Grandpa's wrath. They had their rendezvous secretly on the golf course each morning at about six o'clock when very few people were abroad. My mother would sneak out of the house by the front door which Florrie had just unlocked as part of her early morning duties. Taking her bag of clubs from the lobby cupboard, she would make her way to the links where my father, who was living at Mrs Varley's at the time, met her. Joyfully, they would roam the course together. This worked very well all through the spring and summer of 1912 until the inevitable happened and one morning they were spotted by a friend of Grandpa's who had come out earlier than usual for his game. Of course Grandpa was soon informed.

"Your daughter and her young man were out early on the links this morning Mr Haydock."

What happened then, I don't know, but perhaps my grandparents began to realise that the courting was serious, for shortly afterwards my parents were allowed to become officially 'affianced', with the proviso that this period must last for at least two years.

"Grandma believed in long engagements," said my father with a twinkle in his eye as he told me the story. My mother used to say that this was because Grandma wanted her to have time to change her mind in case she were to meet someone during those two years who was a little more affluent than a mere school-teacher. My mother was very attractive, if somewhat plump. Her fair skin, dark hair and dimples caused Grandma to think that her daughter was capable of making a really good catch and marrying well!

The other cupboard in the lobby was much more exciting for it contained the croquet set. There were four wicked looking mallets with huge round heads, painted hoops, gaily coloured balls and a garish totem pole called 'The Peg', to make up the set. Croquet was still played occasionally at Primrose Bank in the early 1920s. I was never allowed to take part but I liked to watch and can well remember the fun the adults had on Grandpa's lawn – the laughter and the shouts of 'Mind the irises', as balls would come spinning across the drive to land in the rockeries. I made up my mind there and then, that one day I would play croquet myself. Looking back on it now, years later and as a member of one of the country's largest croquet clubs, I have come to the conclusion that they must have been playing golf croquet, or something very much like it. Golf croquet is a 'fun game', and they were certainly having fun.

The lobby was separated from the inner hall by an imposing glass door with a brass knob handle which was polished daily. Tiny squares and diamonds – shaped panes of blue, red and white, took the light from the oval window above the front door and filtered it in multi-coloured patterns on to the floor of the inner hall which was itself beautifully tiled in yellow and black flags. Here, quite often, I fell foul of Uncle Jimmy. When he was unemployed and forced to be at home all day, he would sometimes 'vent his spleen' on the hall floor.

Mother and I, entering from the lobby, would find him on hands and knees beside a bucket of soapy water, mop at the ready and floor cloth to hand.

"I've just washed these tiles," he would say menacingly. "Be careful!" My mother, who was quite unafraid of her youngest brother, would take no notice of the injunction.

"Hello Jimmy," she would say. "Glad to see you're making yourself useful." And on she would sail without even trying to avoid the wet patches. I was left marooned! The floor shone glistening and slippery, before me like some vast soap-sud ocean. Somewhere, I had heard of a mysterious Yellow Sea. This must be it, and Uncle Jimmy was the Yellow Peril, lurking at its centre like some evil-intentioned pirate. Holding on to his yard arm of a mop and flicking his cat-o'-nine-tails-floor-cloth, he waited to pounce on the unwary who dared to cross his watery domain.

"Keep your dirty feet off my clean tiles," he growled. "They'll leave marks." I could see my mother's back disappearing down the passage at the far end of the hall. My heart rose into my mouth with fright, but I screwed my courage to the sticking point, and made a dash for it. Uncle Jimmy yelped and hit out at my bare legs with the wet floor cloth as I passed. If I skidded or slipped, he would succeed in hitting me, to leave a stinging red mark across my calves.

Apart from the occasional menace of Uncle Jimmy, the hall was a pleasant place to be. It was square and spacious. On the left as you entered from the lobby, was an enormous hallstand. When all the uncles, aunts and cousins came to see Grandma and Grandpa at weekends, it was completely covered. Its fussy Victorian decoration was hidden by a heap of hats, coats and macs, whilst in addition, galoshes, wellington boots, Russian boots, leggings and gaiters spilled around it during the winter time. Opposite stood a stout square table, in the middle of which was a large vase patterned with roses and a Grecian maiden embracing an Ionian pillar. In front of the vase stood a silver salver, where, so I was told, in the days of plenty, calling cards were received into safe keeping when Grandma was 'at home'. Above the table, hanging on the wall, was a gong with an attached striker – its hammer-head swathed in leather. The gong was still used in my time, to call the family together for special meals and occasions. The striker was out of reach when my cousins and I were very small, but sometimes it would be lifted down and we would be allowed to use it, one at a time, in strict rotation.

At the back of the hall, opposite to the lobby door, rose the staircase. Shallow, graceful steps led, first to the lower landing, then to the main landing and then, on and up into the attics. The stairs were clad in a patterned carpet which had once been thick and of a rich red colour. When Tommy, Charlie and I used to race up and down, it was faded and in places, almost threadbare. Brass stair-rods held it in position. They were taken up once a week for cleaning, laid out on newspaper on the kitchen table, there seemed to be hundreds of them! The bannisters were carved and elegant, but what I remember most about the staircase, was the handrail. Its smooth polished mahogany flowed dark red and gleaming from top to bottom of the house. We, the grandchildren, helped to keep it polished. Led by Charlie, with me in the middle and Tommy bringing up the rear, we would slide happily from attic to hall – speeding up on the steep bits and propelling ourselves along the horizontal levels with our feet and hands – we would finish the last downwards lap at a tremendous speed. There was no carved pillar or rounded knob to halt our descent. The bannisters and handrail just curved in on themselves forming a beautifully shiny spiral in a horizontal plane, for all the world like a great flat snail. Charlie was good at putting on the brakes, but, if he failed, we all ended up, laughing and breathless, in a heap on the hall floor. Tirelessly, we would sort ourselves out and race for the top floor, to start all over again.

As you faced the stairs, on your left, opening off the hall, was the dining-room. It was large, light and airy, with big square windows overlooking the croquet lawn. All the main rooms at Primrose Bank were lofty. Their ceilings were decorated with elaborately carved cornices and centre pieces in white moulded plaster. Leaves and scrolls curved across the corners, and around the central light fittings were radiating circles of plaster flowers which caught the shadowy gas flames and reflected them in such a way that the blossoms seemed to stir and sway once the lamps were lit. In this room was a chandelier lamp which hung down from the central rose. What seemed to me to be hundreds of oval crystal pieces, were strung together in loops and twirls along golden chains. The lights from the gas mantles which it contained seemed to split into all the colours of the rainbow.

The furniture was massive and solid. Bought at the end of the Victorian Era, it had stood up stoutly to the onslaughts of five children and seven grandchildren. In the bay window I can remember two big armchairs. Grandma had her special one here with a footstool nearby. Two further easy chairs flanked the hearth with its bordering glass-fronted book cupboards, its black-leaded grate with green and gold patterned tiles protected by a big shiny fender on which rested an assortment of fire irons. A huge mirror of Venetian glass reflected the ornaments and the black marble clock which stood centre-most on the mantelpiece. Here, flanking the clock on each side were, to me, the two most fascinating objects in the whole room. Each had a little ornate roof, from which were suspended long triangular crystals of cut glass about the same size and thickness as a small Toblerone bar. Any slight draught or upward rush of air from the fire would set them in motion, clinking and chunking against each other and sending out shafts of coloured light. On the adjacent wall opposite the bay window stood a heavy mahogany sideboard full of cupboards and drawers. It took up the whole length of the wall. Shelves and ledges filled with vases and jars, sprouted from the attached mirror which backed its surface. This polished top held silver tureen dishes, piles of Grandma's best Royal Doulton plates, tiered porcelain cake stands, plated toast racks and silver-gleaming Edwardian teapots and hot water jugs.

A long sofa with one rolled-over arm occupied the remaining wall, but the great central piece of this room was the huge dining table. It could be extended by the insertion of heavy panels and much winding of iron handles, until it reached from the sideboard to the bay window. When I was small, it was extended for special occasions only, so that normally there was quite a large space at each end. This enabled wonderful games of chase for my cousins and myself. Round and round we would dash, choking with laughter, until the head of the line caught up with the tail and we would all fall face downwards on to the green chenille tablecloth. I remember one occasion after supper when the table had been cleared, our parents were gathered round the fire talking and we were engaged in our customary pursuit. Grandpa, instead of moving to a fireside armchair had remained seated to read his book at the sideboard end of the table. This rather hindered our circumlocutory progress, and Charlie, perhaps to register a protest every time he passed by, tipped Grandpa's book which he had propped up before him, so that it fell face downwards onto the table. Grandpa had enormous patience with his grandchildren and stood this indignity for several minutes, but after his reading had been so disturbed for the fifth time, he rose, and as Charlie, passing by, was preparing to make it a sixth time, Grandpa suddenly lost his temper and hit Charlie hard, over the head with the open book. Charlie reeled, staggered, and finally collapsed onto the floor. The rest of us stared at him aghast. The silence was shattered by an explosion of wrath from Aunty Gertie. She dashed round the table, picked up her small son who was rapidly recovering his senses, shook him to see if he were still intact and then directed the full force of her anger at Grandpa. A family row ensued. Everyone had a go. No one waited for his neighbour to stop talking before other opinions were expressed, and finally, the storm blew itself out. No permanent damage had been done to Charlie and soon, he became as irrepressible as ever, but we children never again played chase round the dining-room table unless Grandpa was well out of the way.

I remember the dining-room as the family's main living-room. Here we gathered on week day evenings and while the adults chatted over a game of whist, Tommy, Charlie and I would play together. We were explorers discovering the vast unknown territories which lay behind the sofa. There we would fight battles for supremacy over the area which lay between the sofa and the wainscotting, or we would take turns to wrap ourselves in the heavy green curtain which hung behind the door. Its purpose was to keep off draughts, but it made a wonderful whirligig. It was green and tasselled and smelt of dust. If you stood in the space between it and the door, gathered its material about you and turned round and round you would become imprisoned in a green and smelly world, then, by spinning round quickly in the other direction, you would shoot out, free and exhilarated, into the brightly lit room.

When Grandpa was the President of the Golf Club and there was plenty of money to spare, the dining-room must have witnessed wonderful feasts and dinner parties. In those days, Grandma had maids to wait on table, and my mother, in her usual dramatic way, used to tell me that she had seen the whisky, 'flowing like water' from the dining-room sideboard. When I was very small, I used to think that Grandpa opened the cupboard door and a river of whisky flowed forth! Grandpa must have made a wonderful host, he was such a 'hail-fellow-well-met' type of man, and Grandma, as a hostess was, I believe, quite renowned in Newton Heath. She was a talented cook and kept an excellent table. In the 1920s, when there was still a little cash left, we used to have big family parties. I expect that all who could, helped out by contributing to the food. I can remember especially, towering castle-shaped jellies and blancmanges, bowls of whipped cream and Grandma's renowned sherry trifle. We all used to wait for Grandpa to have the first taste, always followed by the same remark:

"My word, Ma," he would say. "You let your hand slip with the sherry bottle, didn't you?"

At Christmas time, two enormous puddings ablaze with blue flames, would be borne in by Grandma and Aunty Gertie. I remember one Christmas when the dining table was so crowded with family and friends that we children had to be accommodated at a side table. We were quite excited. It hadn't happened before and unsupervised, we foresaw lots of opportunities for silly jokes and face pulling, I sat between Charlie and Tommy with Joan and Phil opposite and Baby John in a high chair at one end close to where his mother was seated at the big table. We were waiting for the turkeys to be brought in. Grandpa was sharpening his razor-edged carving knife on the steel, glasses and cutlery gleamed against the best linen tablecloth, crackers made great red blotches on its whiteness and there we sat hardly knowing how to contain ourselves. No cracker pulling was allowed before our plates had been filled and grace had been said. We waited, serviettes tied in knots at the back of our necks. Charlie, picking up his knife, looked around our little table.

"Feel this," he said, running his thumb lightly along the edge of his knife. "Coo, it could cut Micky's tail off."

His brother, who knew him well, and Joan and Phil, who must have been less naive than I, looked at him suspiciously, but I, anxious to please, always gullible and naturally clumsy, ran my finger heavily down the knife's edge. I wasn't prepared for the spurt of blood which followed. It came out in gushes, redder than the crackers. It stained the tablecloth, went right through my serviette and flowed down the front of my best dress! Tommy turned white and looked as if he might faint. Aunty Gertie rushed to support him and to stick his head between his knees, boxing Charlie's ears as she passed. Joan and Phil both began to talk at once and Baby John banged his spoon viciously on the side of his high-chair.

"Hold your arm *up*," my mother shouted across to me.

I did so and the blood ran up my sleeve. Finally, I was removed for bandaging and re-dressing. When I came back, the turkeys had arrived, grace had been said and the feast was proceeding merrily. As I sat down, Charlie winked at me.

"Sorry our kid," he said.

All was forgiven, if not forgotten.

Sometimes, after a festive meal, Grandpa would keep his grandchildren at the table, holding us spellbound there whilst our parents helped Grandma clear away the dishes. He would tell us one of his wonderful stories about the 'King of the World'. The King of the World, a mythical figure, was really a figment of Grandpa's imagination. We always thought that he took the stories from some wonderful book he kept hidden away from us. Charlie and Tommy claimed to have seen it once in Grandpa's shop, full of spidery writing, which they couldn't understand. It had been whisked from under their prying noses before they had been able to make anything of it. Charlie told me years later, that what they had actually found must have been a dusty old accounts' ledger lying forgotten under the counter at the back of the shop.

The 'King of the World' always arrived in an aeroplane when he visited Primrose Bank. He would land neatly on Grandpa's front lawn in a special machine which had rotary blades! (Grandpa must have foreseen the coming of the helicopter!) He would knock loudly three times on the front door and ask for each of the cousins by name. When told that we were waiting for him in the dining-room, he would come in and sit down at the table with us. Out of the air above us, he would produce his famous 'Bombshell Pudding'. Growing into a huge football, it would float down and settle on the table 'before our very eyes,' which were by this time enormous with expectation. The 'King of the World' would then take up Grandma's longest silver serving spoon and help each one of us to a spoonful of Bombshell Pudding. Out of that spoonful came an abundance of magical gifts. There were long silk dresses with matching Queen-Mary-type diamond-tiaras for Joan and myself, whilst the boys were laden with suits of armour, or entire cowboy outfits made from leather and decorated with real gold studs. A second helping of pudding gave us all our own means of transport. These varied from graceful white horses, to powerful cars, ships, aeroplanes and, sometimes, even submarines. Each possessed extraordinary properties, and within minutes we had sailed down the Manchester Ship Canal and across the Atlantic Ocean, flown high over Alpine peaks, dived to the depths of the Indian Ocean, motored upside down, the length and breadth of Australia or galloped swifter than sound along golden beaches where surf-laden waves flowed endlessly across the sands. Wherever Grandpa's fertile imagination led him, we followed, drinking it all in – eager for more.

Grandpa was especially hot on Norway. I think it was his favourite country. My mother told me that when she was small, he had paid for many of his friends to accompany him there on a holiday trip. He had hired, not just a compartment,

Beryl at six months.

Father as a young man.

Mother, a year before her marriage.

Grandma and Grandpa Haydock, just engaged to be married.

Mother and Father's wedding party on the steps of Primrose Bank, 22nd July 1914.

Uncle Jimmy Haydock.

Aunty Gertie with my cousins
Charlie and Tommy, 1923.

Grandpa Haydock's shop on the Oldham Road.

My Great-Grandmother Hellawell in bed at Primrose Bank.

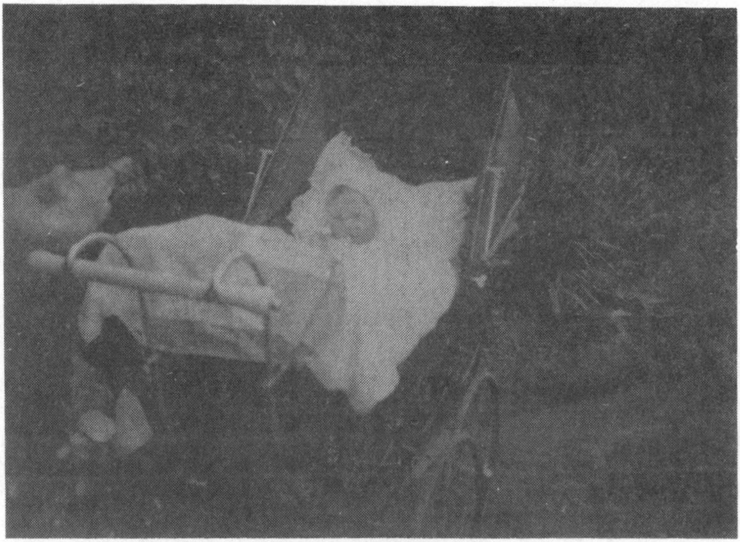
Beryl in pram at Primrose Bank.

'Baby John' in the backyard of
the house on Moston Lane.

Mother and Father in 'Clara', 1927.

but a whole coach on a train which set out from Piccadilly Station in Manchester. She had been taken to the station as a little girl to see the party leave and remembered the big label on the coach which read, so she was told, 'Reserved for Mr Haydock's Party'. Now, in the 1920s, Grandpa was happy to take his grandchildren with him instead. He flew them in the 'King of the World's' own special aircraft over black and fathomless fiords, over snow covered fields alive with reindeer in a land where every tree was a Christmas tree covered with silver bells, where the midnight sun blazed red along the Arctic Circle and the Aurora Borealis splashed its multi-coloured lights across a vivid sky. The fairy tale magic never failed to hold us spellbound until the table had been cleared and all the dishes washed and put away – then we would be returned to the dining-room in Primrose Bank. The King of the World would depart with the promise of another visit providing that his aerial telegraph communication system sent him reports of our good behaviour in the meantime.

By the late 1920s Grandma had become really deaf. She wouldn't admit it, and when in irritation, we shouted too loudly at her, she would draw herself up in a regal manner and proclaim indignantly, "You needn't shout, I'm not deaf!" But she was; and the day came when she admitted it.

One afternoon whilst she was sitting in the dining-room window patching a sheet with her wonderfully neat little stitches, and I was reading nearby, Mrs Carter came to call. Mrs Carter was Aunty Katie's mother and she and Grandma had known each other for many years. Mrs Carter, like Grandma, was also deaf. When greetings had been exchanged and the two ladies had settled down for a good chat, Mrs Carter produced from her capacious leather handbag, a wonderful contraption which she proceeded to attach to her ear. It was made of real tortoise-shell, resembled a trumpet and curled gracefully at its open end like an arum lily. Mrs Carter heard every word without strain. Much impressed, Grandma asked if she could have a go. Conversation continued happily, the trumpet being passed backwards and forwards between the friends. After Mrs Carter had left, Grandma lost no time in describing the hearing aid to Grandpa when he came home from the shop.

"I would dearly love one of those trumpets, Arthur," she said. "I must be a little deaf because I could hear so clearly when I used it."

But there was no spare money to buy Grandma a trumpet, and since she continued to talk longingly about it we did the next best thing. Uncle Jimmy found a length of flexible rubber gas-piping and little Charlie went 'rooting' in the old stable and produced an enamel funnel which he and Tommy managed to fix to one end of the pipe. We presented it; Grandma obligingly put the tube end in her ear and we took turns to speak into the funnel. It worked well until Charlie, who could think of nothing to say when it was his turn to speak, unfortunately whistled down it and put Grandma off using it again.

One of my last memories of Primrose Bank also has a dining-room setting. It was winter time, probably late in 1930. The fire was blazing, the curtains drawn against the cold and dark outside, and Grandma, Grandpa, Uncle Jimmy, Mother and myself were sitting round the hearth – waiting. It was nine o'clock. I remember the black marble clock on the mantelpiece striking the hour.

Grandpa got up – "I'll make t'back up Ma, and let Micky in," he said.

At the dining-room door he paused, looked back and remarked, before going out, "Sam should be here soon if his train's not late."

As he was returning across the hall from his nightly lock up duty, there were three loud bangs on the front door. My tummy somersaulted; I leapt up and ran into the hall. Grandpa was just letting my father in. I rushed to fling my arms about him; he stooped to kiss me and then, without taking off his heavy winter overcoat, holding me by one hand and with his brief-case in the other, he followed Grandpa into the dining-room. Everyone was standing up, even Grandma.

"Well?" said my mother. It was all she said.

"I've accepted," answered my father kissing her.

She just went quiet – Grandpa slapped my father on the back.

"Well done Sam lad."

Uncle Jimmy was shaking my father's hand. I jumped up and down. "Hoorah, Hoorah," I shouted unfeelingly. "Now we shall be going to live at the seaside."

Grandma burst into tears.

My father had just come back from Torquay where he had been offered the post of first principal of the South Devon Technical College. The new building there was not yet finished and it would be his job to recruit students and to arrange courses ready for the opening in September 1931. We would have to leave Manchester for good and move down to Devon in April. A new house would have to be found, a new school for me, and of course, new scholars for the new college. That evening in the dining-room at Primrose Bank, I knew instinctively, marked the beginning of the end of my Manchester days.

Across the hall from the dining-room, lay the 'best' room in Primrose Bank. We called it the drawing-room. The family used it less than they did the dining-room and my memories of it are not so clear cut, nor so detailed as they are of the latter. It gave me the impression of lightness. Blue and white Wedgwood ornaments and clock under glass domes were on the mantelpiece. The furniture was more elegant but less comfortable than that of the dining-room. This room had the same beautifully moulded plaster ceiling and central crystal chandelier, but there were additional lights here – delicately wrought iron brackets carried gas mantles, shaded and discreet, on either side of the fireplace. The wallpaper was thick, almost like silk, it was white and had regency stripes running vertically from the deep white wainscotting up to the picture rail. I remember no specific paintings in this room, but the 'wall' opposite to the big bay window (which, incidentally, was never opened, or the room would have been black within minutes) was covered in family portraits and photographs. This 'wall' was not a wall at all, it was a series of folding panelled doors which rose from floor to ceiling and stretched across the whole room. At one time, they had been folded back regularly, opening out into the morning-room which lay behind them and the two rooms became one large area with windows at each end. Here, my parents' engagement party and wedding reception had been held. After feasting in the dining-room, guests had wandered in here where furniture had been pushed against the walls, rugs rolled back and there had been space for dancing in this big combined room. There had even been a little 'three piece' orchestra established in the bay window.

"Of course," said my mother grandly, when she was describing those parties of long ago, "for really big occasions, Grandpa would hire a room at the Midland Hotel in Manchester."

I wasn't impressed by this last piece of information. The Midland Hotel in Manchester meant nothing to me, but I longed, just once, to see those white panelled doors pushed back to reveal the morning-room beyond. I never did. Instead, I would spend hours studying the photographs which covered them. Some, placed high, were out of my range of vision. I suspect they were portraits of my great-grandparents and their families. But there, lower down hung Uncle Charlie and Uncle Tom, resplendent and handsome as cavalry officers; all three wedding groups were there: Uncle Charlie and Aunty Gertie, Uncle Tom and Aunty Katie, and my mother and father. They gave me hours of contemplative pleasure. Those were the days of long dresses, enormous hats, black stockings, stiff starched wing collars and frock coats. One hat in particular always intrigued me. For years, I seriously thought it was the wedding cake itself. It rose in tiers above its owner's head and was decorated at the very top with a cluster of tiny bells! Here also were framed photographs of my cousins and myself as babies. Charlie and Tommy with their arms about Aunty Gertie's neck; Tommy in a cradle with Charlie holding the pillow beneath his brother's head; Joan and Phil with Aunty Katie, Uncle Jimmy as a little boy and myself standing wide-eyed and doll-like on a chair, embroidered socks and a bow in my hair, and there were many other portraits to enjoy.

Christmas times at Primrose Bank were wonderful for all the cousins. We had such generous grandparents and although the money was dwindling away, between 1926 and 1930, Grandma and Grandpa managed to give us a series of festive seasons which we have never forgotten. From Christmas Eve, when we would all assemble, up to and including New Year's

Eve which was Grandpa's birthday, there would be one evening party after another. A huge meal in the dining-room at six o'clock would be followed by all manner of games in the drawing-room. In the evening of Boxing Day 1927, we had a Fancy Dress Party which I remember as clearly as if it were yesterday. After the meal had been cleared away, we all dispersed to change into our costumes, and when the gong sounded, we assembled in the drawing-room. Tommy and Charlie came as Red Indians. They had been given complete outfits for Christmas and they ran around with brown boot polish on their faces, hitting everyone with toy tomahawks. Aunty Gertie came as a Japanese lady in a silk kimono, carrying baby John in a sling on her back. She had made me up to play the part of her daughter. I had slit eyes, very black eyebrows and a cut-down dressing-gown with a dragon on the back. Grandpa came as the King of the World. There had been much turning out of old trunks in the attics and he had found a truly impressive helmet to which he had attached two enormous birds' wings. He carried a kind of wand and looked rather like Mercury, the messenger of the gods. My father came as Charlie's Aunt – goodness knows where he had obtained the various items of his costume. I suspect it may have been part of my great-grandmother's wardrobe which, for sentimental reasons, Grandma couldn't dispose of. Anyway, my father looked and acted the part admirably – fooling about in elastic-sided boots, a long black skirt, a beaded bonnet complete with veil and a feather boa! My mother, in contrast, was dressed as a little girl in a short frilly frock with white stockings and with a pink ribbon in her hair. I don't remember Uncle Frank being present. After supper, he and Aunty Kathleen had disappeared. They were courting at the time, and I suppose fancy dress parties must have seemed rather pointless to them.

We were all assembled in the drawing-room, when the door was flung open and in stepped a truly fairy-tale couple. We all gasped. It was a Dresden Shepherd and his Shepherdess. His pale blue satin breeches and jacket matched her panniered dress. They wore snowy white wigs and carried tall, be-ribboned crooks. They were utterly beautiful and completely unbelievable for they were my Uncle Jimmy, and Edith

Turner. They bowed to us all, bowed to each other and executed a graceful little dance across the drawing-room floor. They must have hired their costumes – they were so perfect.

Uncle Tom and family could not have been with us on that occasion, or I would have remembered them – but one important person who should have been there was missing – Grandma. Where was Grandma? Suddenly, the King of the World made an announcement.

"If you will all step into the hall, I have arranged for you to meet a very well known popular figure."

We all trooped out and arranged ourselves under Grandpa's direction, round the foot of the stairs. We looked up; lights glowed out brightly from the upper landing which had been in darkness, and suddenly, down the stairs, with a swish of silk, in a froth of lace, swept the Gainsborough Lady. Her head inclining gracefully beneath the plumage of her feather hat, Grandma was the 'pièce de résistance' of the whole evening. We all clapped, received her into our midst as she reached the bottom step, and swept her in triumph through the drawing-room door.

The evening proceeded with Charades, Names on Backs, and Charlie's favourite game, The Parson's Cat. Finally, we all grouped round the piano, my father played, Aunty Gertie whistled and sang for us – *Dear Little Jammy Face* and *When Roses are Blooming in Picardy*, my parents rendered a duet, *When You Come Down the Vale*, Grandpa, looking at Grandma, gave us *There is a Lady Sweet and Kind*, and then we all belted out, *Oh No John* and *On Ilkley Moor 'Bout 'At*. I recited while Tommy and Charlie rolled about on the hearth-rug and pulled faces until Grandma put a stop to it with "It's time for all you children to climb the wooden hill to Bedford-shire."

And so ended for us a wonderful party, but it didn't matter, there would be another tomorrow – we children could bank on it!

The morning-room was as dark and heavy-looking as the drawing-room was light and airy. It was at the back of the house and looked onto a flagged yard. This room was little used in my time, and by 1929, Grandma was forced to let it out together with one of the bedrooms. To make ends meet, she had been forced to take in paying guests. I remember a young doctor and his wife being there. They were jolly people, they became fond of Grandma and Grandpa and were soon very much at home at Primrose Bank.

Everything in the morning-room seemed to be red, dark red; the Lincrusta wallpaper, the plush armchairs and sofa, the chenille tablecloth, the curtains and even the seats of the high backed dining chairs. Uncle Jimmy kept many of his books here. They were housed in deep cupboards against one wall. He had covered them all in the same heavy, purplish paper, which I suspect, must have come from Grandpa's shop. I had to open each book in order to discover its contents – no clue could be gained from its exterior. There were old school text books, various collections of poems, copies of an old annual called *Chatterbox*, and a whole set of Dickens' novels. Before the paying guests came to occupy the morning-room, I would often browse for hours in there, seated cross-legged on the floor. Absorbed in the exploits of the young David Copperfield and riveted by the illustrations of Marley's ghost and the Skating Party, I would nevertheless, manage to keep a wary eye on the door in case Uncle Jimmy should enter and chase me away. Above the bookcases was a picture which intrigued me. It was called 'When Did You Last See Your Father?' Once I learnt the story behind the depicted scene, all my sympathies, like those of the Haydocks of old were for the cause of the Cavaliers.

My father and Uncle Jimmy, had between them, made a crystal wireless set, which, after the collection of an adequate number of 'cats' whiskers, they managed to operate in the morning-room. They would sit at the table with headphones and serious expressions, listening intently. When I was allowed to put on the headphones, I was disappointed. I thought at least a message from the King of the World would come over the ether – instead, I heard nothing but crackling noises and I was glad to take the contraptions off my ears.

In 1926, Father Christmas came to the morning-room. That year, we had a huge tree in there – beautifully decorated and dazzling to behold. In the middle of Christmas afternoon, we all gathered in front of the tree. There were as usual at these times about twenty of us. I remember sitting on the floor between Charlie and Tommy and feeling rather frightened. Father Christmas was expected any minute and the excitement of anticipation was becoming too much for me. Suddenly, a loud knocking echoed through the house. I grabbed Charlie's arm, "I don't like it," I said, "I'm scared."

"Aw, ger off," and Charlie jerked his arm away as Grandpa rose.

"That will be Father Christmas," he announced and went to open the front door.

I froze with fear as an enormous figure appeared – all red and white and black, he seemed, and he was dragging a huge sack into the room. But, after that, it was wonderful. He was so kind, knew each of our names and had presents for all of us. Finally, after accepting a glass of wine from Grandpa, and a piece of Christmas cake from Grandma, he drank our health, wished us well and said that he must get back to his sleigh which he had left on the front lawn, since by this time, he was sure that his reindeers would have become very restive. He stood framed in the morning-room doorway, waving good-bye to us, then he turned and was gone. Grandpa followed him into the hall. My father closed the morning-room door behind them and remained planted firmly in front of it, blocking the exit. We cousins were all dancing up and down, trying to escape from the room. We just had to get to the dining-room window to see Father Christmas depart – but my father said it would be rude to rush out after him, Grandpa was the host and was seeing him off properly. When finally my father opened the morning-room door, we flew across the hall and gazed out of the dining-room window. Too late, he had gone. It looked cold and wet outside, the lawn was empty and it was going dark.

At the back of the hall, a narrow passage between the stair well and the morning-room wall, led through a green baize door to the back of the house. Here were three more doors. One led outside into the backyard and was always locked by Grandpa at nine o'clock every night. One was kept permanently locked and Grandma thought she had the key well hidden but, of course, one day when we were 'rooting' we found it. We waited until no one was about, opened the door and crept through. There was an immediate drop to a flight of wooden steps – no bannisters and no light. If you missed the first step, you could go head over heels into the darkness below. The cold dank air made us shiver as we crept gingerly down into the cellars – 'the dungeons', as Charlie immediately named them. There were two or three separate rooms into which light filtered uneasily through the gratings where, at one time, coal had been tipped. Coal dust and filth covered the shelves and the damp ran in little black rivulets down the thick stone walls. A dank and musty fog hung in the chilly air, and huge black spiders sped madly across the floor on jerky, jointed legs – indignant at the disturbance and ready to inject any number of poisoned bites. Strange-looking rusty implements of torture, no longer recognisable as the household gadgets which they must once have been, lay on the shelves between innumerable wine bottles, empty and roped together with thick and sticky spider webbing. Not a place to linger, and especially for me, since my mother, in an effort to discourage me from ever going down there, had told me a true and frightening story about the cellar.

Long before I was born, when my mother was only nineteen and Uncle Jimmy a small boy of seven or eight, Grandma and Grandpa went away for a short holiday together. My mother, with the help of a maid, was left to care for her brothers and her own grandmother, at that time an elderly widowed lady who had come to live at Primrose Bank. One afternoon when it was the maid's day off and everyone else except my great-grandmother was out of the house, my mother decided to make some toffee in the kitchen. She was in the middle of doing this when Uncle Jimmy came home from school and immediately decided to help her. They were so engrossed in their task that they didn't hear their grandmother come down the stairs, across the hall and along the passage towards the kitchen – her stick tap-tapping against the wainscotting as she approached. What they did hear was a cry, followed by a sickening thud. They ran out of the kitchen. Someone had left the latch off the cellar door; it was wide open and they could hear my great-grandma moaning at the bottom of the steps. Mother, with Jimmy frightened and clinging to her, reached her as quickly as she could. Great-grandma was bleeding and in great pain.

"Quickly, Jimmy," said my mother who could think of only one thing to do in the circumstances. "Run as fast as you can to Mrs Varley's and fetch Sam." She couldn't have known my father for any length of time then, but it was long enough for her to realise that he would be a tower of strength in an emergency. Uncle Jimmy ran without stopping – down Dean Avenue, along Dean Lane and into Mrs Varley's front sitting-room where my father was preparing his next day's lessons. As a small boy, Jimmy couldn't talk properly, especially when he was excited. He tended to leave the initial letter off almost every word.

" 'Am 'um 'ick, Grandma 'umbled down 'ellar 'eps," he blurted out breathlessly.

My father outran Jimmy back to Primrose Bank. He found my mother still sitting by her grandmother. She had taken off her apron to try to make a pillow for the old lady who must have been bleeding badly all of the time. My mother's blouse was soaked in blood and Great-grandma had lost consciousness, which was a blessing, for it meant that my father and mother, between them, could manage to carry her out of the cellar and up to her own room. It was lucky that she was such a light old lady and that they were both young and strong. Poor Great-grandma never really recovered from that fall. She spent the rest of her days confined to her bedroom. She had broken her collar bone as well as having other injuries. I think that her grandchildren must have loved her very much, for everyone in the house saw to it that she was not lonely up there. In fact, my mother said that she became rather imperious, rapping loudly on the floor with her stick whenever she wanted attention, until Grandpa, if he were in an irritable mood, would shake his fist at the ceiling and call for 'a little peace', in his own home. My mother often told me this story, meaning it, I am sure, to be a salutory lesson – also, it gave her a chance to show off her 'streak'.

"Look," she would say. "This happened a week after your

great-grandma Hellawell fell down the cellar steps when I was only nineteen!" She would lift the front of her dark brown hair, and there, underneath, close to her scalp, was a thick line, completely white, running from the front to the back of her head! "It was the shock, you see, and I wouldn't like anything like that to happen to you."

My Uncle Frank discouraged Bryan from going anywhere near the cellar steps, with another story. He invented a family called 'The Plushes'. Bryan was very young, in fact almost as soon as he could walk The Plushes came onto the scene. Bryan believed in them implicitly and became scared of even passing the cellar door, let alone venturing into its depths. The Plushes were very, very poor, and, taking pity on their impecunious state, Grandma had allowed them to live in her cellar free of charge. They had no money, no food, very few clothes and were dirty and so horrible to look at from having to live in the cellar, that they never came out except at the dead of night when no one was about. If ever anything were missing, The Plushes had taken it; one of Grandpa's slippers, Grandma's thimble, even a jam tart and a piece of mutton pie from the pantry. It was surprising how often The Plushes made forays in the night, and it always encouraged Bryan to pack away his toys safely before going to bed in case Jimmy Plush, the youngest of that numerous family, should get his hands on them.

Adjacent to the cellar door lay the kitchen – the work-room of the house where the women toiled and the men enjoyed the fruits of their labour. A busy, no-nonsense room, it had an enormous fire-grate with double ovens on each side of the hearth – solid, strong black ovens which closed by means of bright silvered steel-bar handles. They terminated in ornamental knobs which became so hot when the ovens were in use, that you had to wrap a towel round your hand before you could open them. Above each oven was a deep recess, where, on baking days, Grandma's tins would be set out to receive her bread mixture and barmy loaves, which rose and bubbled soundlessly in the gentle heat, filling the kitchen air with the alcoholic fumes of working yeast. On wash days a big clothes maiden blocked off the fire from the rest of the kitchen, 'dressed overall' with sheets, bolster slips and pillow cases of snowy whiteness. Above, hauled to the ceiling by ropes on a squeaky pulley, was the longest clothes rack that I have ever seen. From it hung festoons of freshly ironed shirts, vests and pairs and pairs of long underpants belonging to Grandpa and my uncles.

In front of the fire was a rag-rug where Mickey and I would sit together on winter afternoons, looking into the flames. Work finished for the time being, Mother would often join Grandma, to sit, feet on fender, chatting about family matters which I didn't really understand, but which did often trouble me. Grandma always seemed to be on the verge of incarceration in a place called 'The Workhouse' – and Mickey was in danger of being sent to the 'Dogs' Home'. I didn't care for the sound of either of these places, and neither did Mickey. Whenever he heard the words 'Dogs' Home', he would get up and slink away into his box in the scullery; his tail between his legs. The country was in crisis; Grandpa's shop had closed down; Uncle Jimmy couldn't find a job; Uncle Charlie was ill again; and Uncle Tom's chicken farm in far away Brize Norton, was on its last legs. It was all very upsetting, but one afternoon, I ceased to worry.

We were sitting as usual round the kitchen fire, when in breezed Uncle Frank. He at least must have been in work, for he came straight up to Grandma, kissed her, took out his wallet and gave her a handful of pound notes.

"There you are Ma," he said, "for bed and board." And with that, he went out again. Grandma rose and took down an old tureen dish from a shelf high in the fireside cupboard. She took off the lid – it was full of money! Putting away my Uncle's contribution, she remarked:

"Just look at this Lily, a few weeks ago it was empty."

"Thank goodness for our Bill then," replied my mother. "That's all I can say."

I can remember now the feeling of relief I experienced then. Uncle Frank had ovbiously saved the day.

The big kitchen table, used for ironing, pastry rolling and cake making during the mornings, was large enough to accommodate the whole family for midday dinner. Often, in the early afternoon, when my grandfather and uncles had returned to the shop, Mother and I would arrive in time to join Grandma in yet another cup of tea – the Haydocks loved to linger over cups of tea. It was on these occasions that my mother would 'tell the leaves'. We would drain our cups, turn them upside down on the saucers and pass them one by one to Mother, who, by interpreting the pattern which the leaves left on the china, could apparently see into our futures. We all took it as just a game, but one afternoon, whilst reading Grandma's cup, suddenly Mother 'saw' Cousin Nellie coming up the front drive to visit her.

"Tell me another one," laughed Grandma. "I haven't seen Nellie in years, I can't see why she would want to visit me now."

"She's there all right," persisted my mother. "Plain as a pikestaff."

"When is she coming?" I asked.

"Right this minute, she is coming up the drive." Mother winked at Grandma and I saw it, but to be quite sure, Mother had seemed so certain, I ran to the dining-room window. A lady I didn't know was just coming through the gates at the end of the drive. I rushed back to the kitchen.

"There's a lady coming," I announced.

"Oh, yes, and I suppose it's Cousin Nellie."

"I don't know, but it's a lady."

"Oh you story teller," said Grandma. "Lily, this child has too much imagination."

With that, there were three knocks on the front door. Grandma opened it and let in Cousin Nellie! No one was more astounded than my mother.

On the wall opposite the kitchen window, above Grandma's treddle sewing machine, hung a portrait of Queen Alexandra in a tiara. There were diamonds on a wide band around her throat. A beautiful blue dress nipped her waist and threw out her bosom into a most challenging posture.

"Poor Alexandra," said Grandma, tut-tutting meaningfully, as she looked at the picture. "She had such a lot to put up with."

Next to Alexandra was King Edward VII (when I was very small, I mistook him for Grandpa). He was equally resplendent in robes of royal red and a white ermine cape flecked with bits of black fur. "The old devil," said my mother.

One summer's day in 1928, Charlie, Tommy and myself were playing together in the kitchen at Primrose Bank when in came my father and Uncle Charlie. They announced that they would take us to the local picture house, 'The Failsworth Pop', for the afternoon. Here, much to my surprise, the two men, after paying for us to go in to the 'first house' – I think it cost 2d each, half price, left us to our own devices, telling us to be good, enjoy the pictures, and they would call for us when the show was over. I think they had been detailed to look after us for the afternoon! I had never been to the pictures without my parents before, but obviously, my cousins were used to being there unsupervised. It was an experience which I never forgot. Their behaviour was awful, even I was shocked! Tom Mix, on his beautiful horse Silver King, was taking on, single handed, the entire Red Indian population of North America. Not only did my cousins shout loud encouragement to him, but they also took part in any fighting there was, by jeering at and punching each other as they rode imaginary horses up and down the central aisle until the usherette, to whom they were obviously well known, caught them, shook them, and returned them to their seats. This happened more than once. Eventually the show was over and we trooped out, Charlie being dislodged with some difficulty as he wanted to wait for the second house to begin in order to see it all round again. However, our fathers were waiting for us in the foyer and took us all straight back to Primrose Bank. There, standing by the window in Grandma's kitchen, they imparted some amazing news to all of us.

"Well," said Uncle Charlie to his sons, "you now have a little brother." I was dumbfounded. A new cousin had suddenly materialised out of thin air. There we were – two men and three children, standing by the window in the shabby, but safe and familiar old kitchen at Primrose Bank and something quite strange and unfamiliar had just come into our lives.

"Where is it?" asked Tommy suspiciously.

It seemed that 'it' was at Charlie and Tommy's home in New Moston and that Grandma, Aunty Gertie and my mother were keeping 'it' company. Charlie was the first to recover.

"I don't believe it, you're 'aving us on," he said. "Come on our kids, let's go out." And he dived through the back door and made for 'the wood'. Tommy followed him, but for once, I remained rooted to the spot. I couldn't get over it. I *did* believe them and the wonder of it all filled my mind for a long time afterwards.

Leading off the kitchen was the scullery – a stone-flagged room, cold, except when Grandma's old gas cooker was alight. Right up against the cooker was Mickey's box to which he was banished when he was too much under Grandma's feet, or kept the fire off the rest of the family by insinuating himself into a central position on the hearth-rug. He was a knowing old dog. You had only to say firmly, "Into your box Mickey," and his stumpy tail would drop as he slunk away. But not for long – he was crafty and soon slipped back unnoticed until Grandma indignantly exclaimed:

"Just look at that dog, Arthur – he's back again!" And once more, he would be banished to the scullery.

At about ten to nine every night, before Grandpa 'made the back up', he would say loudly "Lav-a-toree, Mickey," and Mickey would go at once to the back door to be let out. He would return promptly at 9.00 pm just before the door was locked for the night.

There was a clothless table in the scullery, on which, Grandma would clean chickens. I saw her once bring six eggs in various stages of development, from one such bird.

"This poor creature should never have been killed, she had a lot of laying time left."

Here, on this table, Grandma also prepared her wonderful sherry trifles, her Sally Lunn cakes, her weekly batches of parkin, tea-cakes and scones, to say nothing of her Yorkshire puddings, made as only a Yorkshire woman knows how. They would rise all airy-fairy, and were always eaten with blood-juice gravy before the roast beef came on. Food was stored in the big larder which opened off the scullery – you could walk right into it. There were four deep shelves containing all manner of comestibles in big white earthenware jars, pots and pots of homemade strawberry and raspberry jam, bottled plums, and on the stone floor, great containers of pickled eggs. There were marble slabs with butter and cheese on them and a big meat safe.

All the aforementioned rooms were downstairs in Primrose Bank, but above, the house, although quieter and perhaps less interesting, was still, for me, very much alive. Here, was a place to be alone, to think, to tell myself stories and to act them out in the high-ceilinged rooms empty of daytime people. At the head of the stairs was a short passage leading to the back of the house. This we called the lower landing. Opening off it were – the loo on the right, the bathroom on the left, and the maids' pantry. The loo at Primrose Bank was quite something – known to the family as 'the Throne Room', it really deserved its name. You stepped up to be seated on a highly polished wooden seat, but the 'Throne' itself was really splendid. Festoons of beautifully painted pink roses and green leaves looped and twirled together all over the pan, both inside and out, and if, after pulling the china-handled chain, you gazed into the depths of this decorative lavatory, the roses would seem to come alive, dancing gracefully for you until the water level settled down once more.

When I came out of the 'Throne Room', I would often slide my back down the wall and sit in silent contemplation against the loo door, gazing long and wonderingly, at a picture on the opposite wall. I wish I knew what happened to that picture after all Grandma and Grandpa's furniture had been sold when they were forced to leave Primrose Bank, years later. I have never come across its like again. It was in a very long, narrow frame, almost a frieze. I think it was called, 'Going to the Races'. Colourful ladies in poke bonnets and fantastically feathered hats waved scarves and handkerchiefs out of overladen coaches; gentlemen in top hats and tight trousers, spurred on their ballerina-horses; pedlars, tinkers, tramps, gypsies and blowsy-looking women in donkey carts, streamed across my field of vision. They were all moving in one direction, all straining and bending their bodies forwards almost at right angles. A common purpose was spurring them on to some destination beyond the left hand framework of the picture, for in that direction presumably, lay Newmarket. They were an eager, motley crew, and the wind was behind them, it was going to the races with them, catching at their coat tails and their skirts, it propelled them forwards, bowling them along in a dust of broken twigs and flying leaves. My most vivid memory about this picture is that of the old, white-haired man. There he sat, in the foreground on a rickety chair, with his back to the viewer, as he watched the passing scene. Attached to the leg of his chair by a rope secured around her waist was a small girl in a long white dress and baby bonnet. She looked about three years old and I knew she was his grand-daughter. She also was trying to go to the races. She was straining with the rest of them as hard as she could towards the left-hand border, but she had reached to the end of her tether and the frustration was showing clearly on her face.

On the other side of the wall where the picture used to hang, lay the bathroom. Its most notable features were the lino with its dramatically large black and white squares, and a beautiful towel rail made of burnished copper piping, designed to keep towels warm and dry at all times. The latter must have been quite 'avant-garde', when Grandpa first had it installed. In the 1920s, Charlie, Tommy and I were not overfond of washing, and sometimes, when we went to see Grandma, she would open her arms to us, saying, "Come and kiss your Grandma, love,"; when we responded and she felt she had us in her power, she would demand to 'look down our chimneys', her word for 'ears', and if she found them to be full of soot, she would remove us to the bathroom for 'a clean sweep', as she put it. Apart from enforced visits, I tended to give the bathroom as wide a berth as possible.

The lower landing was joined to the upper landing, which was at the front of the house, by three shallow steps. Here was a lovely place to be silent and to dream dreams. Directly above the hall, it was wide and very light, for there was a tall window at the far end of it, over the front door. There I would sit by the hour on the broad window-ledge, gazing at the patterned carpet, which glowed yellow and red in the weak Manchester sunlight. The big square space became a prairie of waving corn. I would leave my castle on the window-ledge and ride across it to the foreign lands which lay beyond. I would visit each bedroom in turn, conquering its domain, making it my own.

Grandma and Grandpa's bedroom was the finest of them all. It was directly over the dining-room and of the same size. The heavy mahogany furniture was well made and expensive-looking. The full length mirrors in the wardrobe doors, sparkled with reflected light, and the dressing-table with its towers and turrets and ornamental scrolls, was yet another castle to be invaded. The huge double bed had a feather mattress, which, once shaken and turned, billowed forth like the sail of some lofty Spanish galleon, running before the wind. Grandma loved a soft bed. I have seen her sink into the depths of this one until only the top of her lace-trimmed boudoir cap remained visible – that is – until Grandpa, in his night shirt, leapt in on the far side and Grandma bounced into view again. I remember sleeping in this room, in a special cot of my own, drawn up alongside their big bed. My father obtained his BSc degree when I was just four years old, and he and my mother went to London together for the presentation ceremony, leaving me at Primrose Bank. The cot was brought down from the attics and cleaned ready for my occupation. It was of intricate wrought iron work in beautiful flower and scroll patterns – all painted in a brilliant white. Delicately balanced, it hung between two slender uprights and swung gently to and fro at the touch of a finger. It had cradled each of Grandma's children in turn. I was really too large for it, but I begged, and my grandparents indulged me.

Grandma always had beautiful, white lace, hand-made duchesse sets for her dressing-table. Standing on a silver tray, sparkling and reflecting in the swing mirror above them, were silver-backed brushes and combs and an assortment of silver-topped scent bottles, powder bowls and hair tidies. Her dressing-table drawers, chests of drawers and wardrobe were jam-packed with all manner of garments. Grandma could throw nothing away! Here, my naughty cousin Charlie would go 'rooting', trying on anything which took his fancy. On one occasion, he came across Grandma's 'transformation'. I suppose that today, it would be called a hair piece. Grandma's hair was thinning and the transformation was meant to add a certain 'bouffant' look to her coiffure. Charlie was mystified, and mistaking it for some form of masculine equipment, he came downstairs and made a dramatic appearance before us all, wearing it attached to his chin as a false beard.

Of the other three bedrooms which were not so grand as Grandma's, the back room over the kitchen – occupied by Uncle Jimmy, and therefore forbidden territory to me – had, at one time, belonged to my great-grandmother, Eleanor Hellawell. Her husband, whom, I believe, had been the first keeper of Armleigh Jail in Leeds, had died in 1873, and I don't know at what stage in her life after this event, she had come to live with Grandma and Grandpa. Like Grandma, she was a Yorkshire woman through and through, having passed many years in a little village in the Aire Valley. After her fall down the cellar steps at Primrose Bank, she had passed most of her time in this back bedroom. She died in 1919, so that I never knew her, but I still have her photograph, treasured by my mother and passed on to me, the photograph of a very old lady sitting up in bed with a shawl over her head. My father would often sit with her in her room. He loved to hear her stories of days long past, concerning the folk of the Aire Valley. He used to say what a grim picture she painted of life in those days, of the poverty and suffering caused each winter by the terrible floods in the deep, steep-sided valley. She knew the names of all Queen Victoria's children and all the ramifications of her family tree. She had a little mouse which would visit her in bed at night to share her supper-time biscuits. Grandpa set a trap, but Great-grandma and the mouse, managed to outwit him. She died at a great age in this back bedroom. She had outlived all of her children except Grandma. My mother, who was with her, told me that just before she died, she came out of a deep coma, smiled in recognition and greeted her husband and each of her dead children, calling them by name, just as though she were meeting them again after a very long time! I have no personal memories of her, but I keep her photograph carefully, and I have also of hers, a delicate china cup and saucer which she used daily, a black silk apron, embroidered with flowers and lace edging, which she wore in the afternoons before she became bed-ridden, and an affectionate letter in faded brown spidery writing, thanking my mother and father, who were away on holiday, for 'the dear sweet violets' which they had packed and sent to her. All these, I treasure.

I remember waking one Christmas morning in the room opposite to Grandma's room. I think Grandma must have had a houseful that Christmas, since I had to share the big bed with my parents. Hanging at each end of the bed rail were; a sock belonging to my father, stuffed to capacity with all kinds of nonsensical gifts, including one of mine to him, a tin toy train; a long black woollen stocking belonging to my mother, rather under-stuffed, and dangling eerily, but, in the middle between them, hung, not a sock, not a stocking, not a pillow-case, but a bolster case, and it was mine, and it was full to the brim!

The remaining bedroom which opened off the upper landing, lay over the morning-room. It holds one memory only for me, and that not entirely a happy one. Again, I woke in a big double bed, sandwiched between my mother and my father. It was early morning, and Mickey was scratching and howling at the door. He made such a noise, that both my parents were awakened. I started to climb out of bed, but my mother pulled me back.

"You're not going to let him in here, he'll jump all over us." With that, she turned over and went back to sleep, and my father was fast asleep again already. Mickey was whimpering now, so pathetically, that I longed to comfort him. Stealthily, I managed to slide out of bed without waking either of my parents. I would just creep outside and sit with my arms around him until he was comforted. I opened the door a crack, and Mickey, in one delighted bound hurled himself against it. I fell backwards onto the bedroom floor. Mickey leapt on to the bed, and prancing up and down in feverish excitement, he lavishly licked my mother's face and playfully bit my father's nose and at the same time, he left ace-of-club patterns from the garden mud on his paws, all over the white crocheted counterpane. Both he and I were in disgrace for the rest of the day.

Half way up the last flight of stairs to the attics, there was a mysterious door. It lead to the tank room and the loft. I never saw any one of the adults go in there, and on the one occasion that Charlie, Tommy and I managed to get the door open, Charlie alone, had the nerve to penetrate further. Tommy and I hung back. It was completely dark inside and there was a howling noise coming from its depths as if a great wind were perpetually blowing through the rafters. In fact, I think there must have been a gale inside, for as we opened the door, lumps of dust and grit flew into our eyes and up our noses! Charlie didn't stay inside for very long. When he reappeared, his person and his clothes were completely black and he seemed to be festooned with cobwebs. I don't think he ever went to the tank room again. I suppose he thought that it wasn't worth the scrubbing which he was later forced to endure.

Beyond the tank room, the stairs made a right angled turn and went on up to the attics. Here, were two large rooms full of the dusty junk of ages; curtainless, carpetless, but a paradise for 'rooters'. Once, when all Grandma and Grandpa's children were young and living at home together with Great-grandma Hellawell and two live-in maids, the attics had been used as bedrooms. One of them came into use again in the early 1930s when Uncle Tom's chicken farm at Brize Norton had been closed down. He, together with Aunty Katie and Joan and Phil, came to live at Primrose Bank. By that time, my parents and I had moved to Torquay, but we came back once or twice to visit Grandma and Grandpa before they left Primrose Bank for good. It was on one of these occasions that I shared an attic bedroom with my cousin Joan. There was a picture of The Laughing Cavalier on one of the walls. Every night before we undressed, Joan would cover it completely with an old vest. "His eyes follow you everywhere!" she would complain. We were beginning to grow up.

It was Grandma and Grandpa who made Primrose Bank into such a warm and welcoming house. None of my cousins who knew it, has ever forgotten it. Even Bryan who was very young when our grandparents were forced to leave it for good, has quite vivid memories of it. As for me, my life in Manchester centred on it, and the first Christmas after we had moved to Torquay in 1931, I realised what I had lost. I can remember crying on that Christmas Day bitterly and secretly, for a time and a way of life which had gone from me forever.

3

61 BELGRAVE ROAD, NEW MOSTON

Each spring the caterpillars came in droves. Whole armies of them marched at speed in animated loops of vivid yellow, stripy green and furry brown. Each tail pushing forwards its own head, each body converting into an agonised arch as on they went, on and up, until every tree which lined the pavements along Belgrave Road was alive with moving threads of never-ending colour. I first became aware of the caterpillars shortly after we had moved in during the early summer of 1923. I was three, allowed to play in the front garden, but forbidden to go beyond the gate of our new house, yet since there was a tree right outside, the agitated bands of brightness soon caught my attention. I watched and watched with a wondering fascination, and as I watched, for the first time that I can remember, the realisation of my own identity dawned on me and began to grow within me. I suddenly knew that these brilliant creatures were separate entities; were living their lives apart from mine in their own way; that theirs, not mine, was the urgent need to climb the tree trunk, to reach high leafy branches. Ideas came then thick and fast bringing comparisons with them for the very first time. Mine was the superior strength, mine was the ability to thwart their drive, mine the superiority of mind and body, mine the power. In a split second, I had depressed the latch on the gate. I would show these moving beads of colour, how I felt. I stood outside on the pavement. Two small steps and I stretched out my arm, brushing my hand along the tree trunk which felt rough and crusty to the touch. Immediately, about a dozen caterpillars fell to the ground. They curled into tight little balls around the bole and didn't move. Perhaps they would taste as nice as they looked. Curious, I bent to pick them up. At that moment, my mother called, and suddenly conscious that I was on the wrong side of the gate, I ran in quickly, forgetting to close it behind me.

After the episode of the caterpillars, every day brought a new awareness of myself in relation to my immediate surrondings, and with them came a memory; the first, I suppose, I ever had, or rather, ever remember having. It was so strange and so vivid, that it has stayed with me all through my life. When I was three, I accepted it utterly and completely without question, neither did I look upon it as anything out of the ordinary. I knew without doubt that it had happened to me sometime between my birth and the age that I then was. I remembered lying in a wooden cradle, a low, dark, close-to-the-floor, hooded cradle, with rockers at each end, and the next thing which I remember is that I had left the cradle and was hovering at the head of a dim staircase about two feet up from the ground. Then I started to descend, flying on my stomach, arms outstretched, my long white nightgown streaming out behind me, as I floated slowly, slowly, towards the bottom step. There was a panelled wall on my right, and I could see the dark sections going past as if in slow motion. That was all; I never reached the bottom, but that I had flown, I was quite sure, I remembered it so vividly. When I was three I sensed that somewhere in my recent past I had lost an ability which would never return to me but it didn't prevent me from trying to recapture it by jumping off walls which were too high for me, and all through my childhood, taking tremendous leaps into the air, even succeeding in making a step in mid-flight!

I grew, awareness grew, and in the year before I started school, impressions came thick and fast, deep and lasting. First, the front garden. A green pocket handkerchief surrounded by a border of dirty-leaved privet, which in the summer time, gave off a sickly smell from its tiny white flowers. It was a prison-hedge, blocking my view from anything beyond. Then there was the house itself; although

I lived there for four years, only one or two parts of it are clear to me now. I have an overall impression of semi-darkness. The trees in Belgrave Road must have been very leafy and tall and kept much light from the front rooms. It was mid-terrace – probably Edwardian with a dark narrow passage leading from front to back. Sitting-room and dining-room, one behind the other, opened into this passage and on the opposite side, the stairs went straight up from it, with no bends, twists or turns.

We had a piano in one of these two living-rooms where Father would sometimes play in the evenings, especially on a Sunday if we did not go to Primrose Bank. I hated the playing. Music, if it wasn't lively, affected me badly, and unlike Grandma and Grandpa and Aunty Gertie, my parents seemed to sing such sad songs; songs with a Sunday flavour, duets in a minor key about shipwrecks and people dying of consumption. I would look out of the window – the street would be deserted – the Sunday look, no one anywhere – empty, empty, and the sound of the church bells just added to my desolation. I would sit down on the hearth-rug and weep, but Mother and Father took no notice, so absorbed were they with their music and with each other.

I remember being carried into the dining-room on the first Christmas morning after we arrived at Belgrave Road, and there it was! The first Christmas tree of which I have any memory at all. I thought I had never seen anything so beautiful before. It wasn't illuminated, there were no fairy lights, and by today's standards it was probably very unpretentious, but there was such a wealth of tinsel, shining coloured balls and little packets and parcels all done up in brown paper and string, that it made me gasp with delight. The dining-room is also connected in my mind with birthday parties, with jellies and blancmange and homemade meringues. I remember one party in particular. The food had been eaten, the table cleared and pushed back against the wall and the room was full of noisy shouting children, running about in rather an aimless manner, when my father suddenly arrived home from school. He stood in the doorway, looking at us all. As we became aware of him, silence fell, and without saying a word, he had become the focus of our attention.

"Well now," he said into the silence, "which of you likes apples?"

"I do, I do," half a dozen hands went up.

"Here you are then, catch," and from his right-hand coat pocket he took a handful of tiny rubber balls. Smaller than the Christmas tree balls had been, they were coloured with streaks of red and green, and very bouncy. He threw them into the centre of the room, and we children, shrieking with delight, leapt after them as they rebounded high into the air like live things. As soon as everyone had captured one of these treasures (my mother saw to a fair division), my father, who hadn't moved from his post at the door, continued; "And who likes oranges?" And the whole procedure was repeated, this time with yellowy-green balls issuing from his left-hand pocket.

We used the front room for very special occasions only – mostly when visitors came. One day, soon after our move to Belgrave Road, Grandma and Grandpa brought Aunt Elsie to see us. I had never met her before, and I never saw her again after that visit, but I never forgot her. She was Grandpa's sister-in-law. She had married his eldest brother George and lived at the family home in Worksop. She had come to Manchester on a visit and was staying at Primrose Bank. Aunt Elsie was noted in the family for her sharp observations and forthright opinions which she never kept to herself. The adults were all talking together when I came running in and stopped dead in the doorway. All eyes turned towards me. The strange lady was very tall. She came over and stared down at me – quite an awesome figure dressed all in black. As she bent her head and put her face close to mine, I was conscious of two enormous gob-stopper hat pins and a black feather Boa which wound round her neck and descended down the front of her coat to my level. She didn't kiss me, she just stared.

"Well," she said, after a long inspection. "You're no beauty are you?" She unbent and turned to my mother. "Really Lily, I would have thought you could have done better than this!"

Everyone laughed politely, but I think my mother must have been very put out, and I was puzzled. Needing the statement to be elucidated, I asked Grandma when later we were alone together.

"I'm no beauty, am I?"

"You're Grandma's Little Pink," she answered, putting her arms around me.

"I'm no beauty, am I?" I asked Grandpa when he was cleaning the silver at Primrose Bank.

"Handsome is as handsome does," came the reply, as Grandpa polished away never taking his eyes off Grandma's best teapot.

I would climb onto a stool, kneel up, put both elbows onto my mother's highly polished dressing-table and gaze into the swing mirror, "I'm no beauty, am I?"

"If you don't stop looking at yourself in the mirror, one day you'll see Old Nick peering over your shoulder," said my mother. I gazed the longer, hoping to make acquaintance with the mysterious Old Nick, but he never materialised, and I remained puzzled and somehow disappointed.

The front room was the scene of many stories either read to me, or told to me by my father who was a wonderful raconteur. Here, he would read *Black Beauty* by the hour and I would laugh happily at the antics of Merrilegs, or cry silently over the unhappy fate of Ginger as he was carted away, a desolate corpse for the knacker's yard. Here, seated in the best armchair, my father would tell me the 'Betty and William' stories. These started long before I went to school and continued for several years. The two children were complete figments of my father's imagination. He had created them specially for me. Day by day, I grew with them and I don't think he realised just to what extent I had become absorbed in their lives. Each evening I would wait for Father to come home from school, and after he and Mother had greeted each other, he would take off his coat, I would seize his hand and lead him into the front room eager for another chapter in the adventures of this highly entertaining couple. Whilst Mother was preparing the tea in the kitchen, I would sit on his knee and drink in his every word.

One evening, just before we left the Belgrave Road house for good, a terrible thing happened which I have never forgotten. My father killed Betty and William! Whether he thought I was getting too old to be told stories, and should be encouraged to read more for myself, whether he was running out of ideas, or whether he had too much on his mind with our impending move and was just bored with the whole procedure, I shall never know. The fact remains, he killed them off. He drowned them. They went out in a rowing boat on a river, their craft was caught in a current, overturned and they were swept out to sea. In spite of William's noble efforts to save himself and his sister, their bodies were cast up on the shore the very next day.

"And that," said my father, "is the end of Betty and William."

"Go on," I urged, "what happened next?"

"Nothing . . . they're dead!" The finality was horrible, the shock was frightening. I leapt from his knee and fled into the kitchen. I buried my face in my mother's apron.

"They're dead, they're dead, Betty and William, they're dead," I wailed. My mother looked over my head at my father who had appeared in the kitchen doorway.

"Oh Sam, you didn't," she said.

I turned my head hopefully to look at him, expecting him to revive them in some way, but all he said was, "Yes I did and the funeral is to be tomorrow."

"Will you go?" I asked tearfully, hoping that he would be able to tell me about it the following evening.

"I'm afraid not. I have to be at school all day long. I have lessons to give and a staff meeting to run – and in any case, only close relatives have been invited!"

I remember our kitchen at Belgrave Road very well. It was quite large, it formed our main living-room, and we all spent much time in it. It had a range, with ovens on each side of the grate which my mother used to blacklead two or three times a week. On one side of the range was a sink. A plain wooden table with a top which could be scrubbed down, stood against one wall. There was a cheap, brown-painted chest of drawers with big wooden knobs for handles, and in its bottom drawer, I was allowed to keep my toys. There was an assortment of non-matching chairs. One of these was an old-fashioned rocking chair on which my father and I would often sit together in front of the fire in the evening just before my bedtime. I would perch on his knee whilst he would either sing to me or tell me stories, rocking gently all the time. One night, however, the song must have been particularly lively and the rocking grew more and more vigorous. We were laughing and singing together and rocking faster and faster until suddenly, the old chair could stand no more of it. All four legs splayed outwards and gave way simultaneously. Down we went. I fell softly, cushioned by my father. Fortunately, he also fell lightly and did not hurt himself, but the look of surprise on each of our faces was something really worth seeing, according to my mother who had come into the room at the precise moment of our downfall.

It was in the kitchen, that my mother caught fire! One morning, just before I had started going to school, she was busy clearing away the empty breakfast dishes, when it happened! Normally, between ourselves and the burning coals, there was a high, wire-mesh fireguard with a brass topped rail around it, but on this particular morning, it had, for some reason been moved aside and as my mother turned quickly to collect the plates from the table, the apron strings which tied her pinafore at the waist, floated outwards towards the fire and were suddenly ignited. As she carried the crockery to the sink, her back was towards me. I sat at the table and watched entranced as two thin and wavering flames began to climb up her pinafore. Then she turned towards me again and made to pick up more dirty dishes. I laughed, "There's a fire going up your back," I announced.

"All right I know when you're having me on," and she laughed with me.

"But there is, I can see it," I persisted.

With that, she turned her head sharply and caught sight of the flames which by this time were growing quite big, to say nothing of the smoke and smell of scorching material. She panicked and did the worst and the best thing possible. She rushed out into the open air shouting, "Sam, Sam." My father, on his way to work, had just left the house, had crossed the backyard and was at that moment closing the back gate behind him. I stood in the kitchen doorway and watched the scene with great interest. In two bounds, he had turned, reached mother, pulled the halter-necked pinafore over her head, and with great gusto, stamped out the flames on the stone flags! Mother flung her arms round his neck and wept with relief whilst I jumped up and down with the excitement of it all!

Our mangle was kept in the wash-house at the end of the backyard. All through my childhood, mangles (as a direct result of having witnessed a strange happening in connection with one of them), held a certain fascination for me. At one of the wonderful Manchester pantomimes, to which I was taken annually from a very early age, I once saw a man fed into a mangle. He was Wishee-Washee's son, who had fallen head first into the wicked Baron's dung cart. After he had been fished out, his mother had hosed him down on the stage, and then put him through the mangle! He came out on the far side of the rollers – a flat board, but a complete replica of himself, even down to his shoe-laces. His mother then pegged him out on the line to dry alongside all the Baron's smalls! I suppose I was hoping for some sort of repeat performance, for I was always to be found in the wash-house whenever there was any mangling to be done. If my father were about, he would help Mother with the big linen sheets and the heavy white honey-combed bedspreads. He would turn the great iron handle as she fed them into the wooden rollers. The bed clothes would appear on the far side, squashed and flattened, just as Wishee-Washee's son had been, but in this case, there was an added attraction, for great chutes of water would cascade into the tin bath beneath the ribbed resting tray which received all mangled remains!

The wash-house held other delights for me, apart from the mangle. In spite of it being a damp smelling, comfortless place, I always found something to interest me there. Apart from the big sink and boiler, there was a dolly-tub complete with 'dolly' standing by. On wash days, my mother would soak the clothes in the dolly-tub. If I balanced on my toes, I could just see over the top as the Blue-Bag went in and the water magically turned colour. Working the 'dolly', said my mother, always took it out of her. I would wait until she had finished slaving and the 'dolly' was removed and put to one side. Then I would leap upon it and, mounted on the little circular platform above the three legs at its base, whilst holding on to the crossbar at the top, I would jump my way across the wash-house floor.

Completely exposed to view, in one corner of the wash-house, was a lavatory pan with a white-wood seat, a high flush cistern, and long chain and handle. The Edwardian architect who had designed the Belgrave Road terraces, must have been in sympathy with the working-class housewife of his day. Knowing full well how many steaming hours she was expected to spend in her wash-house pouring over her boiler to the constant accompaniment of the sounds of running water, he had catered for her bodily needs accordingly. The curious thing is that he had afforded her no privacy whatsoever in which to attend to them! His design had not allowed for a door on the wash-house, and even in the 1920s, his lavatory pan still lay exposed to all who passed by in the backyard.

Outside the backyard gate lay freedom – of a kind – for from here, I was allowed to leave the precincts of the house in order to cross the wide dirt lane which connected all the backyard gates. Here, on the other side of the lane, each house had its own extension in the form of a long, narrow strip of earth which we called the back garden. I soon learnt to leave our plot and to wander unsupervised up the lane, staring into other people's strips. It was interesting – such a varied collection of old sheds, dog kennels, some with chained occupants, and hen coops full of bright-eyed, tawny birds, with here and there, a magnificent and brilliantly hued creature moving amongst them.

Our next door neighbours had a very large shed which they had converted into a garage for their lorry. The two sons of the house were truck drivers and sometimes they drove away early in the morning, leaving the garage door wide open. I was intrigued by what I found within. Three huge blocks of ice, taller than I was, stood on the garage floor! So cold to touch, colder to lick; so clear and clean-looking, with strange linear patterns deep inside them. It never occurred to me to ask why there were miniature glaciers in next door's garage. Whenever I had the chance, I would inspect them. They melted very slowly; when they reached half size, they would disappear as if by magic and the next day, wonderful new, big ones would have taken their place.

We also had a large shed which we had inherited from the previous owners of 61 Belgrave Road. My father renovated and enlarged it, and then decided that the time had come to buy our first car! What excitement! We were celebrating – for Father, ever since my birth, had gone 'all out' to improve his position in the educational world, to bring in more money, and to make life easier for his little family. He had taught maths all day long, and for three evenings a week, he had stayed in Manchester after school and lectured at night school. At the weekends, he studied, working far into the night and now, at long last, his labours had been rewarded. He obtained his BSc from the University of London and shortly afterwards, he was offered the headship of a Building Trades' School in Manchester. So came about our 'first-ever' car, and there could have been no more wonderful way for any of us to mark the occasion of his successes.

The new car was a nine horsepower, chocolate brown Citroen. Father, who knew all about engines, had already inspected under its bonnet whilst Mother and I had prowled around its exterior. It had solid wheels and two wide running-boards which I jumped on and off several times just to test them. Its rear end was almost pointed and it looked to me, for all the world, like a friendly chocolate bumble-bee. The three of us stood now in a little cluster, gazing somewhat apprehensively at our latest acquisition.

"See if the seats are comfortable," invited the salesman. My parents got in and completely filled each of the two bucket seats. There was no room for me. The salesman closed the doors and erected the pram-like hood over them, and there they were, Mother and Father, in a world of their own. Cut off, left outside, I began to wonder, to be afraid.

"Where do I go?" I whispered, urgently tugging at the

salesman's trouser leg.

"Oh . . . You!" he looked down from a great height. "You sit in there." I looked in vain for a seat as he nodded indifferently to the pointed posterior of the car. I immediately concluded that I was to travel behind my mother and father battened down beneath the rear end of the bumble-bee. I burst into tears! My parents, laughing at my dismay, got out of the car. Father scooped me up in one arm, and with the other pulled a handle on a panel at the back of the vehicle. Wonderful, the panel was a box-lid. It opened out and a padded single seat complete with back rest came into view.

"There you are – that's where you sit. You didn't really think we'd shut you up inside did you?" He lifted me into the open box and I was happy again.

The next day the car was delivered and waiting for Father in the garage when he came home from school. Father had never learnt to drive, but with the help of a manual, he spent the next hour and a half happily backing it out of the shed and then driving it in again, until Uncle Bill Haydock arrived at six o'clock. Uncle Bill knew how to drive and had offered to teach Father. Off they went together, there and then. As there wasn't room for four of us in the car, and since I couldn't be left alone in the house, Mother and I stayed behind. Father was plunged in at the deep end. Uncle Bill made him drive straight away from our house, all along the Oldham Road, right through the centre of Manchester and then all around its outskirts. They came back triumphant two hours later, and Uncle Bill pronounced Father a proficient driver!

It was the start of the Easter holidays and my father was anxious to be 'on the road', so the very next day we set off for Barrow-in-Furness where my father's parents lived. It was a journey of a hundred miles! No driving test had to be taken, there were no motorways, no by-passes around the big towns, no traffic lights, no white lines or cat's-eyes, nothing to restrict us and little to help us for that matter – except long stretches of almost empty roads where we caught our breath and sighed with relief to have emerged unscathed from the hazards of our passage through Bolton, Blackburn, Preston, Lancaster and Carnforth. It took us all of six hours on that first long journey to reach Barrow, but we made it!

Oh the adventures we had in that little car! For my part, I became aware of a whole new world, a beautiful new world and one of which hitherto I had had no notion. Born in a city in the north of England, I had known only dirty and seemingly endless streets, rows of begrimed houses, scrubby gardens, sooty trees and slimy canals – but now, sitting aloft in the 'dicky', wrapped to the eyebrows in rugs and eiderdowns, my chest protected by an enormous wrap-over scarf, my hat clamped firmly on my head with another scarf and an elastic band, I was driven along scented roads between meadows rich in buttercups, past woods full of bluebells, up hills bordered by flowering hedgerows where wild roses twined amongst the blossoming hawthorn. We drove past tiny thatched cottages with latticed windows, and on the skyline the ruins of a great castle would sometimes appear. This was the country. I hadn't realised that it existed and I loved it with all my heart and with a love which has persisted until this day. Best of all was the space. Perched high, I could see forever – mile upon mile of green unbroken space, as on and on the little car bore us right to the edge of the world.

But, she was such a little car, and she sometimes found her load a bit too much for her. Then she would protest with a series of shuddering jerks. Sometimes, she would boil in fury and we were forced to stop wherever we were. My father would get out, and taking a glove which he kept for such occasions, he would open the bonnet, unscrew the radiator cap and leap clear. Boiling hot steam would eject high into the air with the hissing as of a hundred geese moving in to the attack. Such was the thrill of the moment, that I could never bear the suspense and inevitably threw the eiderdown over my head, rather than watch the volcano in eruption! At other times, the 'chocolate bee' would grow tired on very steep hills – more and more slowly she would crawl, with my father audibly coaxing her onwards.

"She's labouring, she's labouring," he would mourn.

Then she would stop altogether, and my mother, who was

a very well built lady, would be forced to get out and proceed uphill on foot. Father would turn the car round, put it into reverse gear and he and I would drive merrily backwards to the summit. I enjoyed this – I could wave to Mother as I watched her toiling along behind us, and the view was usually lovely.

Three months after we had bought the Citroen, Father announced during the summer holidays, that he had always wanted to see Land's End, that he felt it was a challenge which he must take. So off we went again and leaving Belgrave Road far behind us, we eventually arrived at our destination after many days on the road and not before we had been forced to spend the last night of the journey in a fisherman's cottage in Sennen Cove. It was growing dusk and we had failed to find accommodation anywhere along the main road. It was then that we were advised to seek out the fisherman. His dwelling proved to be right on the beach, at the bottom of the steepest hill we had up to that time ever encountered. Fortunately, his wife took us in, fed us and slept us three in a bed in the only upstairs room of the cottage, and it wasn't until the next morning that we realised just how steep a hill the little car had to tackle to get us out of the cove. My mother, carrying one of our two suitcases, was forced to walk the entire way. It was raining and I can see her now, good-humouredly traipsing along the empty road with a rug over her shoulders, an umbrella held aloft in one hand, the other clutching the travelling bag, whilst far below the wild Atlantic breakers beat against the walls of the fisherman's cottage.

In 1924 even the main roads were very quiet. I suspect nowadays, that the country folk must have resented the few noisy, smelly machines which rattled and jerked through their hitherto undisturbed villages. Certainly we noticed the surliness of farmers and their unwillingness to concede any part of the road to us. We soon learnt patience. If we were travelling in their direction, we would crawl along at a snail's pace behind a herd of cows or a flock of sheep which would completely block the road sometimes for half an hour at a time. When we met them coming towards us, Father would pull in to the side, turn off the engine and we would wait patiently until they had all lumbered past. I was scared of cows. The dicky seat was open to the road, and I felt vulnerable. One day, we encountered a particularly frisky and curious herd in the charge of a very aggressive cowman who, by hitting and shouting at his beasts, was inciting them to quite uncharacteristic behaviour. As they came galloping along the road towards us, we pulled in to the side and as usual stopped and waited. The leading cow reached the car and promptly sat down on the front, offside mudguard! My father was furious. He leapt out of his seat and tried to dislodge the offending animal. By this time, the other cows were all round the dicky seat. I sat bolt upright, petrified, frozen with fear as one young heifer took a fancy to my new summer hat. She approached warily, sniffing and slobbering and exuding an earthy, milky kind of smell. It was a pretty hat – no doubt she was attracted by its bright yellow-straw and band of vivid-blue cornflowers. Suddenly, she lifted her head and bit a piece out of the brim! I screamed and my mother bravely rushed to my rescue. She shooed the cow away by hitting it on the nose with her handbag and snatching the remains of my hat from my head, she waved it under the cowman's nose.

"Look what your cow has done to my daughter's hat!" she exploded. "Just look at that." And she brandished the ravished headgear in his face. "This hat cost two and sixpence in Lewises!"

The cowman was unmoved. He walked solidly onwards, chewing the cud with the rest of his herd. Neither my mother's anger nor my father's threats of court action disturbed him in the least. I was the only one to whom he spoke.

"Stop tha whining lass," he remarked in a toneless voice as he went past me. "Nobbut 'th'at's 'urt." And he went on his way, leaving us to expostulate over a dented mudguard and a badly bitten hat!

We kept the Citroen for a year or two after this event, but gradually, we began to outgrow it and to feel the need for a larger car. Since the hood covered only the two front seats, Mother would never allow me to travel in the 'dicky' if it was raining. She grew tired of changing places with me every time there was a shower, to say nothing of becoming soaked through in spite of the makeshift mackintosh canopy and the umbrella which she erected over herself and the exposed back seat. On one occasion, the umbrella blew away and we had to wait whilst Father dismounted and chased it down the road in a howling gale! So now, decided my parents, was the time for a new car, one in which I could travel with them inside, in shelter and safety, free from bovine attack; one large enough to take Grandma and Grandpa for a ride, and one which was strong enough to tackle all hills without having to shed some of its load en route. So, whilst we were still living at Belgrave Road, we said good-bye to the 'little chocolate bee', and we bought 'Clara'.

'Clara' was a Singer. My mother named it so after Clara Butt, whom she said, was well known in the musical world. Who was Clara Butt, and what she was like, I neither knew nor cared, but our Clara was big and busty, over twelve horse-power, with a tall grey body and a bulbous, ferreting nose. Suddenly, with the advent of the new car, motoring began to lose its thrill for me. I'm sure my parents were relieved to have me safely inside with them, but, for my part, I sorely missed the wind on my face, the sun in my eyes and the fly-past view over hedgerows and into cottage gardens. Clara had such tall sides, that unless I were seated on innumerable cushions, I could not see over the top, and kneeling up on the back seat, gazing out over the down-folded hood at the receding countryside, proved very tiring after a while. Worse, there were detachable windscreens all round. Their iron prongs slotted into holes at the top of the car's doors. Made of dirty yellow celluloid, they were about two feet high and obscured my view even further. When they split, which was frequently, we all had to suck special round gelatine tablets which, when thoroughly wet would adhere to the cracks and hold them together. It was all very messy. I became bored on long journeys and finished by taking along a pile of picture books to help me while away the time.

There was one compensation, however, in having a larger car. Sometimes we would take Aunty Gertie and Charlie and Tommy for a ride. We four would all squash together in the back and Aunty Gertie would tell us jokes and stories and sing and whistle to us. We would play 'I spy' and 'The Parson's

Cat', or yell in unison, *One Man and His Dog*, always followed by *Ten Green Bottles.* Aunty Gertie would even turn a blind eye when we three children would kneel up on the back seat and pull terrible faces over the top of the hood at any hapless motorist who might be following us. Charlie's faces were awful, he could pull down his eyes and push his nose upwards with his fingers further than any of us. Then, when Aunty Gertie was leaning forwards, engrossed in conversation with Mother in the front seat, we would hold a spitting competition to see if any one of us could score a direct hit over the back onto the windscreen of the following vehicle, but when one driver shook his fist at our car as he went past, my father realised what must have been happening and soon put a stop to it! But the outings with Aunty Gertie and my cousins were limited and I was destined never again to feel the real adventure of motoring until many years later when, for my seventeenth birthday, I was given my first Learner's Licence and my father taught me to drive, but even that never resulted in quite the same thrill as had my first sight of the English countryside in the early 1920s from the dicky seat of the nine horsepower chocolate-brown Citroen.

School! In the autumn of 1925 it loomed large on my horizon, and the day came when, holding tightly to my mother's hand I was led up Belgrave Road past the corner shop which sold aniseed balls, liquorice bootlaces and sherbet dabs, over an open space between houses and into a side road where big houses faced fields in which cows belonging to Mr Schofield's farm were grazing. At the bottom of this road we came out onto Moston Lane almost opposite one of the Manchester Board Schools which I came to know as New Moston Council School. My mother was all for private education and had begged for me to attend Miss Teggins establishment, but my father was adamant. He said that he had been right through the state system and could see no reason why his only child should not do the same. Neither parent considered my opinion, so there I was, on a chilly Monday morning, heading towards the Infants' Department with forty-nine other five year olds.

I quite enjoyed my first two years at school. It had its ups and downs, but on the whole, there were many more ups than downs. I enjoyed the company. I must have been naturally gregarious, and being an only child, I was probably 'hungry' for friends of my own age. Then, there were the pictures – bright and colourful and everywhere. Big shiny cut-outs were on the walls, full-page illustrations in the books, huge drawings on the blackboard – a different one awaited us each morning, coloured transfers on each tiny chair and even on our cloakroom pegs (mine was a hen). There were toys placed on a corner shelf, to be taken down only when permission was given. There they sat – each toy under its own name, printed large so that we soon learnt to spell it, and until we could do so, we were never allowed to touch 'teddy' or 'dolly' or 'train' or 'car'. Another wonderful memory is of the swing. We none of us noticed it at first, then, one day just before 'home time', our teacher went into the far corner of the big classroom and untied a looped rope and down into the middle of the room fell a little rounded armchair made of wood with a wooden bar across the front of it. It didn't reach the ground, but dangled on two chains just above our heads. We watched entranced, we sat up straight with folded arms whilst the first of our number was chosen, lifted into the seat, secured by the bar, told to 'hold on'. He was then carried backwards as far as the chains would stretch – the teacher let go, gave a push and launched him into space. Right across the room and back again he flew to be carefully removed and replaced by the next in line. By the time it was my turn, I was in a state of almost inebriated excitement. The realisation proved just as thrilling as the anticipation. Soaring above the upturned faces of my small companions, I was reliving the memory of my dream; I was flying again. But it was all too short lived. Suddenly, with a violent jerk, I was down to earth. I was twisting and swinging slowly a few feet from the floor and the teacher was lifting me out of the chair! I resisted. I clung to the chains. My fingers were prised off. I clung to the sides of the chair.

"Another one, another one – please."

The teacher laughed. "Everyone may have just one swing each," she said, kindly, but firmly, and then, because she was a wise teacher, she told me why. "If I let you have more, everyone would want more and it would be long after 'home time' before we had all had a turn. We should all be late out of school, now wouldn't we?" In the face of such reasoning, I reluctantly let go and allowed myself to be lifted down.

We wrote on slates with a thin all-lead type of crayon and rubbed out with a rag which we dipped into a big communal jar of water, or used spit if we were in a hurry. I loved it all and could soon read and write, say the alphabet phonetically at great speed, skip and dance in time, to *Oranges and Lemons*, or *The Big Ship Sails on the Alley Alley O*, but I was no good at singing. Always off key and always on one note which I chose at the beginning of the song, and although the others went up and down, I remained solidly where I was. Another disappointment was 'numbers'. We learnt to count by moving highly coloured beads along wires inside a wooden framework. It was all very lively and enjoyable until one day, the frames were not given out and we were required to write two numbers on our slates and add them together. Confidently, I did this.

"Who has the answer? Hands up."

I had it before anyone else. My hand shot up. I gave the answer, and it was wrong! I shall never forget the sensations which flowed over me in rapid succession. Utter amazement; complete disbelief; strong dislike – first for the teacher for saying I was wrong, secondly for any of the others who were right and finally for 'numbers' themselves which had let me down so badly. I never really trusted 'numbers' again after that and they have continued to mislead me right up to the present day.

After a year in the 'babies', I moved up into Miss Britten's class. Miss Britten had what it took to make every child love her – and I was no exception. We flourished, we grew. Tiny tables gave way to small double desks; slates and crayons to ruled exercise books and pencils, but we still danced and sang, listened to stories, learnt poems, read aloud and chanted our one-times, two-times tables, now reaching seven times! I gained confidence but no discretion – at six, it's hard to come by. One morning after prayers, our headmistress was giving her usual little pep talk before dismissing us.

"Children," she said, addressing all one hundred of us. "You must never, never jump off a tram-car whilst it is moving. It is a very dangerous thing to do and you could be badly hurt." My hand flew up. "Well, Beryl?"

"It's quite all right. You can do it. My Daddy always does it and he is never hurt."

One morning, when the infants were again at prayers, eyes closed, hands folded together, there came a knocking at the outer door. The headmistress continued to busy herself with our devotions, but I opened my eyes and saw my teacher creep out to answer the summons. Then I heard my mother's voice.

"We have come to see if you need help with the children in case any of the staff couldn't get through this morning. The trams have stopped running and Manchester is cut off now!"

It was 1926. The General Strike was escalating. It seemed that our two lorry-driving neighbours had arrived back home at nine o'clock, cut and shaken. A stone had been thrown through their windscreen, their way had been blocked, they had been called 'Blacklegs', and so they had retreated and brought back a graphic account of frozen services and angry mobs in the streets. My mother had at once gathered a posse of women and marched to school. Although their offer was declined as all our teachers were present, I think Mother felt that she had done her bit.

For two years I was happy and making reasonable progress in the little tin and wood building at the bottom of the 'big-school' playground. Then, suddenly, everything changed. After the summer holidays of 1927, I returned to school and was immediately absorbed into a particularly bleak and soulless system. My mother took me through a gate in the high iron railings towards the forbidding red brick establishment. She pushed open a door, thrust me through it and would have followed, but was turned back by an official 'on duty'. Unfortunately, I had heard tales of the goings on in Standard I of the big school. Apparently, it was in the charge of an extremely severe teacher who was out to 'lick 'em into shape'. The children were frightened of her, and one child in particular, so much so, I had heard it whispered when grown-ups thought I wasn't listening, that she had to be removed from school suffering with St Vitus Dance. The old question of Miss Teggins' establishment had come up again during the holidays and caused much argument between my parents, but as usual, Father had his way, and here I was, back again at New Moston Board School, only this time in the big school, very frightened as to what might happen to me – and my fears were not unfounded. From the very first day, I hated that 'big school'.

My mother had left me just inside the Girls' Cloakroom door. The official disappeared and a small group of us from the Infants' stood huddled and bewildered where our mothers had been forced to abandon us. The cloakroom was filled with what seemed to me to be very big, noisy children. Suddenly they were all round us. We were punched and pinched – our hats were snatched from our heads and thrown or kicked over the tops of the pegs. No one allotted any one of us a peg and I can't think why we didn't turn tail and run. Eventually, from somewhere far away, a whistle was blown – silence fell and a fierce looking 'girl' bore down upon us. I was astounded to learn that she was Standard I's teacher. She barked out orders at us.

"Get into line. Answer your names. Not 'Yes', 'Yes Miss', anyone who forgets the 'Miss' will be slapped!" Her hair was Eton Cropped, she wore her skirt high above her knees and her waist-band round her bottom. On her feet were patent leather shoes, black and shiny with overstraps and very pointed toes. Her stockings were of light coloured lisle. She arrived at school every morning on a racing bike with dropped handle bars. I can't remember her ever smiling at us and I think she disliked us as much as we came to dislike her.

She taught us almost every subject in our curriculum. Forty of us – lost in double desks, we spent much time with arms folded, or hands on heads chanting poetry, tables, historical dates, geographical facts, school rules, anything which took her fancy – and woe betide anyone whose attention strayed! I managed to avoid corporal punishment for some time by making myself as insignificant as possible, until one day I was called out in front of the class and shaken hard for some misdemeanour which I cannot recollect. I do remember, however, the horrible feeling of my head falling uncontrollably backwards and then jerking forwards again until I felt sure something was about to snap. I very quickly lost any confidence I had gained in the 'Infants', so that I became poor at almost everything and it was soon evident that I was completely hopeless at anything practical. I was labelled as 'clumsy', and my almost constant state of fear did nothing to rectify this.

One afternoon, we were given a pair of scissors and a square of paper – brightly coloured on one side, sticky on the other. We were shown once, and once only, how to cut the paper, lick the sticky edges and join them together to make a box. We were told to get on with it! I hadn't a clue. I fumbled about trying to look purposeful – trying to copy my neighbour who meanly put her arm protectively around her paper so that I couldn't see a thing, and all the time I could feel our teacher's eyes upon me. Suddenly, she came striding down the gangway between the desks, walked past me, stopped, turned and stood behind me for a few seconds. I knew she was looking over my shoulder. I knew I was 'in for it'. My hands trembled, my tummy turned over, and then it happened. She thumped me several times in the back with her doubled fist, calling me clumsy, stupid and inattentive. Tears of pain and humiliation came into my eyes. I tried hard not to let them flow, especially when my unpleasant neighbour whispered, "You're crying aren't you?"

Mother kept a zinc bath-tub in the wash-house and every Friday night it was brought into the house so that I could have my weekly bath under supervision in front of the kitchen fire. That Friday evening, a day after the thumping, my bruises had come out good and proper. My back was black and blue! Mother noticed it for the first time and was horrified. She called my father, and after much questioning and many tears on my part, the story came out. In the middle of Monday morning, my father stormed into school. Our teacher was summoned to the Headmaster's study where she was confronted by both Father and the Headmaster. Many years later, Father told me what had happened.

Apparently he had managed to frighten her thoroughly. I expect he used 'The Look' on her, whilst pointing out the error of her ways, and after wiping the floor with her, left her with the final threat that if ever she laid a hand on his child again, he would personally report her to Mr Spurley Hey, the Director of Education for Manchester, with whom he was well acquainted. I knew nothing of all this at the time except that, although she never touched me again, I was 'got at' in much more subtle ways which I didn't recognise then, but which now, in hindsight, I feel sure were calculated to be hurtful.

For instance, immediately after this episode, an innovation was made in our usual classroom routine. Every morning we still had to copy six sums off the blackboard, work out the answers and then mark them according to the correct figures which were read out to us, but whereas before we had marked our own work, now we were required to change books with our neighbours, since our teacher had announced that she was sure there was cheating going on. She wasn't wrong either – we were nearly all of us cheating. Now, however, the possibilities were fewer and when the usual order came for anyone with three or more sums wrong to stand on the seats of their desks and await punishment, many more children than previously, climbed shakily aloft. Our teacher then came round with the cane and we received one stroke on the hand for each incorrect sum. So far, by fair means or foul, I had managed to escape the canings but now there was no escape; I awaited my turn with the rest. 'Miss' worked her way round the class with obvious enjoyment at having caught so many more poor fish in her net. I braced myself as she came nearer, but when she reached me, all she said was "You sit down, I'm not allowed to touch you." This special treatment made me very unpopular with my classmates and I began to feel isolated as well as frightened.

Again, a strange thing happened at the end of the first term. There was to be a special exhibition of work and two of the best modellers from each class were to be chosen. They were to miss all lessons, to sit at special desks in the hall and to make models from Plasticine all day long. Imagine my surprise when from our class, I was one of the two chosen! I had no desire to be chosen and couldn't understand why I had been singled out for special treatment. Now, at this late day, I can think of several reasons. I was hopeless at anything practical and couldn't model for toffee, as everyone including our teacher well knew. However, there I sat for a whole week, from 9.00 am until 4.00 pm with a break only at dinner-time. The 'modellers' were not even allowed out at playtime. I achieved nothing. Whilst my fellow modellers created little masterpieces including a farm with every sort of domestic animal imaginable, I tried to model boats and trees, but at the end of each day had produced nothing except a long Plasticine sausage! Eventually a teacher from another class took pity on me and more or less made my boat for me. At long last, it was over, and bored out of my mind, I was almost glad to be able to rejoin Standard I.

During the next term there was another seemingly inexplicable incident. Sometimes, on fine days, we were taken into the playground for drill. On this particular occasion the girls in our class joined forces with the big girls from Standard VI and we were all drilled by our teacher. Towards the end of the session we played a game which seemed very exciting to us little ones. It was called 'Flying Fairies'. The big girls made two lines and faced each other, joining both hands with their opposite partner across the line. 'Miss' lifted up her class one by one. The first 'fairy' to go had to lie face down on the extended arms and at the given signal was tossed along the line from one end to the other, where it was up to the last couple to set the 'flyer' on her feet again. As soon as one came to earth at the far end, so another was lifted up at the beginning of the line. It was very dangerous, but quite thrilling and we did enjoy it. My turn came; I was hoisted up, lay full length on my stomach and was immediately thrown into the air. Experiencing sensations which amounted to a cross between exhilaration and complete helplessness, I proceeded in parabolic fashion along the line, when suddenly, as I reached the middle, a pair of facing partners deliberately let go of each other's hands and I fell through the space where their arms should have been, face-downwards on to the tarmac playground. I was completely and utterly winded – the only time in my life so far that this has happened to me. I was too surprised to cry, but I have never forgotten my desperate efforts to regain my breath. Miraculously, I wasn't injured in any other way. Our teacher came along the line, picked me up, said, "You're not hurt, go to the back of the line and take your turn again after the others!" I went, but how I reached the back, I don't know – my legs were so wobbly. I stood there gasping and moving slowly to the start of the line as my turn came round again, but fortunately, the whistle went for the end of the lesson before I was due to be hoisted aloft once more.

I said nothing of this incident at home because I didn't want to be forbidden to take part in the flying game should we ever have it again. Actually, we never did. Shortly afterwards, however, something happened which I was unable to keep from my parents; something which I found just as inexplicable. Sometimes I walked home after school over the 'White Stuff'. This was a strange area of low hills and valleys. Apparently they had been formed from chemical waste dumped from a Miles Platting factory and spread all around the New Moston area. Nothing would grow on the white stuff; it gleamed in the sunshine, but was a very eerie place to be at dusk. There was a patch of it, as I remember, near our school and in the middle of the patch was a pond. I don't think the water was very deep, but I was forbidden to go anywhere near it and Aunty Gertie had tried to frighten off Tommy and Charlie by telling them that a wicked woman called Jenny Greensleaves lived in the pond. Her teeth were black and her hair trailed in slimy tresses over the surface when she rose to suck naughty children into its depths if they ventured too close to the edge of the pond. It was really out of my way to go home over the White Stuff, but I had a small friend who lived on the other side of it and I liked her company. We always kept strictly to the path, but it did pass quite close to the pond and on this afternoon, as we drew level, a big girl suddenly appeared over one of the hillocks and bore down upon us. I couldn't remember ever having seen her before, but my friend later told me that she was in Standard VI at school. She came straight for me, grabbed my arm and pulled me towards the pond. I resisted.

"Come and look at your reflection, come on, come on,"

she said, pulling me by my sleeve and coat collar. Gradually, in spite of my struggles, we arrived at the water's edge. I managed to turn round to look for my friend, but she had taken fright and gone. The pond wasn't fenced off and there was no drop to surface level, it was just like walking into the sea, and now the water was lapping over my shoes! Thinking she meant to drown me, and terrified of meeting Jenny Greensleaves, I kicked out at her violently. Before I knew what had happened, she let go of me, nipped nimbly behind me and pushed hard from the back. I fell flat on my face in the murk! She took to her heels as I picked myself up – I was soaked through! No one was about, the White Stuff was all round me and menacing. Suddenly I felt very cold. I started to run, crying, in the direction of home. At the edge of the White Stuff, I met a workman coming towards me on his way back from Moston Pit.

"Ee lass, tha's wet throo," he exclaimed. "Cum'ere." He took hold of my coat and with strong hands wrung the water from it. "Tha'd better get thee 'ome, tha muther 'll be non too pleased when she sees thee."

Neither was she! She was very cross. I had no right to be walking home over the White Stuff and was in disgrace. Moreover, since I was wet to the skin, pneumonia was a foregone conclusion but this would be nothing apparently compared with what Mother was threatening to do to my assailant should she ever be able to find her and lay hands upon her.

During that unhappy year in Standard I, I was much occupied with clothes. Due to my mother's over-protective nature, they assumed a disproportionate importance in my life and I have extremely vivid memories of the garments I wore and of various unpleasant incidents connected with certain of them. Mother was so protective of me and so certain that I would never survive the rigours of each Manchester winter, that she enveloped me in layers and layers of 'really warm' clothing. The first thing I had to don was a six-inch wide knitted woollen body-belt – 'To protect your kidneys dear'. As the warmer weather came, rather than discard it suddenly and risk a shock to my system, Mother cut a narrow strip from it every week until

I was left with just a fine piece of thread around my waist. I was allowed finally to dispense with this string at the end of May! On top of the body-belt came a Chilprufe vest with elbow length sleeves. A piece of Thermogene Wool was laid on my chest between my skin and the vest. Next came Chilprufe combinations with long sleeves, a liberty bodice which buttoned down the front, two pairs of knickers, a flannel petticoat, into the hem of which were sewn little oblong lozenges of camphor, 'to keep infection at bay dear', a cotton petticoat, a long sleeved frock, woolly socks, coat, hat, gloves, a long scarf crossed over my chest in front and tied in a great knot at the back and sometimes, leather leggings with innumerable buttons to be fastened at the side with a button hook which quite often hooked on flesh as well as the buttons! If ever I had just the hint of a sore throat (which apparently, I frequently had), Mother would wrap a piece of flannel around my neck twice, pinning it at the side with a large safety pin.

Should I be invited to a party, a wide white silk hair ribbon was tied all round over the top of the flannel strip and tied into a big bow which hid the safety pin. My party frocks were often crocheted by my mother in a kind of silk cord. They were usually white with elbow length sleeves and scalloped hems. They were quite pretty I suppose, for Mother crocheted well, but they were so heavy that once they were lifted on over all my other clothes, I used to feel quite weighted down.

In the 1920s nearly everyone wore headgear of some kind or other. A lady never ventured abroad without her hat and gloves. My mother used to put hers on even when she went out to the milkman's cart when he stopped his horse every day just outside our front gate. Here, the neighbours would gather, each lady sometimes gloved and always hatted, held forth her porcelain jug and chatted as she waited her turn from the milkman's churn and ladle, whilst the children would pat and feed the milkman's horse with scraps of bread and sugar lumps. Morning hats tended to be neither so elaborate nor so highly decorated as afternoon 'tea' hats. The former were often of the easy-to-pull-on Tam o'Shanter type and the gloves were of cheap felt rather than leather

Bringing home the horses – Tommy and Charlie are mounted, Uncle Charlie and Beryl are on foot.

The 'Timps' on right, camping with Aunty Gertie, Baby John and Tommy – also Nobby the dog. (Charlie took the photograph.)

Grandpa Smith and Beryl in 'Clara'. Outside the butcher's shop at 73 South Row, Roose. Aunty Mill is in the doorway.

Mother and Father at Roose during the First World War.

Uncle Bert outside Roose Village School in 1929.

73 & 74 South Row, Roose –
entrance to butcher's shop.
Aunty Mill and friend in bedroom
window of No. 74.

South Row, Roose, 1929.
Uncle Bert, Father, Lady (the dog) and 'Clara'.

Aunty Mill, Grandpa and Uncle Sam in the garden
at 73 South Row, Roose.

Washing day on the Green – along the backs at Roose, 1928.

Grandpa Smith, Beryl and 'Clara'. Roose, 1926.

Overlooking Roose village – July 1929.
Father, Mother, Beryl, Aunty Mill and 'Clara'.

Grandpa Smith and Aunty Mill in the backyard at Roose.

Grandpa, Aunty Mill and Uncle Sam in
Grandpa's garden, 73 South Row, Roose.

'Three men in a boat' at Roa Island, near Roose.
Grandpa Smith, Father and Uncle Bert, 1929.

Mother, Grandfather Smith and Beryl at Biggar Bank,
Walney Island, Barrow-in-Furness, 1931.

chamois. There was also a variety of hats for men, from cloth caps for gardening and motoring, to trilbys and bowlers for more formal occasions. Boys and girls from good families wore velours in the winter and panamas in the summer, and even the mill girls wore their shawls over their heads. A hat constituted the only piece of uniform for girls at New Moston Board School. It was an optional buy and looked like a parlour maid's cap with its turned back, flattened-against-the-head-brim, both front and back. District nurses were often seen cycling around New Moston wearing the same type of hat. Our school cap however was made out of dark green felt trimmed with braid whose colour varied according to the 'House' to which you belonged: Red, Green, Yellow or Blue. Mine was trimmed with green braid. This hat was a constant source of worry to me. It was very warm to wear for it came down as far as my eyebrows in front and completely covered my hair and ears! I was continually instructed never to try on anyone else's hat and on no account was any other head than mine to be inserted into my hat. I never told my mother how this school cap was regularly snatched from my head and either passed round and tried on indiscriminately, or used as a football in a playground game. She would have worried more than ever. As it was, she was terrified of 'nits'. Several children at school had dirty heads and ring worms were also quite common. Once a term 'Nitty Norah', a nurse-like woman came to school armed with combs and a bowl of strong brown disinfectant. She spent an entire day hunting her happy way through the highways and byways of our scalps. She never found anything interesting in my hair, but Mother wasn't satisfied with this once-a-term inspection. Every afternoon, therefore, after I had arrived home, my hair was thoroughly combed with a double sided small toothcomb which my mother kept specially for the purpose of 'nit-cracking'. Nothing ever crawled, wriggled, or jumped out, but my mother remained unconvinced. She would pull individual hairs from my head and exclaim in triumph when she found a white speck adhering. This she would declare to be 'AN EGG'. I was sure then, as I still am, that it was only dandruff, but Mother could not be persuaded. She would insert the offending hair with 'egg' attached, into an envelope and place it on the lowest shelf in the oven.

"Give it very gentle heat for an hour or two, and it will hatch out," she said. She was doomed to disappointment however, for nothing ever did hatch out.

When I was seven, apart from doing up leggings and shoelaces, I had been able to dress myself for some time. Looking back, I feel this must have been quite an achievement considering the number of garments which had to be accounted for each morning. However, one particular morning, when I had probably got up late, or was feeling more sleepy than usual, I quite forgot to put on my liberty bodice. I left it on the bed, where my mother found it when she went upstairs to 'do' the bedrooms. I hadn't realised its absence until suddenly, Mother's face appeared at our classroom door! Through the glass panel, she was beckoning to our teacher, who, threatening us with dire punishment should we dare to speak to our neighbours whilst her back was turned, went outside. She came back with a smirk on her face.

"Beryl Smith, your mother wants you. Well, go on then – what are you waiting for? NOW."

I rose. Forty-nine pairs of eyes bored into my back and followed me to the door. My mother, holding the abandoned liberty bodice beneath her arm, was very irate. She had been busy and had more to do than come trailing to school after me, but she felt she had to come since I would probably have caught pneumonia if I had been left all morning in a half-dressed condition. As it was, I was sure at least to get bronchitis! She took me into the cloakroom where the missing garment was replaced and I was then returned to class. Another teacher was talking to our teacher as I slipped back to my desk. They looked at me, whispered together and then laughed. I knew they were talking about me. At playtime, my desk companion came up to me.

"You forgot your knickers didn't you?" I hotly denied this, but she ran off shouting, "Beryl Smith forgot her knickers, Beryl Smith forgot her knickers!"

More than once during that unhappy year, I pretended to be ill rather than have to face school. My actual physical surroundings have always had a great effect on my ability to cope with life, and I could find nothing attractive about that brick building erected in 1902, set behind tall railings, its windows placed so high in its walls that if you were on the inside, you could see nothing but a patch of grey Manchester sky; its inner walls tiled in drab lavatorial fashion; its lack of pictures; its smelly toilets at the bottom of the playground; its headmaster, just a distant figure who took prayers every morning, afterwards to wield the strap on all late-comers who were required to mount the platform for punishment (my cousin Charlie seemed always to be in that queue), and worst of all, my own class teacher on whom I silently vowed revenge once I was big enough to stand up to her. And I'm sure that I wasn't the only child to feel like this, for when I joined the regular four o'clock stampede towards freedom and surged with a few hundred others through the gate, there were always those who had beaten us to it. Already, on the other side of the road stood a great line of boys – backs to us, legs apart, singing and shouting jubilation and peeing with a kind of symbolic defiance – making great fountains rise and fall over the fence into the cow-field opposite.

All was not doom and gloom during that year in Standard I, for it was punctuated by high days and holidays, by week-ends, by visits to friends' houses on winter evenings and by 'playing out' in the streets after school whenever the weather permitted. I think we had days off school whenever Oldham and Failsworth Wakes' weeks were on, and at Whitsun for St Chad's Church procession and the crowning of the Rose Queen. I loved to watch the maypole dancing and envied the girls and boys in their fresh white dresses and suits, weaving their brilliantly coloured ribbons into a pattern which gradually transformed the pole into a vivid sheath of multi-coloured moving light. I was never chosen to dance, and even should I have been, my father would not have allowed it, since at the time, he thought organised dancing was sinful. Neither did I ever succeed in dancing along in the wake of St Chad's Rose Queen procession, for not only were we Methodists, but procession following also seemed to be frowned upon. Manchester people love processions. I suppose they brighten the surrounding drabness. All manner of firms, companies and institutions, were represented on the splendidly flower-bedecked and horse-drawn floats – and the bands were wonderful to hear. One band always lead the marchers and the dancers, there was usually another in the middle of the procession, and one bringing up the rear. I would have given anything to have been able to follow those bands, but all I could do was to dance up and down on the spot as they passed along Belgrave Road.

I remember clearly an evening in early summer when a procession came down our street. Mother, Grandma Haydock and I were all watching from the big front bedroom at No 61. We thought it wonderful, quite the most elaborate procession we had seen to date. Grandma was particularly loud in her praises. The first group of floral wagons had passed by and we could hear the approaching band heralding the central part of the show when suddenly, we all noticed two young boys dressed as Red Indians dancing along in front of the advancing instrumentalists. They were carrying a banner advertising in huge golden letters on a red silk ground: FAILSWORTH CO-OPERATIVE SOCIETY. The boys were my cousins, Charlie and Tommy Haydock. I had never seen Grandma Haydock so indignant. It wasn't their costumes, their dancing, or the fact that they were taking part in the procession at all – oh no, all that was quite all right with Grandma. The unforgivable thing was that they were advertising – advertising, and here Grandma shook with suppressed rage – advertising the Co-op! It was the Co-op that was ruining Grandpa's business, it was the Co-op which had a stranglehold on Grandpa himself bringing him to the verge of bankruptcy with its competition. Whatever was Gertie thinking of, she wanted to know, allowing those children to have anything to do with the Co-op? Just wait till she told Arthur about it. Arthur, who was being undermined at this very moment by the Co-op. Oh no, she wasn't staying to watch any more of the procession – no, she was off to Gertie's at once to find out whether Gertie was aware of what her children were up to and to demand that they should be extracted from the procession. With that, she put on her hat and gloves and departed. I never heard the outcome, but Charlie and Tommy continued to follow bands and walk in processions for as long as we all lived in New

Moston. How I envied them.

Although I was restricted when it came to dancing and procession-following Father and Mother never tried to control my choice of friends, nor, within reason, to limit my roamings around Belgrave Road. I could play with anyone and everyone, and provided that I was indoors by the time the lamplighter came around no questions were asked. Consequently, as soon as I had reported home from school in the afternoon, and had my hair combed, I was out again – in the streets, over the White Stuff, in and out of my friends' houses, anywhere and everywhere. There was a boy called Fred who took a fancy to me, and I to him. He was older than me, quite big in fact, for I can remember him taking me for rides all round New Moston perched happily on the handlebars of his big bike! Strangely, no one ever questioned his motives, but nothing untoward happened and no harm ever befell me. He was just a friendly boy being kind to a little girl who didn't have a bicycle of her own.

There was another boy of whom I was very fond. He was Douglas Grainger, originally a school-mate, but eventually our families became friends and one year, we all went on holiday together to Rhyll. To start with it was lovely. I sat in the back of our 'Clara' between Douglas and his older sister Isobel. (Mr and Mrs Grainger went by train I believe, since there wouldn't have been room for us all in the back of our car.) Douglas and I held hands all the way.

My happiness was short-lived, however, for we were soon joined by another New Moston family already known to the Graingers. They had a little girl of my age who deliberately alienated Douglas's affections, stealing him from me by taking his hand and wading out to sea where I could not follow. They were each wearing a bathing costume which was something which Mother had forgotten to pack for me. However, I tucked my clothes into my knickers and strode after, shouting for them to wait for me but when the sea reached the elastic round the tops of my knicker legs, I was forced to give up. Seething, I walked up the beach meeting Mrs Grainger and 'the other girl's' mother, both frantic with anxiety, both standing at the water's edge, alternately commanding and then imploring their offspring in loud voices, to return. Douglas and the 'other girl' paid no heed until the water was up to their necks, and only then, since neither could swim, did they think of returning. Then, of course, from being up to their necks in cold water, they were up to their necks in hot water and I couldn't help feeling overjoyed when the 'other girl's' mum dealt her a few well aimed slaps – and I added my disgust by throwing sand in her eyes! Of course, then, I was in trouble – my mother declaring: "Whatever are you thinking of? You could have blinded your little friend for life!" Since then, I have never again thrown sand into anyone's eyes but at the time so bitter and uncontrolled was my jealousy that I secretly wished the 'other girl' had been blinded as well as drowned!

On the opposite side of Belgrave Road from No 61, and further down towards Moston Lane, lived Edgar Shanks. He often came to play with me and I remember him especially because he insisted on bathing all my dolls all together in the kitchen sink. There were so many dolls, so much soap-sud and the water was so warm that we did not notice that the wax doll's face had melted and that two of the jointed hairless ones had lost their eyes. However, I wasn't at all worried – I didn't really like dolls and anyway, Mother fished the eyes out of their heads and Father took the dolls to the Doll's Hospital in Manchester and they came back repaired. I also remember Edgar for the horse which he didn't have. I was quite convinced that his father owned a pony which he kept well hidden in a garden shed, for often, when Mother, Father and I planned a trip over the White Stuff to the pictures at Failsworth, Father announced that we would all go 'on Shanks's pony'. Many times I looked forward to the ride, and was always disappointed when it didn't materialise.

Across the road also, lived Nancy Whittaker – a very pretty, dark-haired little girl with ringlets. I was often in her house, for in the kitchen she kept an enormous rocking horse with which she was generous in the matter of rides. To me, it was the most wonderful toy I had ever seen and I sometimes spent twenty minutes at a stretch riding the great wide-open spaces until I was called back to Nancy's fireside by vociferous demands to 'change-over'. Nancy was not only pretty, friendly and generous, she also came 'gift-wrapped', for her mother made her the most beautiful frocks – all silk and frills and coloured ribbons. I longed for just such a frock as one of Nancy's. I thought that it would transform me and that I would become as beautiful as she was. Imagine my joy, when, for my seventh birthday, Mrs Whittaker actually made me a frock. I was a little sad that there were no frills, but it was delicately made of pink silk with white collar and cuffs and inset panels. Alas, it didn't transform me. With my straight mousey hair, bulky underclothes and big nose, I remained just a 'plain brown paper package'.

I used to call for Lily Whittles on my way to school. She lived on Parkfield Road and walked in St. Chad's processions. We had a kind of love-hate relationship – quarrelling violently at times and then making it up with equally violent affection. I think Lily must have inherited her violence from her father, for she often showed me bruises on her arms which she said he had inflicted. Mrs Whittles, according to my mother, was a quiet and lady-like person, but Lily's father scared me. He was a miner and worked at Moston pit and he seemed never to be at home when I went to play – but one day he was. He was sitting on a wooden chair by the kitchen fire when I went in. He appeared to be covered with coal-dust. His hair and his eyes were black with it. His voice was gritty with it, and he was shouting at Lily who was fetching him a mug of tea from the scullery. As she reached him he grabbed it from her and some of it spilt on his hand, making little black rivulets of coal-dust run down his fingers. The tea must have been very hot, for he jumped and let out a roar. I didn't stay to see what happened next!

Being allowed to play out on the streets whenever I wished, meant that not only did I have these special friends, but I also roamed about with a small gang. Hopscotch chalked on the pavements, ball-bouncing 'exercises' against high brick walls, skipping with a group, in and out of someone's discarded clothes line, top-spinning, conkers and marble-throwing, came round with seasonal regularity. My equipment was always of poor quality. My tops were cheap wooden affairs which never seemed to spin properly no matter how hard I hit them with a leather bootlace attached to the end of a piece of stick. I really envied the tin multi-coloured and pump-activated humming tops which used to appear from time to time – but which I never owned. As for marbles, mine were always small, solid and dull-coloured. In spite of this, I was good at the game and succeeded in winning several beautiful glass marbles with streaks of vivid colour running through them. Unfortunately, my father noticed them and made me give them back since he didn't like me 'playing for gain'. I lost interest in marbles after that!

My favourite games became the imaginative ones which we played on the White Stuff, or on the piece of waste ground at the end of our terrace of houses. The latter was quite a large area, as yet not built upon. There were dirty hawthorn bushes around its perimeter and in its centre was scrubby grass alive with frogs in the spring time. Here we galloped our horses to victory, here we explored distant lands – discovering the hedges to be full of discarded pots, pans and rusty old prams. Here we rescued beleaguered knights and be-towered princesses. From here we set forth to comb the neighbourhood for 'magic pools'. New Moston puddles, and there always seemed to be many of them, held special fascination for us. Invariably, upon inspection, they appeared to have blue, yellow and heliotrope rings encircling their edges. Some were much more vivid than others and if you jumped into them and splashed about a bit with your feet, all the colours split up and floated about in bead-like globules.

Another joy of my life at that time was our weekly visit to the pictures. Mother loved the cinema, and so did I. I don't know if Father was really interested, but he always came along. I must have been taken at a very early age to the Failsworth 'Pop', for I can remember walking along between my parents on cold moonlit nights, holding tightly to a hand on either side. The White Stuff gleamed pale and mysterious on one side and a tall wooden fence loomed high on the other. This fence cast deep shadows across the dirt-track which we followed down to the canal. Since I was so much nearer to the ground than my parents, the shadows appeared to me as great chasms in my path, and I involuntarily leapt over each one, swinging on Mother's and Father's arms until I was told to 'walk properly'. As we crossed the canal, so still, deep, and evil-looking, there always came the same injunction: "Keep well away from this place when you play, and never try to walk along the towpath." In the distance, right on the water's edge, I could see the square shape of what looked like an old deserted mill. I longed to explore it, but never dared. My parents were right, it was too far from home, and the canal made me feel creepy, anyway. Once over the bridge and under the railway, we came into the huddled streets of Failsworth and soon exchanged their cheerless cobbles for the bright and scented warmth of the 'Palace'.

Those old, silent films with their dramatic piano-played accompaniment, left lasting impressions on my mind. Rin-Tin-Tin, Tom Mix and Silver King, Mickey and Minnie Mouse, and Harold Lloyd were easy favourites until I fell in love with Reginald Denny's full lower lip. It impressed me so much that all my life I have retained a preference for men with full lower lips. As a teenager, I was to worship Maurice Chevalier, and in the real world, I have always been haunted by the attraction of those members of the opposite sex whose lower lips measured up to Reginald Denny's standards.

Continued visits to the pictures at such an early age soon made me realise that all married couples were in danger from 'The Eternal Triangle'; that into every happy marriage came a third person, breaking apart the 'love nest', and forcing the children into terrible decisions as to which parent to favour. So much did these films affect me that I would watch intently for any signs of disagreement between my parents. No couple could have been more faithful to each other than my father and mother, but there was a time when their slightest argument threw me into agonies of anxiety, and once, after watching the harrowing experiences of Al Jolson in 'The Singing Fool', I interrupted their mildly heated discussion over the possible removal of my tonsils, by bursting into tears and begging them not to have a DIVORCE – adding for good measure, that if they were to do so, I shouldn't be able to decide which one to live with. My parents were utterly astounded and after that were, I think, more careful over their choice of films which we saw together.

Just round the corner, at the end of Belgrave Road, where it ran into Moston Lane, lived Uncle Charlie and his family. We visited very often, and with them I spent some of the happiest times I ever had whilst living in New Moston. Aunty Gertie was young-at-heart, pretty, bubbly and always ready to join in games with Charlie, Tommy and me. She read us stories, she made us sets of false teeth out of orange peel; she made me a fairy frock and wings out of old curtains and wire; she produced swords and shields for us all out of three-ply and cardboard. When Charlie and Tommy insisted that we played 'wars', and I could see myself being left out as 'a girl and therefore not able to shoot straight', she made me a Red Cross nurse's apron and cap and converted the cupboard under the stairs into a military hospital where I received casualties and performed such miracle cures that Tommy and any other small male friends and neighbours who were 'wounded', were almost immediately restored to the firing line. Charlie was never wounded. He strutted about in an enormous black busby – his pride and joy – but, where it came from or what eventually happened to it, I do not know. My cousins' greatest friends were 'The Timps' – Alan and Leonard Timperly – who lived nearby and went to New Moston Board School with the rest of us. Charlie and Tommy and the Timps were in and out of each other's houses whenever they could be and, sometimes, at weekends Aunty Gertie would take them all camping. My cousins rigged up a telephone line between the Timps home and theirs. Charlie was very proud of this – it was a contraption of cotton reels and taut string. (I could never make it work, but Charlie insisted that he was receiving messages of the utmost importance all the time!)

My Manchester cousins were 'young devils', always up to something and every week there was some new piece of mischief to be reported. They were forever playing tricks on 'Old Ma Healey', the elderly washerwoman who came each day to help Aunty Gertie. On arrival, she would leave her clogs in the scullery where she changed into carpet slippers for work in the house. At the end of the day, as she plunged her feet back into the clogs, the poor soul would find that some 'varmints', had filled them with 'cowd watter'! I don't think the 'Varmints' tried this too often, however, for Mrs Healey became very adept at swiping the calves of their legs with a broom handle. One day, they waited until she was outside sweeping the back-yard and then they lit a bonfire in the middle of the scullery floor. Fortunately, the floor was stone-flagged and nothing caught alight, but poor Mrs H. made a terrible mess in her haste to extinguish the fire with several buckets of water.

One Sunday evening in the summer, after Tommy and Charlie had been put to bed, Aunty Gertie and Uncle Charlie were sitting in the window of their front room downstairs watching the people from St Chad's walking home along Moston Lane after the evening service. As they passed by, many stopped and looked up, smiling and laughing. Aunty Gertie was pleased.

"They are admiring my new curtains in the front bedroom," she remarked – Uncle Charlie was not so sure. Finally, one of the strollers, a friend of Gertie's, walked up the garden path and knocked on the front door. Gertie opened it.

"I don't want to alarm you, Mrs Haydock," said the friend, but your two boys are sitting on the outside sill of your top window, in their nightshirts, dangling their legs, waving their arms and pulling faces at people passing on the pavement. They look most insecure and they should be brought in at once, or they might fall off the ledge. They are right outside, you know."

Gertie ran up the stairs two at a time. The last thing she wanted was to startle them. Swiftly and silently, she crossed the bedroom floor, and suddenly, plunging her arms through the open window, one round each boy, she hauled them into safety, bumping their heads and scraping their bottoms, 'accidentally-on-purpose', as it were.

We were all very innocent in those days, so much so, that when Charlie on one of his 'rooting' expeditions through his mother's dressing-table drawers, found several packets of 'balloons', we were all delighted.

"Might as well blow them up now, as wait for some silly party," said Charlie, producing a tangled mass of dirty string and a murderous-looking knife from his pockets. I thought they were rather boring as balloons went – all cloudy white in colour and all the same long thin sausage shape. However, we blew them all up, tied their ends and floated them out of the window, where they settled gently in the front garden, and one or two which cleared the hedge into the road were picked up by grateful children who gathered hopefully around the gate, some even venturing inside to snatch a prize and retreat!

Mother and Aunty Gertie were great friends. Gertie was the guiding light, and Mother followed in her path. Gertie was the first to exchange black woollen stockings for white cotton ones and subsequently for fawn lisle ones. Gertie shortened her skirts above her knees and dropped her waistband to her hips and wore fringes and tassels and swinging beads long before Mother ever dared. Gertie was bobbed and then shingled soon after Tommy was born, but I was six before Mother finally overcame the Methodist disapproval emanating from my father's side of the family. Her long dark hair was irrevocably shorn at Lewises' in Manchester. I watched in tears as it fell in thick chunks around her, and on the way home, had to be bought a 'flying-bird-on-a-stick' as consolation for what I considered to be a personal loss. Aunty Gertie was the first to learn the Charleston. Mother and I discovered her one afternoon practising alone in her front room. We joined in – she taught us the steps which I have never forgotten and which I still love to dance whenever the opportunity arises.

Mother and Gertie would try out all kinds of facial experiments, the instructions for which were to be found in Mother's weekly copy of *Home Notes* which she would exchange with Gertie for her copy of *Home Chat*. They would retire to Gertie's bedroom, lock the door behind them and make surreptitious attempts to pluck each other's eyebrows and rouge each other's lips and cheeks with papier poudré. There would be much laughter, but when they emerged, they had removed the evidence for they looked just the same as ever. One day, they forgot to lock the door. Charlie and Tommy and I sneaked upstairs and stood listening outside, as usual.

"They're up to something different," said Charlie. "It's

too quiet."

Slowly, he turned the door-knob just to test it, and since we were all three leaning against the panels, suddenly the door burst open and we fell into the room. Mother and Gertie were standing side by side with their backs to us. They were looking intently into the dressing-table mirror. At the noise, they turned abruptly – said not a word, but came silently towards us. Their faces were bright green and crusty all over. Their mouths had disappeared, and only two slits remained where their eyes had once been! I screamed, Tommy turned pale, and Charlie's mouth fell open in amazement. We stood, all three of us, rooted to the spot.

"Go away, go away and don't make us laugh." The dreadful gurgling sound came from somewhere deep inside Gertie.

"It mustn't crack or it won't stick," hissed my mother through clenched teeth. "Go away, go away, we shall be really beautiful when we're done, just you wait and see." And Gertie gave each of us a push on to the landing and closed the door behind us, locking it firmly this time.

"Coo, they didn't 'arf look 'orrible," said Charlie. "Come on our kids, let's play out." And we all three rushed for the backyard.

"You did look horrible," I remarked to my mother accusingly, as we walked home.

"Yes," Mother laughed, "but it was worth it, my face feels really soft now, and next week, we are starting on Monkey Brand. It'll take years off us."

During my five years in New Moston, we took as many holidays as my parents could afford, and as Father's job allowed. Being a teacher, he had substantial breaks at Easter, Whitsun and mid-summer, and once we had acquired a car, we never stayed at home on these occasions. For our big summer holiday, we always went to Devon, sometimes for the whole month of August, but at Easter and at Whitsun, we would often travel north to visit my father's family. They lived in a strange little village called Roose, just outside Barrow-in-Furness. Here, it was so unlike New Moston and Newton Heath, both in surroundings and people, that my memories of it remain clear to this day by the very nature of its contrasts with my Manchester world. Here I came to know yet another house, whose inhabitants with their different way of life enfolded me and left their mark upon me all through my childhood – and after.

4

73 SOUTH ROW, ROOSE

If Manchester was black, Roose was red, for here there was haematite ore in the earth. It turned the rain to blood as it collected in sticky puddles along unmade roads and trickled in rich red rivulets down the blocks of old red sandstone from which the houses had been built. A strange village; it had no centre. There was a school, but I can't remember a church of any kind and its only claim to a village green was the enormous length of grassed area which lay between the backs of the long, parallel lines of houses called North Row and South Row. These houses were terraced, all of the same pattern, red slabs rough-hewn from local stone. There was nothing smooth about their walls, they were bumpy and scratchy if you leant against them, and in summer, the absorbed heat of the sun would almost scorch your back. No picture-book cottages these, nothing pretty or pretentious about them – no bay windows, no porched doorways, nor thatched roofs here. These dwellings were functional, built for Cornish tin miners who had flooded into the Furness area in the last half of the nineteenth century. Hungry for work and food, here they came with their families, rapidly filling the houses built specially for them, they brought their own way of life with them and for a generation at least, the soft burr of the West Country could be heard along the Rows and in the Backs of Roose, until it was gradually suppressed as the harsher accents of the North took over and began to fill the mouths of younger generations.

Each parallel row was divided into four or five blocks,

with about twenty-four houses to a block. Every two houses shared a lobby which ran from the front pavement back into the gloom for the whole length of the walls between the two neighbouring front rooms. These long, narrow passageways were windowless and echoing. Their concrete floors led back from red-earthed pavements to two facing front doors which opened in the dark on the right and left at the far end of each chasm. If you came out of the front door of one of these houses, it was like stepping into a cold dark tunnel where a light glimmered in the distance. Coming in from the street, as a child, I was always frightened by the blank wall which towered in the semi-darkness straight ahead, and I had to keep looking back towards the light in order to give myself courage to go on. I avoided using people's front doors in the village as much as possible and I believe most of the villagers opened them only on special occasions – back entrances were much more popular.

At the end of each block was a wide crossroad which cut the village into sections. Producing a rectilineal pattern, these side-roads crossed right over the Green and joined North Row to South Row by means of their red-puddled, bumpy surfaces. Every house had a backyard which opened straight on to the Green. Some backyards were bricked, some were concreted, but all had a lavatory on their back walls, for although in the 1920s main drainage had come to Roose, there were at that time no indoor toilets or bathrooms. You still had to go 'down the yard' to the loo. Next to the lavatories, big, wooden hatches inset into the thick sandstone walls of the yard, were reminders of the 'Midden Men', who when my father was small, would come down the Backs at night in a cart. Through the hatch they would shovel out the night soil from each family's earth closet.

The Green itself was a great feature of the village. Forty to fifty feet wide and over half a mile in length, it separated the two Rows. It was a wonderful place for the village children, generations of whom played here in complete safety apart from the occasional attack by the geese. These fierce creatures lived on the Green and roamed at liberty from end to end. They terrified me; they wouid rush at me with their long necks stretched into a horizontal line hissing hatred at the human race. I think they belonged to a man who lived near the beginning of North Row, and at Christmas time, their numbers were rather diminished, but at other times, there were often about a dozen of them. They paraded slowly, and with great dignity, in close formation until suddenly and without warning, they would launch an attack.

On Mondays it was difficult to locate the geese, for on Mondays, the Green was transformed. It became a great white sailing ship, half a mile long, alive with sheets billowing as far as the eye could see and straining before a following wind. On other days, when the washing had been taken in and clothes-lines neatly coiled onto masthead posts, another interesting feature of the Green became visible. Erratic boulders! I had no idea then of their geographical name, or origin, but I always thought there was something strange, misplaced, almost magical about them. Like huge grey mushrooms, remarkable in their green and red surroundings, there seemed to be at least one to each block. They were big – about three or four times the size of an ordinary football, beautifully rounded, smoothed, polished and striated, they must have been rolled along for miles by some primaeval ice sheet, or peri-glacial stream and left abandoned when the ice retreated, or the stream dried up. Deposited far from their parent rock, they were pieces of Lakeland granite in an alien sandstone world, but to me and to my village playmates, they became the centre of most of our games.

"Meet you at the stone," we said, referring to the extra large one at the back of No. 74. The grass around its perimeter had long since disappeared – worn down by the successive poundings of small feet – for round the stone, we played tag; we climbed to its summit and jumped off; we took refuge on it when the geese attacked; we sat in friendly communion around it, leaning our backs against it, and picking winkles from their shells with the aid of a pin whilst we discussed matters of great importance. The stones intrigued me.

"How did they get there?" I wondered.

No one seemed to know, and when I asked Mother, she guessed the fairies must have brought them. This satisfied me for a while. After all, if the fairies brought babies, I supposed they could have been capable of humping a few boulders around!

Grandpa Smith's house – No. 73 South Row – was situated on the lower of the two streets, at the beginning of the last block and about four fifths of the way up the village if you started from the main road into Barrow. It was a corner house and had two front doors, one faced the last crossroad which joined North and South Rows, and the other opened onto South Row itself. The latter was a shop door, for Grandpa Smith was a butcher and the front room of his house had been made into a shop, with a display window let into its side wall. On hot summer days, Grandpa used to draw a heavy linen sail-cloth blind over the outside of this window to keep the sun and flies off his meat and there would be strips of brown sticky paper hanging from the ceiling inside, and usually covered with a variety of winged insect life, dead, or struggling helplessly to escape death. Immediately inside the front door of the house was a flight of stairs leading straight up to two bedrooms, one over the shop on the right and one on the left overlooking the back-yard – and that was all on this floor – no bathroom, no toilet. The bedrooms were small, each contained a huge double bed, high standing, brass railed and knobbed, and covered with a thick, white, tassled quilt. Beneath each window was a marble-topped washstand with china basin, ewer and soap dish, whilst on a shelf beneath it, rested a slop-pail with a lid, and a jerry. There was just enough room to stand between the washstand and the bed, and if you were washing, you had to be very careful not to splash water on to the bed. Pictures of Jesus and framed religious texts decorated with scrolls of ivy and painted pansies were on the walls. A mirror, a small hard chair and a cupboard let into the wall, were the only other furnishings, except for the linoleum on the floor – very cold to bare feet!

On the ground floor behind the shop and to the left of the front door was Grandpa's living-room, almost completely occupied by a big central, chenille-covered table. Against one wall, stood a very old organ, complete with pedals and stops. On it, Grandpa played by ear and sang hymns and Juanita.

There was a very black coal range with the usual ovens on each side and a horsehair sofa where Grandpa always had forty winks after dinner every day. He would cover himself with an old tartan rug, and once or twice, when I was very small, I can remember being placed alongside him in the vain hope that I also would take a short nap, but the horsehair prickled me, Grandpa's beard tickled me, and Grandpa himself complained that I fidgeted!

The back kitchen-cum-scullery opened off Grandpa's living-room. It had a brick floor and a stone sink with one tap only which dripped cold water all the time. The back door opened from here into a sunless yard. The scullery was a draughty, cheerless place, so cold in winter, that when my father was a boy, he and his brothers had to break the icicles from the tap and melt them in the sink before they could wash in the mornings, and I think that many a time they just didn't bother. Here, they grew up, tough, used to cold water, earth closets at the bottom of the yard, oil lamps downstairs on dark winter nights and candles to light them to bed.

Eventually, as Grandpa's business began to flourish and his family to increase, he rented the adjoining cottage also and converted the two houses into one dwelling-place by having a passageway knocked between the two living-room walls so that you could walk beneath a curved archway from No. 73 to No. 74, but instead of a shop facing South Row, there was a front parlour.

When I was small, No. 74 belonged to my father's youngest sister, Millicent, whom everyone called 'Mill', and to her husband, my uncle Sam Pearson. No. 74 always seemed to me to be more civilised, warmer and less gloomy than No. 73. Although not so comfortable as my own home, full of Edwardian and Victorian nick-nacks, it was less austere than Grandpa's house and it didn't smell of animal fat. The front parlour was rarely used. The armchairs were over-stuffed and unyielding and there was a tall bamboo plant-stand with an aspidistra which stood in the tasselly-curtained window. I can't remember the family ever sitting together in this room, and I can't recall a fire ever being lit here to dispel the musty smell. Since the Smiths were such a musical lot, its main feature was an upright piano set against the wall facing the window. I think it had been far more in use when Grandma Smith was alive than when I used to visit Aunty Mill and Uncle Sam.

Aunty Mill's living-room was so crowded with furniture that when we all sat down for dinner or tea, I had to take the place at the head of the table because I was the only one small enough to slip into the space between the end of the table and the enormous mirrored sideboard which ran the length of the back wall. Aunty Mill would preside at the opposite end, nearest to the scullery door, whilst Grandpa, Uncle Sam and my parents sat two to a side. An iron-framed, treadle sewing machine stood under the window next to a walk-in larder, and on one side of the kitchen range was a cupboard where Aunty Mill kept a box of odds and ends designed specially to amuse visiting children. There was space for only one armchair. This, standing near the fire on one side of the range, and made comfortable by years of hard wear, was the only semblance of luxury in the entire room. This was not a house where people sat around and chatted much. On rare occasions when all of us assembled after a meal, the table was pushed back and the hard wooden kitchen chairs drawn round the fire in a semi-circle, otherwise the adults rarely lingered and I went out to play as soon as I was allowed to 'get down'. I would go straight out, through Aunty Mill's scullery which was the same size and shape as Grandpa's, but which had a covering of linoleum on its brick floor and a bath! You wouldn't have suspected the existence of the latter, for it was well hidden beneath a big wooden table top on which Aunty Mill used to bake batches of wing cakes for sale in Grandpa's shop alongside the meat. I never remember anyone using the bath, I certainly didn't, even though sometimes we stayed for a whole fortnight at Roose. In any case, since no hot water was laid on, it must have been quite a problem to fill it.

The backyard at No. 74 was concreted and sunny, and the high wall which divided it from No. 75 was covered all over with thick ivy-like creeper which in late summer turned to a brilliant red colour. Due to the creeper, the only place left for ball-bouncing was against the lavatory door at the end of the yard. This favourite activity of mine must have been rather disturbing for any loo-visiting adults, for once I started bouncing, I didn't let up no matter who was inside – I ceased only for a moment to allow them to enter and when they had finished and wanted to leave, they were forced to shout. I would pause for just long enough to allow them to exit in safety. The grown-ups tolerated this pastime of mine, since they must have realised there was just nowhere else suitable for it anywhere round the two houses; the front lobby was too dark and narrow, the side wall was too bumpy and uneven with its huge sandstone blocks, all rough and powdery, and the garden was completely filled with Grandpa's precious vegetables and flowers, with not a wall in sight, for although every house on South Row had its own long, narrow stretch of garden which lay across the road from the houses and sloped gently down to a beck and a railway embankment at the bottom, the land was divided by thin wire fences, through which you could see from one end of the village gardens to the other.

On their wedding day in 1873, Grandma and Grandpa Smith came to Barrow-in-Furness from a little village in Somerset, called Draycott. There could have been few prospects for Grandpa in Draycott. His father owned the butcher's shop there, but there were a brother and a step-brother older than himself to carry on the family business, so he must have decided to take his chance with the Cornish miners and to follow them to Northern England. He worked for a year or two in a butcher's shop in Barrow, then when the opportunity arose, he branched out on his own, renting No. 73 South Row in Roose village and moving in with his young wife and first little son. The journey from Draycott to Barrow, made at one go on their wedding day must have been quite an undertaking, but they were young and tough. They led fervently religious lives, devoted to the teachings of John Wesley. They were Bible Christians who had each 'grown a backbone', very necessary to survive the poverty of the day.

I was five when Grandma Smith died, so my memories of her are few, but vivid. She had been born possibly in Cheddar on July 1st 1852, the eldest daughter in a family of eight children. My great-grandfather, Samuel Spencer, subsequently kept a draper's shop in Bristol. Grandma was christened Harriet Alice and as the family grew and the living quarters over the shop became more and more cramped, she was sent to live in Draycott with her mother's parents and sisters. Grandma's mother, Frances, must have been a resourceful and courageous lady, for in the early years of her marriage, a splinter from a broken mixing bowl went into her arm and blood-poisoning set in. Finally, her arm had to be amputated, but Frances carried on regardless, bringing up her large family in the Methodist faith, coping with an alcoholic husband, which, considering her religious persuasion, must have been especially difficult, and at the same time managing to produce some wonderful needlework including a large and beautifully made patchwork quilt which has been handed down through the generations and which I hold treasured in my home today.

Grandma herself thrived in Draycott where her grandparents and aunts worked in the village store – still there today on the main street, which leads to Cheddar. The Week's family, who owned this shop, were all staunch, God-fearing Bible Christians, formerly Bryanites. Obed and Margaret, my great, great grandparents, born in the 1820s were Somerset people and had moved during their early married life to become well known and respected figures in Draycott. They were leading lights in community worship at the little Bethel Chapel there. Obed founded its Sunday School. Obed and Margaret had many children, mostly girls. Their eldest son Jesse inherited the family business and passed it on to his son Earnest who is still remembered in Draycott today. The girls married and at least two of them emigrated with their husbands to America. I like to think that Harriet Alice helped her grandparents in their shop by working alongside her aunts and uncle and earned enough to be able to send a little home to help her parents also. Somehow, somewhere, she must have received an education, for she was clever with a distinct flair for imaginative writing. I believe that at one time she ran a small school in Draycott which was in some way connected with the chapel there.

Of course, she had grown quite elderly when I was a child.

I could have been no more than three when I first became aware of her. We must just have arrived on holiday from Manchester and were all clustered in the little lobby at No. 73. Much kissing and greeting were going on between my parents and Grandpa, and growing bored, I strayed into Grandpa's living-room. I couldn't see much, it was a dark room, and anyway, my head barely reached above table level. In the gloom, I gradually realised that an old lady was struggling to rise from a chair by the fire on the other side of the table, she hauled herself up slowly and what must have been very painfully on two sticks, and stood facing me across the vast chenille-covered space. She had rosy cheeks and suddenly she smiled so brightly that I felt interested and not at all afraid.

"My little one," she said, "I have been waiting for you. You and I are going to play a game together."

I was astounded and overjoyed that this hitherto unnoticed old lady really wanted to play with me, before I'd even had my coat taken off. She held on to the table, first with one hand and then with both as she placed her sticks right across its width, leaving a narrow track between them. Then, from her pocket she produced a little white ball.

"Now," she said, "I will roll this ball to you, you must stop it and roll it back and see that it stays between my sticks." I was enchanted and deeply engrossed in this new game when my father came striding around the table, took his mother in his arms, kissed her long and lovingly, and lifted her back into her chair. During the next two years, she must have spent more and more time in bed, for I cannot remember seeing her ever again downstairs. My father would take me to her room when it was my bedtime. Before I was lifted up to kiss her goodnight, I was usually requested to recite a little poem and then to kneel at her bedside to say my prayers. *Gentle Jesus Meek and Mild* was always followed by a list starting 'God bless Mummy and Daddy', and followed by the same request for all the relatives, friends and acquaintances who, up to that moment in my life, had made any impression on me at all. The list was lengthy and delayed my bedtime considerably. Grandma never grew impatient and always appeared interested – sometimes asking after I had finished, "Is so-and-so a new friend dear? I haven't heard you mention her before." If my father hadn't been present, I would have been tempted to invent many further names!

She had suffered from rheumatoid arthritis for many years – as a result, my father said, of driving with Grandpa in the pony-trap every Sunday of the year, no matter what the weather, to Roose Road Chapel. She would sit through morning service, often in wet clothes, eat her lunch sandwiches in the vestry, lead the Sunday School in which she taught her class of senior girls during the afternoon, and stay on for evening service, after which, she would drive home again with Grandpa who would come to fetch her in the trap. At one stage, when my father was a boy, the progression of Grandma's rheumatism was so rapid that it was decided she should go to Bath to 'take the waters'. Grandpa was desperate to see an improvement in his wife and Grandma was willing to try anything. When she left home, Grandpa had to lift her into the pony trap. He drove her to the station and lifted her into the train. One of my uncles drove the trap home, but Grandpa accompanied her to Bath, saw her installed and left her there. Six weeks later, she came home on her own and although Grandpa met her at the station with the trap, she made him stop half way up South Row. She got down and walked the length of the last block home, just to show her waiting family how much better she was. Sadly, however, the rheumatism returned until finally she became bedridden.

Grandma's father had been an alcoholic and having witnessed him picked insensible out of the gutter and brought home in a drunken stupor on the very day that her brother became ordained as a Methodist Minister, she had decided there and then to become a lifelong abstainer. However, she had once confessed to my father that many a time she felt the desire for strong drink and had been forced to resist it. For many years she had fought against this weakness with all the strength and determination of which she was capable – she was made of stern stuff and had never succumbed. Therefore, towards the end of her life, when the doctor recommended that she should take a bottle of

Guinness stout every day, Grandma was horrified. Grandpa, however, went out specially and brought back the first bottle. It proved to be the last; Grandma refused to let a drop pass her lips. As a member of the Band of Hope, her main drink had always been 'water bright', and ever mindful of the inherited tendency in her blood, she pressed her lips firmly together and turned away her head on the pillow as Grandpa proffered the glass. Grandpa, however, deciding that good money should not be wasted, himself took a huge mouthful of the 'dark satanic brew'. The taste was apparently so awful that he rushed to the bedroom window, flung it wide open and spat the lot onto the pavement below – narrowly missing a customer about to enter the shop! He then emptied the remaining contents of the bottle down his scullery sink and alcohol of any nature never again entered No. 73.

When Grandma died in 1925, a plaque to her memory was erected on the inside of the Roose Road Chapel wall. I used to study it through many a long sermon. I learnt that she had been a founder member of the Chapel and had died on the 15th May 1925 at the age of 73. I doubt if the plaque is still there – perhaps the Chapel also has gone.

When I was very small, I used to confuse Grandpa Smith with God. He had brilliantly blue eyes, a high noble forehead, snow white hair and eyebrows, a long white beard and my father always spoke of him with great respect. He wasn't a tall man, but very strong. He would carry a huge side of beef, half a beast at a time from a wagon parked in the road outside No. 73. He would heave it into the big cold store in his shop and hang it there on a vicious-looking meat hook before returning to the vehicle to pick up another half carcass.

Grandpa had been born in the little village of Draycott in the county of Somerset on April 15th 1852. He was the youngest child of George and Rebecca Smith. It was George's second marriage, made in Bristol in 1841 at St Nicholas church, so Grandpa, who was christened Edward George after his grandfather and father had a half-sister, and a full brother and sister, John and Sarah. Brother John and sister Sarah lived and died in Draycott, but his half-sister, I believe, emigrated to America and was tragically burnt to death there in a Prairies' fire.

The Smiths were butchers and farmers. Great Grandpa George Smith kept the butcher's shop in the village for many years. He and Rebecca must have been quite prosperous for they managed to send young John and my grandfather, Edward George to boarding school at Shebbear in North Devon at the time when the well-known Thomas Ruddle was headmaster. Grandpa had many tales of his school days, the chief of which concerned the arduous journey from Draycott into North Devon, finishing with a long ride in a horse-drawn cart from Bideford to Shebbear. I don't know how long Grandpa was at this school but I think he must have started there prior to 1864 when Thomas Ruddle took over. In those days, the school was run for the sons of Bryanites – the forerunners of the Bible Christians. Many of the older pupils were training to become ministers of the faith. The Bryanites were known as 'plain folk with plain houses, plain dresses and plain living'. Gradual improvements were made when Mr Ruddle took over, but Grandpa and Great Uncle John must have found their school life very spartan indeed. However, they were young and tough and managed somehow to enjoy the rigours of the regime imposed upon them. They were full of energy and mischief and Grandpa would often recount tales of fights in the dormitories, and of how on one occasion, his brother John was pushed backwards so vigorously that he fell right through the dividing wall of lath and plaster into the adjoining dormitory and all his caution money for the year was used up to pay for its repair. In addition, other dire punishments which Grandpa would not specify were also meted out!

When Edward George left school, he found work for a time as a clerk in the railway booking office at Radstock and in his spare time he must have helped his father and brother John in the butchery business. Grandpa told me that often he would walk into Cheddar with produce or to collect letters and packets from the Post Office there. Many a time, he said, he ate his noonday piece sitting in an old cart which a farmer kept at the entrance to what is now one of the famous Cheddar Caves, but at that time was just a cleft in the cliff face. The Smith's butchery and shop were on the main village street almost opposite to the Week's general store where Grandma lived with her grandparents, aunt and uncle. Apparently, from the Week's upper windows above their stores, you could look straight down into the Smith's front parlour. When Grandma and Grandpa started courting, they were allowed to use the front parlour, but the curtains had to be left un-drawn and a strict watch was kept on Grandma from the house on the other side of the street!

When Edward George finally married his Harriet Alice in 1873, it must have been quite an occasion, for a cousin of the bride who was present at the wedding and who later emigrated to America, wrote of it: 'A very pretty wedding, the bride being attired in white silk, tulle veil and orange blossoms. A very good looking and worthy couple. They went immediately to Barrow-in-Furness to reside'. There must have been a great and joyful wedding breakfast at the General Stores, after which all the guests followed Grandma and Grandpa down the village street to the railway station at Draycott, to see them onto the train for Barrow. Unbeknown to the bride and groom, their friends and relatives placed fire-crackers on the line; as the carriages pulled away they ran over the fireworks and off went my grandparents to the accompaniment of tears, laughter and explosions!

For the rest of their lives Grandma and Grandpa Smith were to live in the North Country, first, for a short while in Barrow itself and then in Roose village. Every year, however, Grandpa would return to Draycott to help his father and his brother John with the cider-apple harvest. For at least a month, he would stay in the old home, picking and loading in the orchards. He must have worked very hard and lived mainly on apples, for when he returned to Roose, my father told me he had always lost a couple of stones in weight. Not that it mattered for he was a big, strong and healthy man and the weight soon came back again. In fact, when I was ten, after never having had an illness in his life, he was suddenly whisked into hospital and operated on for suspected appendicitis. When he was opened up, however, it was found to be merely a twisted loop in the intestine. It was untwisted, he was sewn up again and all was well for the rest of his days. In fact, the doctor told my father then, that for a man of Grandpa's age (he was eighty at the time), he was abnormally healthy with enough fat and muscle on him to last for three months should he ever be stranded on a desert island! What a fate for a man who, every morning of his life, cooked himself two eggs on a rump steak for his breakfast!

He hated hospital and couldn't wait to get home again. He had been put on a diet and was perpetually hungry, also, he had been quite outraged, shocked to the core. Young unmarried girls, he told my father, in a scandalised whisper, had subjected him to all kinds of indignities; treated him with uncalled for intimacy and taken unimagined liberties with his body! Two of them had even given him a bath! It was the first he could ever recall having. He didn't believe in bathing. It diluted all the natural juices in the skin and he was very annoyed that this should have happened to him at his age and in such circumstances.

In spite of his dislike of bathing Grandpa always looked strangely clean to me, even on workdays when the big white apron which he wore over his overall would become quite stained with blood, and on Sundays, when he donned his best black suit for chapel, he looked positively impressive. With it, he always wore a special tie. I never knew him to wear any other sort. Grandpa Smith's ties were like no one else's, they were very old-fashioned and could be bought only at a certain shop in Manchester. My father obtained them for him twice a year and we took them to him when we went on holiday to Roose. They were made of stiff black silk and always cravat style. To protect these precious ties, Aunty Mill fashioned for him a large bib which he clipped on to his suit at mealtimes, but of course that didn't prevent his beard from harbouring stray bits which fell from his fork – and since all of his life he had used only a two-pronged fork, the bits were plentiful. As a result, I found that kissing him was not only a ticklish process, but one redolent of meals long past! In addition to the bib and two-pronged fork, he also used a special cup. It was unusual in that it had a kind of extra lip running half way around the rim inside the main lip and at a lower level. We called it Grandpa's moustache cup. I think its purpose was to prevent his moustache from becoming saturated every time he took a drink.

I always stood somewhat in awe of Grandpa. Although his bright blue eyes twinkled and he used to wink at me a lot, I never felt quite at ease in his company. When he wasn't working, or attending chapel, he would read the Bible, *Pilgrim's Progress* and *The Meat Trader's Journal* and for recreation he played the organ. He had never had a lesson in his life but he was distinctly musical and passed on his gift to many of his descendants.

Grandpa was a popular butcher with always a cheery word for his customers. He was also something of a tease especially with children who were sent on errands to his shop. One day, to his great delight, one child really got the better of him. "Well, little maid," he said to a neighbour's daughter. "What would you like today?"

"Please, Mr Smith, Mummy would like three lamb chops."

Grandpa cut the chops, parcelled them and passed them over the counter with a smile.

"How much will that be sir?"

Grandpa winked. "Just one kiss my dear," he said.

"Thank you." The child picked up the chops. "Mummy will call and pay you tomorrow!"

Grandpa's sausages were renowned in the village. The recipe was a well-guarded secret. They were the tastiest sausages I have ever eaten. Aunty Mill often cooked them for tea, but they invariably gave me hiccups and I had to keep very quiet whilst eating them. Meat was plentiful at 73 and 74 South Row when I was a child. Huge roasts, sometimes twice a week and wonderful steak and kidney pies were no novelty. In those days I had no qualms of conscience about the slaughter of animals for food, in fact, I once accompanied Grandpa and my father to a slaughter house but I had to come out – overpowered by the sight of gutters full of blood and the dreadful stench which made me vomit once I reached the fresh air.

Food had not always been plentiful in Grandpa's family. My father remembered times of depression in the village when folk just couldn't afford to buy meat and in order that his large family should survive, Grandpa, working his way over on a cattle boat, had been forced to go to America to work on a farm in the Mid-West which belonged to Grandma's aunty and uncle. He took his two eldest sons with him – Uncle Bert and Uncle Art. They were so full of devilment, apparently, that Grandma felt she couldn't cope on her own with them plus her five other children, the house and the business. I believe Grandpa stayed out in the States for about a year and was able to send enough money home to keep his family from starvation, although, according to my father, it was a near thing once or twice.

Apart from selling meat, Grandpa often sold fruit. He had boxes of beautiful apples, pears and plums delivered in season and when he was in hospital, we would always take some of the choicest specimens for him to give to Matron and the Ward Sister. In his garden over the road, on that long generous strip of ground sloping down to Roose Beck and the fields beyond, he grew enormous peonies and gladioli which were also sold in the shop, but the biggest and best of them were always taken into the chapel for decoration and after Grandma had died a pilgrimage was made every week in the summer to take a bunch of flowers to the lonely, windswept grave where she lay in the churchyard at Rampside, looking out over the treacherous sands of Morecambe Bay.

At one time, Grandpa had kept cows and a pony and trap in the huge, black draughty shed at the bottom of the garden. In my day, it was empty, so that when we visited we were able to garage, first the Citroen and then Clara inside. My father could remember driving Grandpa's six cows up the village street to a pasture at the end which opened off the lane towards Yarlside. The cows wintered in the shed and Father would often describe to me how joyful and skittish they were the first time they were let out each spring after their long confinement.

In those days Duncan the pony, and Jess the cat shared the shed with the cows. Grandpa loved cats and dogs. He had only to step outside his shop door and four or five of them would be immediately there to greet him, lovingly nosing into the palms of his hands for the scraps he held concealed. There was one dog I particularly remember called Lady. She would sit all day on the shop step and was always rewarded for her vigil.

Jess, Grandpa's favourite cat, had long departed from the scene when I used to visit Roose, but memories of her lingered on. Jess had never been spayed and produced large litters with great regularity. Grandpa disposed of them quickly and kindly by giving each new-born kitten a sharp tap on the head. Poor Jess, it seemed that she would never be allowed to fulfil her role as a mum. However, being an intelligent animal, she eventually became wise to Grandpa's actions. One spring, after the litter had been despatched in the usual way, Grandpa noticed that she would never quite finish her dinner scraps, but would make off with her mouth full of the last bits. Down the garden she would go and disappear into the cowshed. This continued for several days until Grandpa finally managed to follow her without Jess knowing it. She mounted the ladder to the hayloft – Grandpa went after her very quietly and standing on the top rung, he saw her disappear far into the hay. When he investigated, he found that buried deep in the dry, sweet-smelling grass, she had made a nest for herself and hidden one of her kittens there. Knowing full well that Grandpa would destroy her new family first thing in the morning, she must have carried it there during the night immediately after it was born. By the time it was found, it was quite big and beautiful and the image of Jess herself! It was uncanny the way she had saved the one which was her double. Grandpa hadn't the heart to destroy it especially after she had gone to such pains to protect it from him, and Jess, just for this once, was allowed to fulfil her maternal instincts.

Grandpa continued to work in his shop until the thirties when he was over eighty, and he never gave up his garden. He was so healthy that he didn't die of any disease – he just grew tired and stopped. He was ninety-three, and on the morning of his death he had pottered down to the old cowshed as usual, looking at his plants en route. He must have known what was about to happen for he came slowly and calmly back to his house, walked through the archway into Aunty Mill's kitchen, sat down in the one armchair and closed his eyes. Aunty Mill found him there when she came in from the backyard. She realised at once what was taking place and knelt down beside him. She was terribly upset and as she went to put her arms around him, he opened his eyes and smiled. "Don't cry Mill," he said. "Don't grieve, we shall all meet again very soon." And then he was gone.

Aunty Mill must have loved her home and her parents very dearly, for she never really left them. She was the only one of Grandma and Grandpa's children to live nearly all of her life in the village where she was born. I believe there was a short period after her marriage when she and Uncle Sam rented a house in Barrow, but her parents, convinced that she was pining for her old home (as indeed she was), and finding two houses too large for them now that all their children had left, made over No. 74 to the young couple. Back home with rejoicing came Aunty Mill and there she stayed for the rest of her days. She was a stolidly upright kind of person, someone you felt, who could always be relied upon, who would do the right and honourable thing and stand by you through thick and thin if you were also trying to do the same thing, but woe betide you if your intentions were at all suspect! She was highly respected both in chapel and in the village, and there was an aura of great purity about her.

Nevertheless, she had a real sense of fun and she and my father were always laughing and joking together whenever they met. Born on December 28th 1882 the fifth child of the family, she was five years his senior. She and Uncle Sam had no children, so there were no cousins for me to play with at No. 74. They would both have liked to have children – they certainly always made me feel loved and wanted, but apparently, so Mother told me years later, Aunty Mill had once expressed to her, much disgust as to the manner of their begetting. I found this sad. It was a shame that her natural fastidiousness had deprived her of the pleasures of motherhood especially as her two sisters appeared to have had no such scruples. They had produced about ten children between them.

Like most of the Smiths, Aunty Mill was of average height, plumpish and rounded. When she sat at table presiding over her very beautiful Japanese-style teapot, her back was so straight that if you had put a yard rule against it, the rule would have touched all the way down. She never made-up. Ladies usually didn't in those days. I knew Mother kept a swans-down puff in a cut glass powder bowl on her dressing-table and I had sometimes seen her apply a light touch, but I never saw her do it at Roose! Aunty's cheeks were very bright with little red, thread-like capillaries clearly showing in them. She had never had her hair bobbed and wore it pulled back into a bun. It was light brown, very fine, straight and whispy, just like my father's and mine. Although my mother liked Aunty Mill very much, I think she was rather frightened of her disapproval, and it took quite a bit of courage on Mother's part to appear for the first time in Roose wearing white stockings! Aunty was horrified, but my mother stuck to her guns and to her white stockings, and the next time we visited, three months later, Aunty Mill was also wearing white stockings.

"For informal occasions only," she told us. She still thought them too frivolous for chapel and there she kept to her sober blacks.

Whenever she had time, Aunty was always willing to talk, or to read to me and to play games – especially the educational sort which helped my dreadful spelling and arithmetic. She would go about singing, hymns and country songs. She tried hard to teach me to sing, but with my congenital inability to move from one note to another, it proved hopeless. I would try very hard and looking back now on my frequent attempts, I realise just how much my musical family must have suffered. One of Aunty Mill's songs still lingers in my memory. It went like this:

Little bird you are welcome
What news do you bring
Of our mothers and sisters?
Now tell us and sing.

A kiss and a letter
I bring you today
If you've nothing better
I'll take them away!

That song always puzzled me. I could never quite understand the little bird's rather negative attitude. It seemed so mean to take away a kiss and a letter from those who had probably been longing for them. I expect it was a Methodist song, for to me, so much seemed to be negative and forbidden in the family's religion, especially on Sundays when 'Thou shalt not' reigned supreme. Grandpa and Aunty were very strict about Sundays. Chapel in the morning, Sunday school or a visit to Grandma's grave in the afternoon, and once I had reached eight or nine years old, chapel again in the evening. In between times there were to be no skipping, no ball-bouncing, no 'playing out' on the Green with the neighbours' children, no knitting, no sewing, no reading of books except the Bible or *Pilgrim's Progress*, no singing except for hymns or psalms and no reciting of poetry. I dreaded Sundays at Roose, but eventually, I found an escape. I would go outside under the pretext of visiting the toilet after dinner when all the adults were snoozing or talking and I would stand alone in the backyard, even in cold weather – imagining, daydreaming. Stock still by the lavatory door, I would gaze into space for half an hour at a time, but my mind was ranging far and wide. There in the back, at the age of seven, I started a serial in my head which continued for years and years, one which I could pick up and secretly enjoy whenever I was bored or restricted in any way at all.

Aunty Mill was a first class cook. She never appeared flustered no matter for how many she had to cater. Wonderful milk puddings, rich and creamy, filled with sultanas beneath a dark brown skin, would come bubbling from her oven. Another of her achievements was her 'Wing Cakes' which she produced in great batches for Grandpa's shop, but there were always a dozen or so left over for our tea. Aunty had been cooking for Grandpa long before Grandma died, she was a good organiser and meals were always on time. When we went to stay with her and Uncle Sam, she managed without neglecting Grandpa or the shop, to come out with us almost every day to the seaside or into the country. She really enjoyed riding about in Clara. She would sit in the back with her arm round me and sing, and she made us lovely picnic teas to take with us. She was fun, but like my father, she could be quite frighteningly stern if the occasion warranted it. I was always mindful of my behaviour and never took advantage when I was with her.

I remember to this day one particular afternoon when I was left alone with Aunty. My parents were visiting some friends, Uncle Sam was at work and Grandpa was selling his meat. I was looking at a picture book by the fire in Aunty's kitchen and she was in the scullery preparing the tea. I dropped my book and as I bent to pick it up I must have let out some very mild expression of exasperation, for I didn't know any swear words except 'damn' which I had once heard Grandpa Haydock use. I had been forbidden to use that word – neither did I. Actually, I wasn't aware that this time I had said anything at all, but I must have done, for Aunty appeared at the scullery door with the same look in her eyes that my father knew so well how to use when he was displeased.

"Don't ever let me hear you use that word again!"

I shrivelled. "What word?"

"You know very well which word and I have no intention of repeating it. It was a disgraceful thing to say and I am ashamed of you!"

I was quite innocent and puzzled and I wish I knew today what she thought I had said. I became even more puzzled when, in private, later, I told Mother about the episode.

"Well, there you are," said Mother. "You must always mind your 'p's and q's' with Millie."

I concluded that the word which I had used had contained 'p's and q's' and that words with these letters in them should in future always be avoided when talking to Aunty!

Uncle Sam was a heart-throb! Tall, handsome and jolly, he appealed to me in every way. He laughed a lot and I never heard him say an unkind or bad-tempered thing to anyone. To me, he was the male counterpart of my Aunty Gertie. In the 1920s, he had black curly hair, fine white teeth and dark brown passionate eyes. He worked at the shipyards in Barrow. I think he must have been a mechanic for when he came home from work, he was always wearing navy-blue overalls and he smelt delightfully and intriguingly and cleanly of metal and machine oils, and although I didn't recognise it at the time, of masculinity. He would breeze into Aunty's kitchen, kiss her and greet everybody present in his friendly way and he would lift me by the elbows until my head touched the ceiling – looking up at me and laughing as he held me there. I would shriek with delight as he lowered me so swiftly that my stomach would rocket into my mouth and I loved the sensation. Strange that I had no fear and yet I was terrified of the same feeling in Lewises' lifts.

On a summer's evening, as soon as he had had his tea, he could always be relied upon to come down the garden. Here he would help me to fly my kite or to get my 'Loop-a-Roo' game going. He was the only one in the family who could spin a rope cowboy fashion. I never mastered it and even my father couldn't keep it up for nearly as long as Uncle Sam could. He showed me for the first time the magic invisible forces which could work so dramatically when a small piece of cardboard with a hole in the centre was fed on to the end of the string which held my kite aloft. I would watch amazed as the cardboard left my hand and went sailing up and up along the string until it almost reached the kite, and there it would stay – floating far above my head. My link, my message to the upper air.

Dear Uncle Sam! I could never get quite enough of him. He had left home each morning by the time I was up, and I could spend only a short while with him in the evening before I had to go to bed. He rarely came out with us on picnics, he was always working, and on Sundays, he was much occupied with chapel-going. I dearly wish now that our friendship could have continued into my later years. As it was, he was just a wonderful playmate to me, but looking back now, I can feel the underlying sadness of his life quite strongly. After we had left Manchester when I was eleven and we were living in Torquay, we visited Roose far less frequently. I saw him for the last time when I was seventeen. We had called in at Roose on our way to Scotland. His hair had turned quite grey and although he still laughed a lot, the old camaraderie had faded.

"Well, I couldn't lift you to the ceiling now," he observed, looking at my sturdy adolescent build. Although I joined in the general laughter, suddenly I felt inadequate, distanced, and I didn't know why.

During the War, my first husband, who was an Observer in the RAF, was stationed on Walney Island. He had never met Grandpa, Aunty and Uncle, so one Saturday afternoon, when he had time off from flying, he made the short trip to Roose. He recognised the village, he later told me, from my description of it and he soon found No. 73. He was immediately made to feel one of the family and given a loving welcome. He stayed with them all until long after tea. When the time came for him to go back to camp, Uncle Sam insisted on walking with him to the end of the village where there should have been a bus into Barrow. It was wartime and buses were infrequent, so my husband prepared to say 'good-bye' and set off on foot. Uncle Sam, however, still insisted on walking with him and my husband told me later that the whole time they were walking, and they had almost reached Barrow before they parted company, he had the feeling that Uncle was trying to tell him something, to confide in him in some way. The sad thing is that he never managed to bring out whatever was troubling him. I wish with all my heart that I could have been the one to have walked with him all those years ago. As it was, he died a little time afterwards and the circumstances of his death were quite tragic.

After Uncle Sam died, Aunty Mill became seriously ill with leukaemia and had to be moved into hospital. No. 74 had been sold when Grandpa died and Aunty and Uncle had moved into No. 73. Aunty never came back from hospital and the old house stood empty for many months filled only with the memories of days when it had been overflowing with noisy, fun-loving brothers and sisters.

In 1887 my father had been born there. He came at the tail end of the family when the stock was becoming weaker. Grandma had been producing children since 1874 and was to go on giving birth until 1890; eleven children in all! My father was the last to survive. In 1886 there had been born a sister Frances, in 1887 came my father, in 1888 a brother Keedwell, and in 1890, twins, Emmeline and Keedwell. Frances must have died when she was about five years old, for my father could just remember her lying wrapped in rugs, pale and ill on Grandpa's horsehair sofa; the other three all died at birth or very soon after, and it was touch and go whether my father himself would survive.

He was a seven month baby and so weak at birth that the doctor held out little hope for him. In fact, the doctor was angry. He told Grandma that she must have no further children, that she should not have had this one and that he must definitely be the last. Indeed, this baby, he said, had such a small chance of survival that he was as good as lost now. The doctor was giving him up, washing his hands of him. Grandma Smith looked down at the wizened little man who had just been put into her arms. He had no fingernails, no toe-nails or hair and he was scarcely breathing.

"I didn't give you up," Grandma told my father years later. "I loved you and prayed for you."

It seemed to be enough, for when the doctor called the next day, to his amazement, my father was still alive. Either there is something very special about seven month babies, or perhaps all Grandma's extra efforts engendered in her son capabilities above the norm. For as he grew, Samuel Wesley, 'Wes' as he became known to his family, developed an intelligence beyond his years, and it seemed in later life, that whatever he turned his hand to, be it practical or intellectual, he made a success of it. Best of all, he inherited his mother's power for love, her strong emotions and her giving, generous nature.

One of his earliest memories, he told me was of a time before he was britched. It was washing-day – lines and lines of white cotton sheets, shirts, petticoats, pinafores and drawers were flapping on the Green. Three year old Wesley toddled across the side-road and into the yard opposite where another mother of another family was busy over her wash-tub. She smiled at him absentmindedly and he watched quietly until she went out of the yard gate with a pile of washing for 'hanging out'. Fascinated that the sloshing sounds had now ceased, and curious to find out why, my father, clinging to the rim of the tub, hauled himself up and managed to get one leg over the side. There, he wobbled precariously, overbalanced and fell in! His dress and petticoats saved him. They spread out around him and buoyed him up just long enough for the neighbour to return from the Green and fish him, miraculously unharmed, from the water. Without stopping to take off her apron, she wrapped him in its voluminous folds and Father could remember being carried back home to Grandma, dripping and shaken.

He went to the village school on North Row as had all of his brothers and sisters before him. When he started at five, his brother Ed and sister Mill must still have been attending there. Father could remember his first day very well. He had a new suit for the occasion. As he stood in the hall for prayers, he suddenly noticed that all the other children were on their knees and that he alone was standing. His teacher came up to him and whispered, "Come along, Wesley, kneel down now with the others."

"Not likely," replied my father in a loud voice, "not in my best suit!"

All England shivered throughout the winter of his ninth year. So intense was the cold that Lake Windermere froze over from end to end. Special day excursions at five shillings a head return, were being run from Manchester to Ambleside and hordes of people came to skate on the lake. There were cheaper trips starting from Barrow, so that the Smith brothers and sisters managed, by pooling their resources, to partake of the fun *en masse*. They must all of them have had skates for my father remembered how they set off as a family group and managed to keep more or less together, skating along the whole length of the lake – some ten miles in all! Before he reached the end, he grew very tired, he told me, so his big brothers and sisters took turns to pull him along between them. He held a hand on each side and 'free-wheeled' for the rest of the trip.

They must have been an affectionate, noisy and united lot. They loved their parents dearly, especially Grandma around whom their world revolved; but the boys were so wild and the girls so high spirited that Grandma had to control her brood, not only with love and prayers, but also with the cane! She kept a special little swishy one hanging on the back of the scullery door in No. 74 and my father would often recount how efficiently she used it and how sharply it stung. He would tell me, with laughter in his eyes, of times he remembered when all of them had been up to some mischief or other, of which Grandma had become aware. She would bide her time, waiting perhaps until the evening when the family gathered in the living-room which later became Aunty Mill's kitchen. Then, she would reveal that she knew all and quick as lightning, she would disappear behind the scullery door. Her children rose as one and made a dash for it, hotly pursued by Grandma lashing out at any legs arms and backs she could reach before they disappeared through the connecting arch into No. 73 and on and out through its back door. Usually she managed to trap one or two of them in the yard before they could get away, and the rest she dealt with later – just to be fair. All was quickly forgiven, and no one bore malice, but Grandma continued to wield her cane until the older ones were almost grown up.

There was 'bath night' twice a week in those days, one evening being set aside for the boys and one for the girls. The old tin tub was placed on the scullery floor and gallons and gallons of water were heated up on the stove and on the kitchen range. When it was the boys' turn, the girls, with "the well-taught decorum of Victorian maidenhood," said Aunty Mill, withdrew, but as the boys grew older, they took a teasing delight in trying to outrage their sisters' modesty. The whole family would tease each other unmercifully, and on the girls' bath night, the three sisters had to organise quite a campaign to keep the lads at bay. "But we managed it," Aunty Mill would say – winking at me and tossing her head at my father. One sister would mount guard over the scullery door and one over the back door, while the third would take a bath. "It was high jinks," said Father. "We never succeeded in storming the fortress – they had too much amunition in the way of loofahs and wet towels and they would stick their flannels into the keyholes and hold up Grandma's baking board when we tried to look at them through the scullery window from the outside yard."

"By the time Wes was ten," said Aunty Mill to me one day as I stood watching her putting cream dabs onto a batch of wing cakes, "Queen Victoria was celebrating her Diamond Jubilee year. Your Uncle Bert and your Uncle

Art had left home by that time and were in America. There were only five of us children left here and Annie was very grown up anyway and courting Jack Mitchell at the time and we didn't see much of her either, so when there was a day's national holiday declared in June, your Grandma and Grandpa took Wes, Ed, Flossie and me out into the country for the day. Grandpa drove the pony and trap and Grandma took a picnic."

"Did you see the processions?" I asked, thinking of Oldham Wakes' Week.

"Oh no, certainly not. Your Grandfather had no time for royalty in those days and wouldn't let any of us join in the celebrations. He forbade us to go anywhere near Barrow where the big shows were on. It was your father's birthday about the same time, so we had a party all on our own. We made a big fuss of him. He was the youngest and delicate, but very clever. He had passed his Scholarship exam by the time he was ten you know and he went to Barrow Higher Grade School in the September of that year. He did really well, became a King's Scholar and we were all so proud of him. He Matriculated early and was quite determined to become a teacher. Your Grandma was much pleased, she could see that he was a born teacher even when he was quite little and she encouraged him. It wasn't easy to find the money to equip him for college, but our parents were used to making sacrifices for what they thought worthwhile and he was entered as a student at the Methodist Training College in Westminster in London."

"Were you all very sad when he left home?" I asked.

Aunty Milly laughed. "Oh he didn't go straight away." She stood back, surveying her half finished tray of wing cakes with a critical eye. "He was far too young. He had to wait nearly four years before he could start at college."

"So what did he do?"

"Well, he went back to school, partly to keep on with his lessons and partly to learn to teach. And that was learning the hard way. It was so difficult for him that we all used to pray together as a family that God would help him in his task."

"Why was it hard?"

Aunty Mill looked at me and smiled. "He wasn't so very much older than you are now," she said.

"How old?"

"He was only fourteen." Privately, I thought that was a lot older, but I didn't say so.

"And he was small for his age," she continued. Then, seeing that I was really more interested in the story of my father's early achievements than in the successful production of wing cakes, she went on: "There was a scheme at the time called the Pupil-Teacher Scheme, and if you were accepted into it, you could stay on at school, continue your lessons and learn to teach at the same time – the hard way." Aunty Mill slapped a big dollop of cream, into the hole in the centre of a wing cake and levelled it off expertly with a knife before going on: "He and another boy – between them were put in charge of a class of school-leavers who were all boys over thirteen years old and all waiting for the day they became fourteen."

"Why?"

"Well, you see, people were even poorer then than they are today and mothers and fathers took their children away from school as soon as they were allowed to do so and put them to work. Any job would do, so long as it brought in something, no matter how little, just to help to buy food for the babies, and little brothers and sisters not yet able to work. You can imagine how the boys in your father's class didn't want to pay attention to their lessons when they knew they would very shortly have to leave, can't you?"

"Was it a big class?"

"Well, there were sixty of them to start with, all about the same age as your father and that is when it was so hard, but the numbers gradually dwindled and it became easier as the year wore on. He managed very well, our Wes, and he never complained." I expect he gave the bad boys 'The Look', I thought to myself.

"Did he like going to college?" I asked.

"Oh yes, he worked very hard. He was the youngest student in his year and in his second year he became Senior Monitor and was in charge of all the other students. He had come top in English and French in the exams at the end of his first year, but he was top in science and maths also and he decided to concentrate on those. Of course, when Grandpa knew of this, he was very worried."

"Why?"

"Well, at the time, a man called Mr Darwin who was a scientist, had just published a book with a theory, that's a kind of explanation, about something which Grandpa didn't agree with. He thought it was against the teachings of the Bible, and he thought that if your father became a scientist and followed Mr Darwin's teachings, he might lose his faith in the Methodists."

"He still goes to Chapel," I said, thoughtfully.

"Of course he does, and anyway, your Grandma was quite sure that he wouldn't lose his faith and persuaded Grandpa to let your father go ahead and take science subjects in his second year in college. He did very well and you know what happened next, don't you?"

I nodded. "He came to Manchester and lived with Mrs Varley and then he met Mummy and they got married."

"That's right," said Aunty Mill. "Once he left college he never came back to live at home again – " She sighed. "Bert, Annie, Floss, Art, Ed, and then Wes – he was the last to go."

"But not you." I protested. "You're still here."

"So I am." Aunty Mill laughed, nodding towards the wing cakes. "There, this tray is finished now. Just help me to carry it into the shop, will you?"

My father talked a lot to me and to all of us really, about my Uncle Ed. He was the next brother up the ladder and only a couple of years older than my father. Between the two of them, of course, there had been the little sister Frances who had died when Ed was about five and old enough to have grown very fond of her. After her death, he and my father seemed to be always in each other's company. They grew up together with a great deal of fun and laughter and a great deal of quarrelling also. They fought like young puppies, and Ed, being the elder and bigger and stronger than Wes, usually had the upper hand. They fought at home, they fought at school, they even fought in the middle of the night, leaping out of the bed which they shared and tearing the old patched sheet right down the middle as they battled for supremacy of ownership! They must have looked very much alike, for on one occasion, someone in the village complained to Grandpa that my father had pushed her daughter into a puddle and run off with her bag of sweets. It was Ed who had done the dirty deed, but my father who took the punishment. Fortunately, their big sister, Annie, had her doubts about my father being the culprit and pleaded with Grandpa not to thrash him. Wes never split on Ed and Ed didn't own up. "I couldn't blame him really," said my father. "Your grandfather's thrashings could be very severe."

"What happened to you?" I whispered, looking at the benign old gentleman now having 'forty winks' on his horse-hair sofa.

"Oh I was only sent to bed for the day, it was nothing compared with what could have happened to Ed if he had owned up!"

One day when I was very small and Father and I were having a paddle together at Biggar bank, I suddenly noticed that his right foot looked different from the left one. The difference must have shown up in the brilliant sunshine for one foot was pink and healthy looking, but you could see right through the skin of the other. It was tightly stretched and quite transparent all across the top and seemed so unnaturally white that even I noticed it.

"Why is your foot like that?" I asked, pointing with my own toes.

"It's been scalded with boiling water – years ago – your Uncle Ed did it. Hold on to my hand and I'll tell you all about it as we paddle.

"One winter's night when I was about as old as you are now, Ed and I were all ready to go to bed, sitting in our nightshirts and warming our bare feet in front of the fire in what is now your Aunty Mill's kitchen. We were waiting for your grandma to hear out prayers and put us to bed but she was busy and we were having to wait rather a long time. I was beginning to feel very sleepy," said Father. "There was a great big black kettle boiling away gently on the coals, the steam was rising in a kind of slow, swirling dance towards the ceiling and whispering with a quiet hissing music as it rose. It was warm and cosy and I was beginning to nod off, when suddenly, your Uncle Ed leaned forward over the top of the fireguard, grasped the handle of the kettle and tilted it towards the hearth."

"That must have made you jump," I laughed.

"It did, but I wasn't quick enough. A great jet of scalding water splashed all over my foot."

"Did it hurt?"

"Terribly. I screamed and your Grandma came running in to see what all the noise was about. She picked me up, carried me into the scullery, held my burnt foot under the cold water tap and at the same time, called for your Aunty Annie to fetch Nurse Maggie who lived further up the village. She soon came back with the nurse, and amongst the three of them they managed to stop me screaming and to treat my foot so that it healed quite well, but it took a long time and the marks never faded away completely. Perhaps the doctor could have done better, but we couldn't afford one in those days."

"What happened to Uncle Ed?"

"Oh," Father laughed. "Once all the panic was over, your Grandma set about him in no uncertain manner, with that swishy little cane of hers."

"Did he cry?"

"I can't remember," said Father, "but do you know, when Grandma asked him why on earth he had done such a thing, he said that he had wanted to find out how loud a sound the water would make if it fell onto the hearth stone instead of going up into the air as steam, and how was he to know, he said, that Wes would put his foot in it as usual?"

One evening some time after this, Father and I were alone together in the Barrel House putting the car away for the night.

"I don't like this place," I remarked, it was a draughty spot. The wind whistled through the gaps in the old black boarding and the roof lifted and clattered as the air rushed beneath it.

"This was the cowshed when I was a boy."

"The cows must have been cold!"

Father laughed. "Oh it was much more solid then, not so draughty – in fact, your grandfather kept quite a valuable piece of farm machinery in here at one time." I wasn't much interested in farm machinery until Father suddenly said, "Your Uncle Ed got the most severe thrashing of his life over that machine!" Of course, I was all ears then.

"Why, who thrashed him?"

"Grandpa of course." We closed the car doors and walked back together up the garden path towards the house. Father talking all the time.

"Ed must have been about twelve when the new machine arrived. Grandpa had it set up in the middle of the cowshed and he forbade anyone, especially Ed to touch it. Now you Uncle Ed loved machines – he was always tinkering with something or other and he kept coming down to the cowshed just to look at the new arrival. It tempted him so much that one day he couldn't stand it any longer. The two of us were down in the cowshed doing the milking and your Grandpa was away 'buying in' at Barrow market, when Ed suddenly said, 'You know Wes, I could take this machine to pieces and put it back together again without anyone knowing anything about it.' I was very afraid that something would go wrong, but he was quite sure of himself," said Father.

"What happened then?"

"I cleared out, I left him to it. I finished the milking, emptied the last pail of milk into the churn, gathered up the empty buckets and started back for the house – just as we are doing now. I didn't want any part of it. I felt sure there would be trouble."

"Go on, go on."

"Well, Ed stayed behind in the shed. He told me afterwards," said Father, "that he knew exactly what he was doing. He took that machine to pieces quite quickly until he had stripped it right down to its bare framework and then he started to put it back together again. All went well at first and it wasn't until he had almost finished when he discovered that he had lost a most important part and that he couldn't go on until it was found. Ed was frantic. He searched the cowshed, every nook and cranny, every cow's stall, even up in the hay loft, but it never turned up. In the end, after everybody in the family had helped to search, and the cowshed had been completely raked out, Grandpa was forced to buy a new part for the machine. He was so angry, he beat Ed severely and stopped his pocket money for weeks."

"I wonder what happened to the missing part?"

"You know what I think?" said Father. "I think that one of the cows ate it!"

To me, the cows seemed 'to have it in' for Uncle Ed, for in addition to swallowing a vital part of Grandpa's machine, one of them apparently once split Ed's nostril wide open. She turned her head to look at him whilst he was milking her, just as he raised his head from her flanks. She couldn't have liked what she saw, for suddenly she tossed her head upwards in aggravation and one of her horns went straight up his nose!

According to Father and Aunty Mill, Uncle Ed wasn't the sort of boy who enjoyed school, yet he was quite brilliant in his own way – an engineer in the making. He was the only one of the Smith boys not to go in for preaching or teaching as his life's vocation. He became an apprentice in the Barrow Shipyards, and carried on studying at night at the local Technical School. He completed his apprenticeship, obtained an Engineering Certificate and began to work on the construction of naval ships. During this time, he met a girl from Walney Island and they started courting. They wanted to marry, but money was scarce, promotion slow and new jobs hard to come by in England at that time. Ed, however, was sure that there would be big opportunities for him in a place like Australia. He said good-bye to his family and to the girl from Walney Island, asking her to wait for him until he could send for her to join him, and off he set at the age of twenty-three, all alone to find work on the other side of the world. He travelled steerage to Fremantle where he remained jobless and penniless and reduced almost to starvation. After a while he heard that there was work to be had in Sydney and he moved on. This time he was forced to work his passage as a stokehold trimmer, wheeling coal from the bunkers to the boilers' furnaces on board a cargo vessel. He was seasick and alone and had no idea of what the future held for him.

Ed must have written home to tell his parents that he was about to move on from Fremantle to Sydney, but he never once mentioned his predicament and the hardships he was facing. Grandma and Grandpa, however, read between the lines. They scraped together as much money as they could possibly afford and wired it out to him so that it would be waiting at the main post office in Sydney when he arrived. And then a strange thing happened. It was going dark in Sydney as Uncle Ed opened his envelope outside the Post Office underneath a street lamp. As he read the glad tidings and realised how much this gift would mean to him, he shouted aloud, 'Hallelujah,' for the sheer joy of being able to live again and for the love which had reached out to him from the other side of the world. The wonderful thing was, so my father told me, that at the precise moment when he had shouted 'Hallelujah' into the Australian night, Grandma had been serving a shop full of customers in Roose village. Suddenly she was filled with such a strong feeling of elation and thanksgiving, that she had to rush away upstairs and cry out aloud to relieve the emotion which was welling up so uncontrollably inside her!

Ed made good in Australia. He sent for the girl from Walney Island who travelled out to join him and they were married out there. They settled finally at a place called Coffs Harbour on the north coast of New South Wales where my uncle over the years invented machines for use in the iron foundry and timber mill which he had established. He and my Aunty Ethel raised three children, had lots of grand-children and founded the Australian branch of my father's family. Ed came back to England only once. It was in the 1960s after both his parents had died. He visited Roose but found it so changed from the village of his childhood days that he told my father he wished he had never gone there to see it again.

It was Aunty Mill who held on firmly to family ties. All through the twenties and thirties she kept each thread closely attached to its central knot by her constant letters to brothers

A visit to Draycott, 1925. Great Uncle John, Mother, Beryl and Great Aunt Nancy.

Roose village.

Grandma and Grandpa Smith in the early years of their marriage.

The Smith girls. Beryl's three aunties: Annie, Mill and Flossie.
Taken in the 1890s.

Beryl's father and his three brothers, also from the 1890s.
Art, Ed, Father and Bert.

Aunty Mill and Uncle Sam on their wedding day.

Mother, Father and Beryl at Dovaston, Devon, 1926.

Uncle Robert and Aunty Kate's bungalow,
near Ottery St. Mary, Devon, 1926.

Picnicking by the roadside – Uncle Robert, Aunty Kate, Aunty Jessie and Eileen. (Uncle Robert's car in background – note rubber tyre attached to spare wheel.)

Mother, Father and Beryl at Dovaston, Devon, 1926.

Beach party, Sidmouth, 1930.

Father teaching Beryl to swim in the rock pools at Jacob's Ladder, Sidmouth, 1927.

Eileen and Beryl at Sidmouth.

A picnic at Sidmouth in the '30s. Aunty Kate, Uncle Robert, Mother and Beryl.

and sisters abroad. She passed on information from one to the other and encouraged them to keep directly in touch with each other. She continued writing well into the war years and was such an interesting correspondent, that many of my Smith cousins who never met Aunty Mill still remember her vivid descriptions of life in Roose village in the first half of the century. Like my father, she could tell a good story and kept me amused for many a long hour with anecdotes about her own life. She had been the liveliest of the three girls in the family and being the youngest daughter, she would tease her sisters unmercifully about their sweethearts. In fact she had once caused Annie, the eldest, to become quite hysterical and the doctor had had to be called in to administer a sedative. Unlike the others, she never strayed far from her home. She was devoted to her parents and had nursed Grandma Smith all through her bedridden days and stayed by Grandpa's side right up to the day he died. Her strict Methodist upbringing made her appear 'Prim and Proper', but underneath there was a warm and loving personality which I came to appreciate the more, the older I grew. She married Uncle Sam in 1907. She longed for a white wedding; a beautiful dress with train and veil such as my mother was to have seven years later, but Grandpa Smith had frowned upon the idea of personal adornment and forbidden any hint of 'gaudy raiments', so that Mill was married in a long grey dress with an up-to-the-neck choker collar. She wore her light brown hair straight and pulled severely back into a bun.

Not only did Aunty Mill tell me about her own life, but also she remembered many happenings in the lives of her brothers and sisters, so that much of the information in the following stories comes from the tales which she told to me so long ago. In particular she remembered a great deal about the brother who came next to herself two years older and two years up on the family ladder – and this is his, this is . . .

Art's Story

My Uncle Art, John Arthur Smith, had been born on January 25th 1880, two years before Aunty Mill. I never met him, but around Roose village when I was young in the 1920s, there were still tales being told of him and his 'wicked ways'. He had been wild and such a tearaway as a boy, that when he was fourteen, and Grandpa decided to find work in America for a year in order to save the family from starvation, Grandma refused to be left with the responsibility of controlling Art and insisted that Grandpa took him along also. Art must have been overjoyed at the decision. What an adventure! They worked their passage out on a trading vessel – an animal transporter. Once there, helping on a farm in the mid-west where his mother's aunt and uncle, Mary and John Masters had settled some years previously, Art must have fallen in love with America, and when Grandpa returned after the year was up, Art was not with him – he stayed for another six years in the USA. Grandma was heartbroken. She hadn't envisaged having to part with Art at such an early age. It took her a long time to forgive Grandpa for leaving him behind.

Art developed quite a degree of charm at an early age. He would sidle up to visitors, smile beguilingly at them, and ask for money! Grandma was horrified and embarrassed when she first caught him at it. She forbade him ever to do such a thing again, but he persisted until finally, she told him that if he repeated the performance, she would have to smack him. He was about five years old when a young visiting minister came to take tea with the family. There was a lull in the conversation, and Art, who was seated between his mother and the minister, slipped his hand into the preacher's. Looking up innocently into his face, "Give us a penny Mate?" he pleaded. The minister laughed and produced the penny. Grandma said afterwards that she didn't know how to keep her hands off him until the visitor had departed! Once he had gone, however, the penny was removed and the threatened punishment was meted out. "And now," said Grandma, at the end of it all, "I hope I have managed to teach you never to do such a thing again!"

"Yes," choked Art, manfully holding back his tears, "you have, so now can I have my penny back please?"

As he grew, so the villagers became more and more aware of him. He always seemed to be in some trouble or other.

He would invade their gardens, steal the eggs from their hen houses and the apples from their trees. On one occasion, he was caught with his head stuck fast in the small entrance to a chicken coop. On another, he was chased the whole length of the village by an irate farmer on whose territory he had been trespassing – no doubt with evil intent. As he ran, the last house came in sight and the man was gaining ground rapidly. Art became desperate and took a chance. He dived headlong down the very next lobby he reached and pushed breathlessly against one of the two front doors at its end. It was locked! The man appeared at the entrance to the lobby as, frantically, Art threw himself against the opposite door. It opened and he stepped through, closing it firmly behind him. The family were all seated round the kitchen table having a meal. "Excuse me," gasped Art to the astonished company. "But there's a man after me!" and he dashed through the room, across the backyard and out on to the Green, where he easily made his escape!

He and Ed were always playing pranks together. One of their favourite tricks was to lean out from the upper window on the side wall of No. 73. From here, using a long stick, they could reach the front door, on which they would 'rat-a-tat-tat' loudly, and of course, when anyone came to answer, they found no one outside. They were also known to have repeated the performance in their friends' houses elsewhere in the village. Poor Grandma, no wonder she wanted Grandpa to take fourteen-year-old Art to America. One day, someone trying to commiserate with Grandma over the conduct of her mischievous sons, shook her head especially hard over Art, sighed, and remarked, "Oh well, Mrs Smith, you must accept the fact that nearly every family has at least one black sheep in it."

"Ah yes," replied Grandma brightly, "but it's the black sheep which causes so much rejoicing in Heaven when it returns to the fold." Grandma's prophecy was to prove right, for once he reached America he was truly 'gathered in'. The fold suited him and he became gentle and caring.

He loved music – his favourite instrument being the piano. When he came back from the States he was twenty years old. He had saved enough money to put himself through college in America and he returned to England full of the idea of taking up a musical career. Once home, however, Grandpa discouraged this ambition. He pointed out to Art the difficulties he would encounter in trying to make a living as a musician and he persuaded him to choose the Methodist Ministry as his livelihood instead. No sooner had Art made this decision than he learned of his selection to sing in a Cathedral choir, which he then couldn't accept. Instead, he went as a mature student to Shebbear College where his father and his Uncle John had been as boys years before. Whilst here, he obtained certificates to teach vocal and instrumental music and he ranked second in all England on Finney's Theological Lecture Tests. He was ordained in England and spent nine years preaching in some very poor parishes in the North. There he met and fell in love with Louisa Coates. They became engaged and after Art returned to America in 1910, he sent for Louisa, and they were married in 1911 in Melvin, Iowa. They had three children; my cousins whom I have never seen.

My father was teaching in Manchester when Uncle Art left England to return to his beloved America for the second time. Father went to Liverpool Docks to see his brother off. My father knew in his heart that he would not see this warm-hearted man ever again, and so strong were Father's feelings of loss, that rather shamefacedly, he told me years later, his grief got the better of him and he shut himself away in his room at Mrs Varley's for many days before he could again face the world.

Uncle Art and his family moved about America, finally settling in Colorado where he continued to serve his church faithfully. He worked very hard in all his parishes to establish the Methodist faith and was greatly loved and respected. In 1931, when he was only fifty-one, sadly, he died after an operation in Denver Hospital; a special man whom 'the gods loved'.

Flossie's Story

In 1877, three years before Art, a little girl had been born to the Smiths, a frail little girl who suffered from asthma nearly all of her life. She was born a healthy baby, the third child of the family, and although Grandma and Grandpa loved all of their children, Grandpa especially doted on this daughter, possibly because she became so delicate and was so brave in facing the sickness which crippled her to the end of her days. They christened her Florence Amy, but the family always called her Floss or Flossie. My father told me a strange story about the alleged cause of her illness. It seems that Grandpa always blamed vaccination for Flossie's troubles. Apparently, in 1877, when new babies arrived in the village, the doctor would wait until a sufficient number of his deliveries had reached between three and six months of age and would then make one round of the houses, taking matter from the suppurating sore of one previously vaccinated child to be used in the vaccination of the others. Aunty Floss was vaccinated in this way when she was a few months old and almost immediately she developed asthma. Grandpa became very suspicious and couldn't rest until he had discovered the source of the vaccine. It had come from an asthmatical child! Rightly or wrongly, Grandpa blamed the doctor ever afterwards for Flossie's life-long affliction, and my father was so worried about it that, in 1920, when it was my turn to be vaccinated (and by that time, vaccination was enforceable by law), my father refused to have me subjected to it and put up quite a fight in establishing his right to do so.

Aunty Floss was too delicate to become a teacher. In order to pay her way and help the family budget along, she may, like many girls from the growing lower middle classes of her day, have, before her marriage, taken in dressmaking or millinery wok. She married a man called Dave Garbutt from Barrow. He probably worked as a fitter in Vicker's shipyards and soon afterwards, she moved with him to Scunthorpe where he had found better employment. They had two children, my cousins Alice and James, and much later on in life, I was destined to meet both of them.

When depression hit Scunthorpe in 1913 all four of them emigrated to Australia and went to live in Coff's Harbour close to Uncle Ed whose timber and Engineering businesses were thriving at this time. Here, Dave, and later James, found work. Cousin Alice trained as a nurse in Sydney hospitals, and when the family moved again to South Africa where they finally settled in Johannesburg, close to one of Grandma Smith's brothers, Alice became a nursing sister in a large hospital there. Aunty Flossie's asthma never left her and my cousin Jim told me how she had to have injections daily to help her to breathe. The whole family had an aversion to needles – even Alice the nurse couldn't bring herself to inject her mother and in the end it was Jim, the schoolboy, who performed the task for her. It took all Jim's determination, he said, to be able to bring himself to stick a needle into his beloved mother.

From the way in which her children remembered my Aunty Floss, she must have been a brave and loving parent. Certainly she had all the firm determination of which the Smiths were capable. Delicate as she was, she decided that she must see her father again before she died and so, in the thirties, all alone, she made the voyage from Capetown to Southampton and I was able to meet her very briefly for the first and last time. Mother, Father and I were on the dockside when the ship berthed and I remember my father trying in vain to persuade this frail old lady to come back with us to Torquay and rest a while before undertaking the long journey north to Roose. But no! She must leave at once for Barrow. We found her a corner seat in what I hope was a through train, piled her luggage onto the rack and into the Guard's van, wished her 'God speed' and waved her a regretful good-bye. She arrived safely and stayed many weeks, scarcely leaving Grandpa's side. I never saw her again, she died in South Africa shortly after she reached home.

In the days before they emigrated with their parents to Australia, Flossie's children often visited their grandparents in Roose, and after Grandpa had closed his shop in the evenings, they had been allowed to play 'pretend shop' on the premises. They served imaginary customers over a real counter, and once, on opening one of the drawers at the back of the shop, they had been delighted to find large quantities of loose 'tea'. This they packed into brown paper bags and 'sold' it along with many other make-believe items. Aunty Mill, coming to look in on their games was horrified when she discovered the contents of the brown paper bags. She threw them on the fire immediately, bags and all, and the children were made to scrub their hands thoroughly, for the contents had been . . . rat droppings!

On another occasion, Aunty Mill gave Alice and Jim two silver threepenny bits – one each to spend at the village shop – just a block away. They set out together and Alice, as the eldest, took Jim's hand. In the other hand, she carried both threepenny bits. On the way she tripped over a loose stone and the money fell to the ground. One of the threepenny bits rolled merrily along the gutter and disappeared down the grating of a drain cover. Alice retrieved the other coin – took Jim's hand firmly in her own again and marched quickly back to No. 73. There she found Grandma Smith sitting by the fire. Without hesitation, my small cousin approached, announcing in a loud voice, "Nanna, Jim's threepenny bit has fallen down a drain."

In 1937 Alice came back on holiday to England. She spent several weeks in Roose looking after Grandpa while Aunty Mill and Uncle Sam took a trip to Draycott together. When we called at Roose to collect Alice to take her on holiday to Scotland with us, I realised just how strong a bond she had formed with Grandpa. She was thirty-two, I was seventeen and I envied her the warm, teasing, familiar relationship she had with him. To me, Grandpa remained an aloof and respected figure – to Alice, he had obviously become a dearly loved friend. In one month, she had come closer to him than I had ever done or was ever likely to do. I think Grandpa must have seen in her the reincarnation of Flossie, the daughter he had loved so well.

Annie's Story

Annie Clarissa Smith, the eldest daughter of the family was born in Roose in 1876. From an early age she appeared to be a very strong-minded young lady. She did well at school, had a bright and capable personality and wanted to become a teacher. Just as she was about to embark on this career, Grandma Smith, worn out with child-bearing and the onset of arthritis, became ill, and obviously the eldest daughter's services must have been much in demand. Flossie was delicate, Millie still at school, little Frances had not survived her long illness, and the three latest Smith babies had just died, so Annie set to work with the washing, the starching and the ironing, the cooking and the cleaning, the shopping and the gardening for a family of at least seven people, to say nothing of helping to nurse Grandma, and serving in the shop whenever she could. I feel sure all the rest of the household would have rallied round – it was in the nature of the Smiths to pull together in a crisis, especially one which involved their dearly loved mother, but in spite of this there must have been enough work to keep ten eldest daughters occupied. So, Annie left her studies and stayed at home. If she had any time at all, she may have taken in sewing for, 'she was an excellent seamstress and did exquisite handwork – every stitch was perfect and she knitted and crocheted extremely complicated patterns.' She looked after the little ones in the family until Grandma grew strong enough to take up the reins again, but all through her late teens, she must, intermittently have played the role of housekeeper and substitute mother. She had a great sense of humour and of fair play, and I know that on more than one occasion she defended my father against Grandpa's wrath. It was as well that alongside an iron will she developed a strong faith and high principles, for she was destined to lead the hardest life of all, compared with those of her brothers and sisters.

She married Jack Mitchell. It was a love match. Jack was a miner who lived on North Row – a handsome, upright man of whom Grandma and Grandpa Smith were very fond. However, Jack was not strong and mining was probably the last sort of job he should have been doing. My grandparents were worried that Annie might have to face very difficult times ahead if she married Jack. Moreover, a friend and classmate of Bert (Annie's eldest brother) who was training with Bert for the Ministry at that time also wanted to marry her. Grandpa was especially worried that Jack had no training for anything other than mining and he forecast a bleak future for his eldest daughter. Strong-minded Annie, however, would not be persuaded. She was marrying the man, she declared, and not the profession! And marry the man she did, but since Grandma insisted that her girls wore plain dresses with plain collars, it is quite likely that Annie, like Millie was not allowed a white wedding.

Annie and Jack set up house together on North Row where in 1900 their first child, my cousin Claire, was born. They were completely happy; theirs was a real life romance, but by the time their baby was a year old, America and the prospect of a better life was beckoning, so the young family decided to emigrate. This must have taken a great deal of courage, but they obviously had plenty, for they severed their family ties, left the village and the friends whom they had known all their lives and with a great pioneering spirit subjected themselves and a young baby to a totally different environment. It is interesting to learn, through my cousin Muriel, their youngest child, that they entered America, not through Ellis Island, but directly at New York Docks. This, she concludes, is due to the fact that they must have travelled as first-class passengers! I wonder if Grandma and Grandpa Smith found the money for those tickets, perhaps Uncle Bert was able to help out also, or had Jack and Annie themselves saved every penny they possibly could?

At first they lived in the state of Michigan where Jack continued to mine coal. They were lovers and were happy. Here, Hubert was born in 1902 and Frederick in 1904, and then they moved to Montana where the copper mines held out prospects of plentiful work and an early death! Here, Edna was born in 1907 and Spencer in 1909, Alice in 1914 and Muriel in 1916. Their family life must have been a replica of family life at No. 73 a generation previously; seven children, loving parents and a firm and guiding faith, but unlike Grandpa Smith, Jack was not strong, neither was he working above ground. He became ill and had to leave the mines. A gentle, artistic and musically inclined person, he was neither mentally nor physically suited to his job. He had always changed his clothes at the mines, never appearing at home in working gear. This was probably due partly to a natural fastidiousness about his appearance, and judging from his photograph he must have been a very handsome man, and probably because he did not wish to bring toxic fumes and dust anywhere near his family. In this way he may have saved his wife and children from an early death, but he couldn't himself escape the price which the mines exacted; his lungs became clogged with the poisonous dust and, sadly, in1921, he died at the age of 47.

My cousin Muriel can scarcely remember him. She was four years old at the time of his death. She has a dim memory of him being in bed and drinking malted milk – but that is all. However, from the rest of her family, she learned much about his capacity for hard work, his courage, his charm and his great love for his wife and children. Now he was gone, and for Annie, his widow, the hard life which Grandpa had forseen began in earnest. It is unlikely that in those days, governments had pension schemes or private companies made compensation for such a one as she, and Annie must have been at her wits' end to know what best to do for herself and her family. Her youngest child was four years old, her eldest twenty-one. Being Annie, she made rapid and firm decisions. Claire and Hubert were already working and could be left in Montana; Alice, Edna and Fred went to Iowa where Mary and John Masters welcomed them as they had welcomed Grandpa, Bert and Art, years previously when times were difficult; Spencer was given a home in Colorado with Art and his family, and Annie, taking Muriel with her, packed up and came back home to Roose. Muriel remembers arriving there. In her words: "When Mother and I arrived at 73 South Row, the first thing that Grandmother did was to hold my hair away from my face and say 'She has Jack's forehead'. I was only five, or four really. I did not know who Jack was and certainly not how I happened to have his forehead, nor why my grandmother cried about it."

During their year's stay in England, Muriel attended the village school on North Row. She had a doll, so my father told me, to which she was much attached and which had accompanied her from America, and which now accompanied her to school. When Annie brought Muriel to visit us in Manchester, the doll came also. Living next door to us at that time in Dean Avenue were the Hollins family. Jacky Hollins was a butch seven-year-old who thought girls existed to be teased and bullied. But in five-year-old Muriel, he met his match. One day he made the mistake of trying to take her doll from her! She set about him with such determined ferocity that she succeeded in giving him a thrashing which he didn't forget, and he never teased her again after that.

At the end of a year, Annie and Muriel returned to America. Annie gathered her family around her again and took in sewing, mending and dressmaking to keep a roof over their heads. She must have made many good friends in Montana who rallied about her in times of crisis. The family's next door neighbours were a Mr and Mrs Jack Harper from England. They had become very fond of Annie and Jack and their children. The Harpers had one daughter, Lili, who was Edna's age and the two girls became firm friends. In 1916, when Muriel was born prematurely at 3lbs 7oz, Mrs Harper took the tiny baby and looked after her, for Annie was very ill indeed. When Muriel and her mother arrived back in Montana, it was to find that Mrs Harper had suddenly died and Lili was in a children's home since her father who was a miner, just as Jack had been, could not care for her and do his job at the same time. Eventually, two years later, Mr Harper and Annie married, Lili came home to live and the family managed to survive quite well for a year or two. Then the mines claimed yet another victim, for Mr Harper also died, leaving Annie to cope with a family not yet completely grown and still largely dependent on her.

In 1928, Spencer, Alice and Muriel were still living at home. At this time, Annie left Montana and, taking all three children with her, went to live in Seattle. I think she stayed here for the rest of her life. My cousin Muriel's account of her final day speaks for itself: "It was June 10th 1963 and she was 87 years old. Apparently, she knew she was not well at all because she did something most unusual . . . she called a doctor and also Spencer's wife, Dorothy. When the doctor examined her, he said she must go to the hospital. She said she did not care to go to a hospital. Dorothy tried to get her to change her mind and said since the doctor wanted her there, she should agree. Mother said she frequently visited her older friends in hospitals and she had no intention of becoming a patient. Doctor asked her what she wanted to do or where she wanted to go, and she said she would go to her son's home – so he told Dorothy that Mother must do just as she wished. They called Spencer and he came right away; Mother insisted upon dressing, although she had very little strength. They took her to Spencer's home. She died later that same day. She had a sense of pride that governed her life, and it never left her."

Bert's Story

Hubert George Smith, the eldest son – the first born and the only child of my grandparents not to be born in Roose village, first saw the light of day in Barrow-in-Furness on August 27th, 1874. He was the only one of my father's brothers and sisters – apart from Aunty Mill – whom I knew at all well, for he came home from abroad when I was eight years old and he spent a whole month with us, holidaying in Devon. He was great fun – a most unusual man, easy to get to know, easy to be with and never, never dull. He must have worked very hard as a lad – humping meat about in Grandpa's shop, working as a counter assistant, delivery boy and general factotum. He, like the rest of the Smith Children, became imbued with the religious teachings and principles of his parents. He went out to Iowa at an early age to stay with Mary and John Masters.

Like Art, he loved America and became engrossed in chapel life there. As his mother before him, he became an ardent Sunday School worker, teaching, educating and bringing the Methodist way of life to young farmers and their families in South Dakota and Kansas where he travelled widely. In 1899 he came back to England – but only for a year. He may have influenced his sister Annie and her husband Jack in their decision to emigrate to America, for they followed him there shortly afterwards. About this time also, Art returned from the States, so at No. 73 the joy of reunion and the heart-break of parting must have been the order of the day.

Once back in America, Uncle Bert started serious training for the Ministry at Mount Vernon School and then at Northfield Training School in Massachusetts. Here he won the Moody Prize for outstanding Bible Study Work and it was here that he first decided to enter the Cuban Mission Field. He moved to Cuba and there he met a missionary nurse – Agnes Smith. They married and the pair of them devoted most of the rest of their working lives to the Cuban Mission. They longed for children, but none came so they adopted a little Cuban orphan boy called Manuela Oropesa, whom they came to love dearly. However, shortly after they had adopted him, Agnes became pregnant and in due course, my cousin Hubert was born. The two boys grew up side by side. Manuela married and had many children and grandchildren.

Hubert went to college and obtained a degree. He married and had two sons – beyond that, I know nothing. Hubert is the only one of my Smith cousins who seems to have disappeared. No one in the family knows of his whereabouts. I remember Uncle Bert mentioning his two grandsons once in a letter to my father. He, Bert, said that he was overjoyed, for Hubert and family had been on a visit to Cuba and as they were about to leave at the end of the holiday, Bert had seen the children filling their sandals with sand. This he explained was an old local custom 'if you fill your shoes with the local soils as you leave, it is a sign to your host that you have enjoyed your visit and wish some day to return.'

Bert and Agnes did outstanding work in Cuba for forty years, first at an orphanage in Gardenas and then at Sancto Spiritus. They had a short rest period in Colorado and Michigan, after which they worked together for a spell in San Angelo – Texas, but finally they returned to their beloved Cuba and in 1950, Uncle Bert was to be found teaching at the Union Theological Seminary in Cuba. He was then seventy-five! Shortly afterwards he and Agnes retired to Windermere in Florida where he lived until he was ninety. He wrote quite often, sending photographs and presents to my parents during this retirement period. Auburn's Birds of America, beautifully bound and illustrated was one of his gifts which still has a prominent place on my bookshelves.

So there they all were – the Smith family at Roose; Grandma and Grandpa, Aunty Mill and my father still physically present in the early 1920s, and the rest of them – lively ghosts seeming still to inhabit Nos 73 and 74, for Aunty Mill was a wonderful correspondent. Her constant stream of letters to Ed and Ethel in Australia, to Art and Louise in America and to Bert and Agnes in Cuba, resulted in almost weekly replies bringing photographs and anecdotes of all the various families to centre on the old homestead. One of our favourite pastimes at Aunty Mill's was to gather round the fire in her kitchen after tea whilst she read out the latest report and photos were passed round, questions asked, and discussions raised on family matters. I remember particularly when Spencer Smith was born in Australia. Up to that time, I had been the youngest grandchild and I can still recollect the vague feeling of resentment which took hold of me at the exclamations of kindly amusement and pride with which everyone else greeted the photograph of this fat baby in process of counting his fingers as he stood in solid contemplation in the midst of vast Australian sand dunes.

I needn't have worried, since at that time I was the only grandchild out of all the sixteen of us who could possibly visit Roose regularly. Of course I was spoilt. They loved having me there – at least Aunty and Uncle did; I'm not so sure about Grandpa. I think Aunty often wished me to stay on alone after my parents had to return to Manchester at the end of the holidays. I could never be persuaded to it. I was so terribly frightened of being abandoned. In connection with this I remember particularly one Easter holiday.

Aunty used to boil eggs in all kinds of dyes so that it was exciting on Easter morning to be able to choose either a yellow or a pale blue egg for breakfast. Of course, there were lots of chocolate eggs also, but on this Easter morning, Aunty and Uncle gave me a chocolate hen as well as an Easter egg. I was not allowed to eat it. Aunty put some feathers in a hole on its back so that it appeared to have a tail.

"Now," said Uncle Sam. "Your Aunty will put it in the pantry for you and because it has a tail, it will lay eggs."

"Is it a magic hen?" I was intrigued.

"We think so," was the reply. "But by tomorrow we shall know." I hardly knew how to wait. All through that day I kept visiting the pantry to inspect my hen, but nothing had happened. She just sat there, a plump lump of self-satisfied chocolate, her tail feathers waving majestically in the draught every time the pantry door was opened. Morning came at last. I rushed straight into the pantry before I had had my breakfast and there she was, more self-satisfied than ever, and beneath her deliciously smooth brown exterior, something silvery was glinting in the light coming through the door. Gently, I picked her up – and there nestling on the shelf, was a clutch of three tiny eggs, one wrapped in gold paper, one in silver, and one just plain and *chocolatey!*

"She's layed! She's layed!" I ran out into Aunty Mill's kitchen with the hen in one hand and the eggs in the other. Everyone was astonished and congratulatory. It was suggested that I replaced my hen, but kept the eggs for future consumption. Well, for the rest of the Easter holidays, the eggs appeared regularly each morning and I consumed them regularly each afternoon. Sometimes there were three, sometimes only two, but she must have laid at least two dozen during my stay. Then came the day before we were due to go home. I began to worry about my hen. Should I leave her with Aunty Mill, or should I take her back to Manchester with me?

"If you bring that hen back to New Moston, she'll stop laying," said my economically minded mother who had no intention of indulging my taste for chocolate eggs out of her housekeeping money.

"On the other hand," announced Aunty Mill, "if you were to leave her in the pantry undisturbed and stay here with her, I am sure that she will continue to lay."

I tried to compromise – "Perhaps she will lay if I just leave her with you?" I asked Aunty.

"I'm sure she won't," was the reply. "She needs you – but you could stay here with me and Uncle Sam until Whitsun. Your daddy has to go back to work and your mummy must go with him to look after him, but you don't have to go back and they will both come up to collect you at Whitsun." I was torn and tempted, but in the end, my terrible fear of never again seeing my mother and father once I had let them go back without me, won the day. On the following morning, I gathered my hen and three eggs from the pantry shelf and departed. When we reached home, I installed her comfortably on the lowest shelf in our pantry and waited. Morning after morning I visited her hopefully, evening after evening I included her in my prayers – but no eggs! Finally, in disgust, I ate her.

The hen episode must have taken place before I was five as did my very first immersion in the sea. Up to then I had paddled regularly at Biggar Bank on Walney Island, my clothes bunched inelegantly into a pair of rubber waders, but except for the time when I had overbalanced and fallen into the sea fully clothed, I had never experienced the joys of salt-water bathing. Although my unintentional soaking had worried and frightened my parents, it had imbued me with a strong desire to repeat the performance, and all through the Whitsun holiday, in 1924, I must have pestered everyone to 'take me swimming', until suddenly, they all gave in and a picnic was planned for the following day.

The great excuse for keeping me from the water was that I possessed no bathing costume, which was as essential to a four-year-old in those days, as it was to a fully grown adult. Someone must have had a bright idea, for needles and thread and scissors were produced and my very first swimming costume was created by Mother and Aunty Mill, from one of the sheep-cloths in which sides of mutton were delivered to Grandpa's shop! It made a good bathing costume, but I might just as well have gone without, as once it was wet, it became completely transparent! However, we seemed to be the only occupants of the beautiful sands at Silloth, where we all enjoyed our picnic and I rolled about the water's edge in my sheep-cloth, thoroughly rejoicing in the fact that at last I was 'swimming in the sea', and what was more, I had the approval of all concerned. I remember that day strangely vividly for one so young; the sands, the sea, the sun and I was even conscious of the backdrop of the mountains, stretching into a kind of vague blue distance. A coastline, as then unspoilt, as today, much of it is spoilt by the shadow of a great nuclear power station.

As well as being 'picnic time', Whitsun was also 'Anniversary' time at chapel and whenever we were staying at Roose on these occasions, my father was always invited to conduct the Sunday School singing. A platform was erected behind the altar and on Whit Sunday about fifty well scrubbed boys and girls filed on to it, to sit on wooden benches facing the congregation. I was always invited to sit with and sing amongst them, and I really enjoyed the opportunity to show off my prettiest dress and my shiny new straw hat with its flowers and ribbons. This I did year after year, from the time I was only four years old, until suddenly, when I was nine years old, I had no further desire to 'perform' with the local children and was quite adamant about it. I wanted to be a spectator and not a participant. Everyone was surprised, including myself, and it wasn't until much later that I realised I had been experiencing the first symptoms of growing up.

I was both loved and teased at Roose. I must have been about three when they sent me for 'a spoonful of sunshine'. We were all sitting round the table in Grandpa's dark kitchen – Grandpa, Aunty Mill, Uncle Sam, my parents and I. Through the keyhole of the back door came a shaft of brilliant light to make a tiny dazzling circle on the opposite open scullery door. I watched and blinked and remarked to such an extent that my father handed me a teaspoon. "It's liquid sunshine," he explained. "Could you fetch me some?" Obediently, I climbed down from my chair and made several abortive attempts.

"It won't come with me," I complained, much to the amusement of the family.

The fact that I loved my food and ate heartily, seemed to give my family great pleasure and also endless opportunities to tease me. I was served with substantial helpings of Aunty Mill's excellent Christmas puddings, but made to eat them very slowly and carefully and to spit out anything which was of a hard and solid nature. One Christmas I succeeded in spitting out three threepenny bits from one helping of pudding and on a different occasion, I spat out a lead bullet from the turkey! These were 'free range' days, so I think the turkey must have been shot!

My father was dexterous in carving a joint of meat – he enjoyed doing it. To him it was a work of art and whenever we visited Grandpa Smith, Father was always given the honour of dishing up the Sunday roast. One dinner-time after the long grace had been said and everyone had been served according to his taste – lavish slices of well browned outer meat, or red and raw-looking pieces, on which, said my mother, "the blood had followed the knife' – there was one plate left before him. It was mine. Again, he sharpened his knife on the steel. My mouth watered in anticipation. He carved. A tiny piece, the size of half a crown was placed in the very middle of my plate and passed in silence down the table. I sat and stared at it for some time and no remark was made. I looked questioningly at my father.

"That's yours," was all he said.

Apparently my bottom lip quivered and my eyes filled with tears. I don't remember that, but I do remember the relief when everyone burst out laughing and my mother exclaimed, "Don't tease the child Sam." My plate was seized, passed back and returned to me again half full of luscious slices, and brimming with gravy.

I was allowed to play out on the Green with any of the village children who would have me in their games – only on Sundays was I forbidden. They were a friendly lot these children with their rough accents and rougher clothes. Next door to Aunty Mill lived a mining family whose mother, Maggie, used to come in to clean for Grandpa when he was busy in the shop. There had been three children in this family, but the eldest had caught typhoid at an early age and had died before I could make her acquaintance. According to Aunty Mill, "the angels had taken Frances to Jesus, for she had been too good for this world"; she had looked like an angel and behaved like one also. Fortunately for me, the angels had left her little sister Margery behind and she and I struck up quite a friendship. Margery was no angel! She would station herself outside the backyard gate when we were having a meal in Aunty Mill's kitchen and chant in a loud, tuneless and raucous voice, "Naow Berill, Naow Berill, Naow Berill" over and over again. On and on it would go, sometimes through our entire meal, with no pause except for intake of breath. On these occasions, I would be encouraged to eat up quickly and allowed to get down and go out to play the moment I had finished my last mouthful. Only on my appearance at the gate would the wailing cease.

Margery and I would then roam the village together. Sometimes we would sit on lobby steps with other children, sharing a halfpenny sherbet dab, which was sucked up through a liquorice tube; only one suck allowed per child, until the liquorice became so wet and sticky that it blocked the tube. Then the original owner would break open the bag, lick the remaining powder off the inside of the paper and devour the liquorice. Sometimes, just Margery and I would sit together on the granite boulder outside Aunty Mill's backyard gate. It was here that Margery first introduced me to winkle picking, showing me how to use a pin in order to extract the little creature neatly from its shell. This occupation would absorb us completely, sometimes for half an hour at a time as we picked our way steadily through a large brown paper bag discarding shells onto the Green as we ate. At other times, as we ran round the block together playing 'horses', we would see and hear the villagers coming across the road from their gardens, shouting in cheerful comment to each other.

"Ows ta bin lass? Tha's looking reet gradely."

"Ee, not bad considering t'weather. Tatty crop's nabbut leet, ist na?"

Sometimes, we would join a crowd of children following an old battered taxi making its slow way up the village street. Once it stopped and its occupants had alighted, they would find themselves surrounded by an avaricious crowd of boys and girls all shouting at the tops of their voices, "Out wee't, Out wee't," in the hopeful expectation of monetary reward. On rare occasions when the taxi brought a newly married couple home from the church, we were rewarded, as custom in the village demanded, by a handful of halfpennies thrown into our midst by the bride and groom. In the mad scramble which ensued, I never remember ever having obtained one of them.

Sometimes I was taken into Barrow to play with the Minister's daughter. She was much older than me and I remember that we always stayed indoors to play, for, in the attic of her big old house near the chapel, she had a trunk full of every kind of fancy dress costume imaginable. I was in my element; we danced as fairies, we pirouetted as Pierrots, we served teas as Nippies in Lyons, we subdued enormous conflagrations as firemen, we became Cinderella and Prince Charming, rabbits and squirrels and sunflowers – in fact I don't think we ever reached the bottom of that trunk. The costumes were glorious and endless.

The Minister and his wife, besides having a daughter with a dressing-up chest, also had two young sons and the five of them would occasionally join Mother, Father, Aunty Mill and myself for a picnic at Rampside or Baycliff, or even on the shores of Lake Windermere. By this time, I had achieved a respectable cotton bathing costume and we four children would walk out over the worm-cast sands of Morecambe Bay to meet the far distant line of sea-edge and then wade into the water for what seemed miles before even our knees became covered.

Grandpa rarely came with us on picnics. He couldn't often leave the shop but also I think he was very frightened of travelling in a car. When he did come, he would sit in front with Father, the brim of his grey trilby hat turned down all the way round. He always sat very still, didn't speak and stared straight ahead. We would take him through the shipyards at Barrow, over the bridge to Biggar Bank on Walney Island, but he wasn't happy and although he said nothing, even I could sense that he was only too pleased when the time came to go home to exchange the hard-ribbed golden sands and warm rock pools which I loved so much, for the familiar surroundings of South Row, Roose.

They are so plentiful and so happy, my memories of Roose – so redolent with the aroma of Aunty Mill's freshly baked wing cakes, with the fatty odour of meat from Grandpa's shop, with the tangy smell of machine oil from Uncle Sam's overalls. They are a sensory gift of family and enduring affection. They are glimpses of long ago – of country life from generations past, implanted in a child's mind to form a picture painted in red, splashed with green and bathed in brilliant sunlight.

5

'DOVASTON' IN DEVON

Once-upon-a-time, a long time ago, there lived, far away in a beautiful land, a fairy godmother and a fairy godfather. They dwelt in a pretty cottage surrounded by green lawns and beyond the lawns were their three big fields in which their three pet horses, who had never done a day's work in their lives, galloped and rolled in the sweet smelling grass. All round the outskirts of these fields, in and out of their bordering hedges, roamed warm brown hens which laid enormous warm brown eggs. Leading in to the cottage through a wide latched gate from the sunken lane outside was a long drive. It stretched towards the house, outlined on one side by tall pines. In the spring time this drive was awash with bordering daffodils, and all through the summer it was guarded by rose-standards, rising tall and graceful between the pines; proud sentinels, flaunting their magnificent heads of gold and red and white. Flowers were everywhere, spilling in great cascades from hanging baskets below the cottage eaves, dripping over the stones of the rockeries, climbing in purple and red confusion over walls and trellises and wafting their scent, high and seductive into the open windows of the cottage. Over the lawns and through the flower beds, three feline familiars, furry and friendly, padded on silent paws to patrol the outskirts of their territory. Beautiful they were; one Persian gentleman, grey and fluffy whose looks were of the squashed-face variety which proclaimed his aristocratic background, and two silky moggies – mother and son. So devoted to each other, and so inseparable were the latter, that they moved slowly in dignified unison, the tips of their erected tails linked lovingly together as they prowled.

Now, although the fairy godmother and fairy godfather lived in such an enchanted cottage in the middle of such a magical land, flowing with cream and honey, as it was, and although they seemed to have everything which their hearts could possibly desire, just one happiness had been denied them. They loved little children and had always longed for one of their own to share their beautiful home with them – but none came, and as the years went by, they realised that none ever would. Instead of being mournful, they wrote letters to their friends who lived in the dark city of the North where they once had also lived. They invited them to come with their children to spend enchanted holidays in their west-country cottage. And so it was in the summer of 1924, I was first made aware of 'Dovaston' in Devon. It became immediately the most magical place in my small world, and so it has remained, an image held secure in a special corner of my mind, safe and unchanging, protected from the sad march of 'progress' and 'development' which has in recent years beset its actual vicinity.

Aunty Kate and Uncle Robert Brown were not really my godparents, for, like my parents, they were strong Methodists and the children of such do not have godparents. They were not even my real Aunty and Uncle. They were, however, great friends of our family and knew my mother and father long before I was born. They had lived in Newton Heath and had attended the Methodist Chapel where Mother and Father were married. They had been guests at the wedding and in fact, outside our immediate family circle, they were my first-ever visitors, bringing a gift-box of very fine toilet soap for the new baby's bath. Uncle Robert had owned a soap-making factory somewhere near Manchester. Mother used to tell me a gruesome story of one of Uncle Robert's workers who had slipped and fallen into a vat of boiling soap and never been seen again even though the vat had been drained!

During the Great War, Uncle Robert had obtained a contract for supplying soap to the Army. He must have made a great deal of money in this way for he was able to retire early in the 1920s, to live the life of a small land-owner, first near Oswestry on the Welsh border-land and then near Ottery St. Mary in Devon. To these two places, we were annually invited; Mother, Father and I. I have only the faintest memory of Oswestry, but vivid and lasting memories of the beautiful bungalow in Broad Oak. Here, for five years from 1924 to 1928, we visited in August, sometimes for the whole month. They were holidays bathed for me in perpetual sunshine and summer warmth.

It took a two-day journey for us to reach Devon from Manchester in the early years. We travelled first in the little chocolate brown Citroen and after 1926, in Clara the Singer. We would put up overnight at 'The George' in Newent where we all three occupied an enormous bed which had been specially made for the previous landlord and his wife who had each weighed over eighteen stones when they died! Along the Welsh Marches we would ride – my father pointing out the sights. Wem and Whitchurch, Ludlow and Shrewsbury, Hereford and Gloucester, Worcester and Kenilworth – so rich in castles, cathedrals and history. My father knew much about them all. Not only had he stories to tell, but he could explain their architectural styles and from him, at an early age, I learnt to recognise Saxon crosses, Norman keeps, Tudor doors, Gothic arches and Elizabethan chimneys.

We stopped frequently to look at this and that. Sometimes a pretty roadside cottage would advertise 'Garden Teas'. After dismounting, Mother would always enquire the price of everything before we settled down to waft the wasps off the strawberry jam. If she thought the prices were too high, she never minded saying so and we would drive on to find the next cottage. On one occasion a whole cream sponge cake was set before us on its doilyed pedestal stand. Three slices had been cut and we demolished all of them. When the bill came, Mother pronounced it 'astronomical'. It was five shillings for the three of us, and Mother demanded a break-down of costs from the lady in charge, pointing out that we had partaken only of a pot of tea for three and three slices of cream sponge.

"Once it has been broken into," said the owner, with a self-satisfied smile, "it is as much for one slice, as for the whole cake."

"In that case," replied Mother, producing an unused paper serviette which she had secreted in her handbag, "I'll wrap the rest of it in this and we will eat it on our journey." And she bore away the remaining confection in triumph whilst Father paid the bill. Few people ever got the better of Mother where money was concerned.

I don't remember the first time I arrived at 'Dovaston'. I was very small and since we nearly always arrived in the evening, worn out with the adventures of the journey, I had probably nodded off. But oh – the excitement of subsequent arrivals! Driving through the scented dusk of sunken Devon lanes; seeing the dim shapes of great pines tower over us as we passed by Woodbury Common; watching out for rabbits caught in the car's headlights; swinging downhill at Tipton Cross on the last leg of the journey over unmade roads where dust and little stones flew up to greet our passage until at last we came to a halt facing the great black gate with the white name-plate on it. As I grew older, it was always my job to descend and to open that gate, holding it open until the car had passed through. Then I would mount its lower rung and 'ride' it back to anchorage.

No city-bred child could have wished for a more magical environment in which to spend a holiday. The cottage was really a 1920s chalet-bungalow. I think Uncle Robert must have had it built, for at the time it was considered very modern indeed. At the back door, housed in a separate building, was a big generator which made electricity for the lighting. All the interior doors were of plain wood – well creosoted. A strong smell of creosote pervaded the whole place so that today, whenever I smell creosote, I immediately recall Dovaston and its pungent doors with their press-down iron latches. There was a large kitchen with a red quarry-tiled floor and a square bay window latticed into diamond panes. A cheerful table filled the bay and here we always sat for breakfast, looking out over the vegetable garden at the side of the house. Here Uncle Robert would carve huge chunks out of a big runny honeycomb and right under my nose, transfer the dripping, sick-smelling mass to his plate. I would heave, turn my head the other way and hold my breath whilst he did it. They soon desisted from offering me honey – the very smell made me vomit!

We were nearly always out on picnics at midday, but often we would have an early supper together *en famille*, in the kitchen. Here, Aunty Kate had a wood-burning stove and an electric cooker in which she roasted chickens galore and made much rabbit casserole. At first, I refused the latter, not out of dislike, but out of compassion for the poor dead rabbit who minutes previously, before Uncle Robert entered the kitchen with his double-barrelled shotgun still in his hand, had apparently been jumping about happily near his burrow in the top field, and who now, held by the legs head down, was dripping blood onto the tiled floor. Eventually, driven by hunger, I was forced to enjoy the rabbit stew, since Father decreed that if I didn't eat it, there was nothing else. I could take it or leave it – so I took it, but with the wisdom of hindsight, I now believe that had I remained adamant, Mother would soon have found me an acceptable substitute, for, like me she loved her food and was fearful of starvation.

The room which opened off the passageway immediately to the right of the kitchen door, should have been the dining-room, but for some strange reason, it had been made into Aunty and Uncle's bedroom, and the dining-room was at the far end of the passage, as far removed as possible from the kitchen. Their bedroom was not exactly forbidden territory, but on the few occasions I entered there, I was always glad to leave as quickly as possible. I never saw it tidy. The bed was never made, the jerry visible beneath it was always full, clothes were thrown in heaps on chairs. On the dressing-table dark hairs filled the silver-backed combs and brushes and the sunlight coming in through the diamond-paned windows broke into floating patterns as it split the dust particles in the air into all the colours of the spectrum. I never understood why there was such a mess in here when the rest of the house was quite reasonably clean and tidy.

At the other end of the corridor was the room which should have been the main bedroom, but wasn't, it was the dining-room. A long polished table, over six chairs and a sideboard almost filled it. The window here looked right out over the vastness of the front lawn. On and on went the breathtaking view – down into the Otter Valley, up again in a great sloping green sweep to where the crest of East Hill ran for mile upon glorious forested mile along the skyline; to the right, the Sidmouth Gap hinted the excitement of seas beyond, while to the left, far off on Dumpdon Hill, you could actually see that mysterious ring of trees which Father always called the 'Honiton Clump'.

"We're passing the Honiton Clump," he would say as we journeyed down to Devon. "Not long now," and my heart would leap with the joy of anticipation.

After morning chapel, we invariably ate Sunday dinner in the dining-room. It was nearly always roast chicken preceded by a very long grace delivered in sonorous tones by Uncle Robert who had a fine voice. Occasionally, on weekday mornings, I would become 'trapped' in the dining-room, for here was a specially remembered cupboard – a built-in treasure house which stretched from floor to ceiling, its every shelf filled with books. Here I discovered *Little Women*, *Good Wives*, *Dear Enemy*, *Anne of Green Gables* and many others. They had been given to Aunty Kate long ago, for they carried her maiden name of 'Berry' and held a loving message written on their flyleaves by their benefactors in old-fashioned, spidery writing. The inner sides of these cupboard doors had their own attraction – photographs – taken by Uncle Robert with his Brownie camera in summers past and kept in position by drawing-pins. They covered every inch of the woodwork from top to bottom. I would stand between the two open panels, studying the pictures for hours. They were mostly of people I knew, enjoying last year's beach parties. When I became tired, I would choose a book, slide to the floor, and sitting cross-legged, was quite capable, as I grew older, of reading the morning away.

Half way along the creosoted corridor, before you reached the dining-room, a latched door led into the lounge. Here, at one end was a Devon brick fireplace and on its mantel-shelf stood a clock with the most musical chime I have ever heard. Considering my complete lack of musical appreciation, it's strange that the sound made any impression on me at all. But it did and I loved it. It could be heard all over the house, chiming every quarter of an hour; four notes, eight, twelve and then sixteen on the hour.

Along the inner wall of the lounge was a very grand, grand piano, for, like my parents, Aunty Kate and Uncle Robert were both musically inclined. Sometimes, after supper, Aunty Kate would accompany Uncle Robert's singing, and sometimes they would sing duets together. I listened to their songs, for they were not gloomy at all and usually told a story like *The First Minuet*, but what I really enjoyed were Uncle Robert's monologues. He was a great entertainer and made us all laugh with his recitations concerning Albert and t'Lion and Little Lulu. Quite intriguing to me were the pieces he rendered in a spoken voice with a background of musical notes from Aunty Kate on the piano. There was one which compared people to pieces of pottery – some were fine china vessels, some old earthenware crocks and some, chipped and cracked, had seen better days. I remember clapping vigorously at the end of this one and voicing my approval of it.

Aunty Kate laughed. "Did you understand what that was all about?" she asked, rather astonished. I was seven at the time.

"Oh yes," I replied. "I'm a piece of Dresden China – Grandma Haydock says so."

Everyone laughed then and Mother exclaimed, "Well, yes she does, but your Grandma Haydock sees the world through rose-coloured spectacles as far as you are concerned." That remark I didn't understand, but couldn't query because Aunty Kate had started to play the piano again.

At the far end of the lounge was a glass door which led into a small conservatory which Aunty Kate grandly referred to as 'The Loggia'. It was so full of plants that you could hardly see out of its windows and if you sat on the bamboo settee, you seemed to be in a thick forest where flowers, leaves and tendrils caressed your every movement. Sometimes, we tried to have Sunday tea in the loggia, but it was much more comfortable to eat our strawberries and cream outside at a big table set up on one of the lawns where Dainty, Matt and Stella, Uncle Robert and Aunty Kate's three horses would poke their noses against the restraining bars of their field-gates and try to join in the feast.

I slept downstairs in a tiny room next to the dining-room. I had never before slept so far away from my parents who were housed in the one and only upstairs bedroom, but I soon became used to it and began to enjoy a feeling of independence. However, Aunty Kate and Uncle Robert were close at hand at the other end of the corridor and I remember Aunty Kate bringing me a sweet in the middle of the night. Apparently, my continued coughing was keeping her awake. I accepted the sweet happily, but was amazed when Aunty Kate sat down by my bed and refused to go away until I had finished it – just in case I fell asleep and choked on it. I sucked slowly, savouring the sweet and relief from my tickles. It took a good half hour, by which time I was wide awake, but I had to shake the round white figure in the bedside chair quite hard to let her know that it was safe now for her return to her own bed. One morning, a few days later, I was awakened by a scratching sound on my window pane. I jumped out of bed and flung back the curtains. It was broad daylight and there was Uncle Robert, laughing at me through the window. In his hand was a big metal bowl about the size of a baking bowl and in it, a fluffy yellow mass – heaving and chirruping and making feeble attempts to overflow on to the window-ledge. There must have been twenty or thirty newly hatched chickens, all fresh from the incubator and all as astonished as I was in their realisation of life.

Only once, during the five years of our 1920s visits, did I sleep upstairs in the room with the dormer window and the polar bear mat. It was to keep Mother company when, for some reason which I do not remember, Father was called away in the middle of our August holiday. Mother was a very nervous lady, very afraid of being left alone in the dark. She was wont to pull heavy pieces of furniture in front of the door – to repel the armed burglars and/or rapists whom she imagined were always lusting after her money or her body. On more than one occasion I have helped her to lug the bedroom wardrobe into position across the entrance to the room! (Years later, when we finally moved from Manchester to Devon in 1931, she became particularly scared of the Spanish onion boys who often peddled their wares at night around the village where we then lived. If they happened to come on an evening when Father was away organising evening classes, I have seen her run upstairs, open the landing window and pour a jug of cold water on to their unsuspecting heads as they stood wearily leaning their onion-bedecked bikes against our front door.) I think Aunty Kate's wardrobe must have been screwed to the wooden floor, for it resisted all our attempts to move it and as there was no lock on the insides of any of the latched interior doors in the whole bungalow, Mother probably didn't close her eyes all night long. I was conscious of her arms about me as I lay drowsing on the edge of the big bed. When I complained of this in the morning, Mother said she had been afraid that I would fall out of bed and that she had been forced to hold me in. Actually I now feel sure that the poor soul had been petrified and was seeking the comfort of bodily contact.

Mother was not only frightened of being alone at night, but she was very suspicious of the motives which activated all men (excluding my father, of course), and indeed, Uncle Robert did behave rather strangely at times. Mother was wary of him. He loved to chase me all over the house and garden, and once captured, I was forced to suffer the indignity of being seized and smothered in kisses. As I grew older and my legs grew longer, I could give him much more of a run for his money. Sometimes I managed to tire him out completely so that he became breathless and had to give up the chase. I didn't mind the kisses too much, but when he rubbed his bristly chin all over my cheeks, it really hurt. It was a kind of a game to us both, executed with much screaming on my part and much laughter on his – but it was a strange kind of game and since it continued well into my teens, eventually I came to resent it.

The day after I had been held in bed all night by Mother, Uncle Robert must have decided to take advantage of Father's absence to play the kissing game with her also. I was following Mother into the bathroom when suddenly Uncle Robert came round the corner and surprised us both.

"Aha," he cried, "now I've caught you. Two for the price of one! You can't call for Sam now," he said, throwing his arms round Mother's waist.

"Go away Robert and don't be so silly," protested Mother, half laughing and trying to push him from her.

"You leave my mother alone," I shouted, tugging at his coat. He turned – I ran and he came after me, but for once he didn't catch me and that night Father came back.

Every day at Dovaston was warm and sunny. There must have been some rainy days, but I don't remember them. I would dash away after breakfast, mount my imaginary horse at the back door and gallop off to inspect my whole estate. I would visit the rockeries. They lay on one side of the house, separated from the main lawn by the driveway. Here, petunias, godetias, antirrhinums, love-in-the-mist, lobelias and nasturtiums, made seas of tropical colour lapping against islands of grey and white stone. Over the lawns and between the rows of prize-winning sweet peas, I would ride, becoming dizzy with the scent and sounds of a myriad insects buzzing in my ears; down to the gate where the pine trees whispered and dropped their double brown needles in a soft mushy mass onto the unmade lane beyond; back along the edge of the horses' fields whinnying in immitation and in answer to their equine greeting; inspecting the vegetable garden, especially the strawberry beds and finally I would finish in the big outhouse where Uncle Robert stored his chicken feed in huge rat-proofed leaden containers. If their lids had been left open, I would stretch up on tiptoe, lean over and plunge my bare arms down and down into seas of free running grain. There was much sensual satisfaction to be had in the feeling of all those moving particles yielding to the pressure of my limbs, trickling through my fingers and caressing my plunging arms.

Uncle Robert employed a full-time gardener and handy-man called Mitchell. He and his wife lived in a cottage on the edge of the far field where it bordered the lane coming down from Tipton Cross. Mrs Mitchell helped Aunty Kate in the house and her husband must have worked very hard outdoors, for the garden was always beautiful. It was Uncle Robert himself, however, who always fed the hens morning and evening. Sometimes I would go with him over the fields helping to scatter the grain and to collect the eggs. There was quite a thrill to be had in opening the boxes at the back of the hen-houses and shooing indignant birds off their nests to discover the treasure beneath. Batteries in those days were military establishments and most hens, like these, were free and happy and laid enormous eggs which tasted richly of fresh air and sunshine. Uncle Robert must have found me more of a hindrance than a help on these occasions. For one thing, I was scared of the horses – they seemed huge as they came running up to us the moment we entered the first field. They followed us very closely wherever we went and I was so nervous of being stepped on that I would stop dead and refuse to move until Uncle Robert had smacked them all smartly on their flanks, and sent them packing. I expect they resented my presence at egg collecting times which they were accustomed to sharing alone with their master, for on the occasions when I watched at a safe distance from the other side of the fence I noticed that they would trot round happily with him from hen-house to hen-house and he would talk to them in a companionable way. Often I failed to understand and act on Uncle Robert's instructions when he was trying to shepherd a straying hen through a gate between one field and another. He became very irritated.

"Come through. Come through," he would shout at me, but I thought he was talking to the hen and I stayed where I was on the wrong side of the gate whilst the hen ran clucking violently into the adjacent field and had to be chased back again by a red-faced and angry uncle.

During the morning, Mother and Aunty Kate would be busy making mountains of sandwiches, filling flasks with tea and coffee and packing two giant sized picnic baskets with enough food for dinner and tea on the beach. This always included a huge jar of clotted Devonshire cream, strawberry jam and splits, and sometimes, carried separately with great care, a big earthenware bowl of freshly picked morning strawberries, for if we were lucky, our holiday dates would coincide with the final days of Dovaston's strawberry season. By midday, all the chores were finished and the big brown, canvas-roofed Austin Sixteen was backed slowly out of the garage and stood ready on the drive. The picnic baskets were strapped on to the luggage rack at the back whilst the strawberries were held carefully on Aunty Kate's knees. Mother, Aunty Kate and I always travelled in the back of the car and Father was in the front with Uncle Robert who drove slowly and carefully through the sunken lanes until we came to the sea. Uncle Robert belonged to the AA and had a shiny chrome badge affixed to the radiator grill on the front of the car. Whenever we passed an AA man on his motorbike and sidecar combination, we would all salute and he would salute back again. Uncle Robert seemed to know the AA man who was on duty by his box at the entrance to Budleigh Salterton town, for here, we not only saluted, but Uncle Robert would always blow his horn as we passed by and the AA man would smile in recognition and click his heels as he returned our greeting.

Before we left Dovaston on each picnic outing, I was usually sent down the drive ahead of the car to open the gate and to close it after the vehicle had passed through. I would ride the gate back to its anchorage, swinging with it on its lower rung until it almost clanged shut, then I would leap off, rush round to its other side and catch it before it latched itself. It almost invariably caught me first and unless I were very quick in avoiding it, it would take the skin off the back of my heel before I managed to leap clear! However, practice made perfect and as I grew older, so my heels suffered less. But it was not only my heels which suffered. Uncle Robert was very proud of his car and I had to be very careful how I behaved in it. I remember him once smacking my bare legs quite hard, because he said, I had put my feet on his recently polished real-leather rear seat, which he had repeatedly told me not to do. I had no memory of him ever having said this and in any case, I felt sure that I had kept my feet firmly on the car floor, so I felt amazed and hurt in more ways than one at such treatment. Worst of all, I was embarrassed and couldn't talk to anyone for quite a long time afterwards, consequently, I was accused of sulking which wasn't really the case at all.

Every day of the week except Sunday, we would head for the beach, for all those delightful spots in East Devon which in the twenties were sheer uncluttered magic; for Seaton, far to the east, for Beer where a little stream ran through the main street down to the fisherman's cove where the cliffs were unusual in being white and having exciting caves in them which Aunty Kate and I once visited with an old sailor who rowed us out to look at them for a pittance; for Branscombe with its long lane winding down between thatched cottages, past the village smithy to finish in a field where we left the car and walked out across the pebbles to bathe in the coldest sea around those parts, looking up as we did so at some of the highest cliffs in East Devon, where the red sandstone gradually turned into white chalk masses; for Sidmouth – dear Sidmouth, it was so 'genteel' in those days, so full of the 'upper crust', amongst whom the old Duke of Connaught could often be seen taking his daily constitutional along the 'prom'; Sidmouth, where Queen Victoria had lived as a baby; Sidmouth, where important cricket matches were held on a beautiful ground overlooking the sea – my father would spend hours here watching the play; for Ladram Bay, a haunt of smugglers in bygone days and in the twenties, still mysterious and hard to reach along narrow twisting lanes which existed long before the new 'no nonsense' road had been driven horribly straight down to the sea – cutting the land about and feeding the hundreds of caravans which now have spoilt the remote loneliness of this once lovely and dramatic cove; for Budleigh Salterton, old-fashioned even then – a place where the elderly dozed in deck-chairs and wheel-chairs, peaceful in 'God's Waiting Room' and untroubled as are the residents of Budleigh today by the constant threat of development to their still beautiful and unique little town. And finally, we would sometimes make for Exmouth – a fun place for little children. There was sand – real sand here and masses of it! Huge dunes of it piled up against the sea road cutting off the view from the long line of beach huts which had been forced to the far side of the road so that their occupants had to cross over and wade through the shifting hills before they could enter the water. Exmouth, where I seem to remember donkey rides and a man with a kind of round canvas topped stall where you could play 'Bubbles' and catch brightly coloured ping-pong balls in a net on the end of a fishing rod. The balls spurted up on a jet of water coming from the centre of a round table. Gaily they danced, dazzling the eyes for about thirty seconds. I never caught one, I never won a prize.

We visited each of these places at least twice during our holiday. I was hooked on the sea and longed to progress from paddling to swimming. I bemoaned the fact that East Devon beaches were mainly a stony lot and apart from Exmouth, couldn't compare in my eyes with Biggar Bank on Walney Island. Then we discovered Jacob's Ladder at Sidmouth, where the tide goes out a long way, uncovering a vast area of sand stretching red, red, red along the cliff line to where the island stacks of Ladram Bay lie detached beneath Peak Hill. Its unspoilt beauty, I didn't then appreciate, but everything else about it fulfilled my wildest dreams of pleasure. The only way down to the beach was by the 'ladder'. In single file we would negotiate its steps. It wasn't a real ladder, more of a very steep wooden staircase. It was so long, that there were three angular turns with platforms where we rested – never on the way down, for we were all eagerness to reach the shore, but always on the way back, lingering to catch our breath and, in my case, trying to take in all the details of sand and sea so that I could keep them in my mind and weave them into the stories which I told myself in bed at night, holding them close in case I was never able to come again to this enchanted place.

Having to cling to one of the handrails, left us with only one hand free for carrying – and we were laden, all of us. Picnic baskets, thermos flasks, bathing gear, strawberries and sunshades, all had to be transported. There were red and white striped tents at the bottom of the steps which could be hired at 6d a time for changing purposes. We had two of them. Uncle Robert and my father shared one, and Aunty Kate, Mother and I another. There was a strip of cord carpet leading down from the tents, over the stones and on to the sand. Out we would come in our cotton costumes and rubber caps. I remember Mother, self-conscious, but dimpling and pretty in a red cap with a big white and red flower on it, and I can remember thinking – she must have bought it specially to match the bathing tents. At this stage, Uncle Robert unearthed his Brownie box camera and we posed for the inevitable. Aunty Kate and Mother always stood nonchalantly behind two deck-chairs, leaning forward and resting their arms on the top rails. In this way, their bodies were well hidden and only their curvacious arms, well-shaped shoulders and smiling faces were recorded for posterity.

On the beach, immediately beneath the clock tower at the top of the ladder, lay the rock pools. They were deep in places, stretching on and on, opening from one into another so that you could wade through narrow, gorge-like passages to emerge into sun bedazzled warm water basins whose many floors wavered clear and intriguing in the bright light. Here, shoals of minute fish darted right and left as one waded through. Tiny, scuttling pink crabs and sea anemones, opening and shutting in slow motion, lived their lives in a world of such liquid sunshine, that strangely and invariably, I was reminded of marmalade and the light passing through the big Golden Shred Gollywog jar as it stood on the Dovaston breakfast table!

It was in one of these safe and friendly pools, at the age of seven, that I learnt to float and to swim my first-ever strokes. My father took off his boots, socks and jacket, rolled up his shirt sleeves and trouser legs and waded in, in waistcoat and cap, to support and instruct me until I could go it alone. When I progressed from the pools to the actual sea, it was always in the company of the grown-ups, and always with an old inner-tube from Uncle Robert's car firmly around my waist.

Aunty Kate and Mother, holding on to each other's hands, would bob and dip repeatedly, at waist level. Father tried to teach them to swim also. He was convinced that they should be able to float easily since each of them was so well built. They allowed him to support their heads, but they would never take their feet off the bottom. After the dip, we all went into the tents and re-dressed – fully, with hats. Ladies and gentlemen always wore hats out of doors – even I wore a hat. Father mostly wore a cap for motoring and on the beach, Uncle Robert had a very expensive looking cream coloured Panama with a black ribbon, Aunty Kate and Mother had wide brimmed straw hats to protect their complexions from the sun and I had a multi-coloured chip-straw hat.

All of our hats sat well down on our heads, the crowns were deep and bell-like and mine reached my eyebrows before the brim sprouted from it! Once dressed, the adults sat in deck-chairs with adjustable hoods, further, to shield their already well-covered craniums, and I paddled in the sea and in the rock pools. I was always alone, but never lonely; my head was too full of imaginary people.

When the picnics had been eaten, the strawberries demolished and the shadows from the cliff faces were beginning to lengthen, Uncle Robert would stir everyone into activity – he must get home to feed his chickens – we must leave immediately. Then it was that the fun would start! Mother and Aunty Kate had somehow to be raised to cliff top level and the only way was via Jacob's ladder. They could carry nothing – they would be lucky if they reached the top alive. Aunty Kate was afraid of giddy spells, Mother of a heart attack. So, I was laden with the inner-tube and the bathing gear; Uncle Robert took both picnic baskets and my father carried thermos flasks and sunshades. The procession set off; Uncle Robert and I led the way, Mother and Aunty Kate came next – the two latter pausing for breath every four or five steps, but wasting it completely by giving each other vivid descriptions of the palpitations, sick headaches and dizziness which each was experiencing – they seemed to be vying with each other as to who was having the worse time of it! My father brought up the rear, offering assistance, encouragement and the constant reassurance of his cushioning presence to break their fall, should they be so unlucky. We always reached the top without mishap but sometimes it took almost twenty minutes since the two ladies halted at each platform level and avowed at length that they would never again repeat this particular performance. However, they always did and in fact, they recovered so rapidly that they were able to sing lustily on the way home in the back of Uncle Robert's car; *Tom Pearce, Tom Pearce*, *Little Grey Home in the West* and *Just a Song at Twilight* were their favourites. I didn't like the last one, it made me feel so sad and weepy that I would cover my ears rather than listen to it.

Back we rode through the dusty, unmade Devon lanes

via The Bowd and Tipton St. John which Uncle Robert insisted should be pronounced 'Tipton Sin John'. As we turned off the Ottery St. Mary road, we approached Tipton village through a very narrow steep-sided lane which was just a cut between red sandstone, cliff-like banks. They rose sheer on each side and towered over our heads. Passing through was scary and dark and we held our breath in case we met another car coming up 'Cheddar Gorge' as we called it but so few were the cars on the roads in those days, that it never happened. Of that fact I am sure for such a traumatic experience as having to back the Austin up the whole length of the 'Gorge' would have provided a talking point for a long time afterwards. When we emerged into the daylight of Tipton village, we often had to stop and wait on the roadside. A man, coming from a cottage, flagged us down, closed the level-crossing gates in front of us and there we sat until the little steam train from Ottery came puffing down the valley and crossed our path on its way to Budleigh Salterton.

After Uncle Robert had fed his chickens and we had eaten supper, we would all gather in the lounge for monologues and duets, but on particularly fine and balmy evenings, we would stroll together round the garden where the flowering night-scented stock perfumed our paths and seemed to permeate every corner of the grounds. Occasionally, on very light evenings we would venture beyond the gate and along the lane outside. As the light faded, bats would swoop down from branches above our heads in a kind of kamikaze flight which made Mother shriek with dismay and caused Aunty Kate to announce that although she didn't mind the little blind creatures themselves, she had a horror of one of them becoming entangled in her hair, unable to escape. As I gazed in fascination at Aunty's head, it struck me as strange that she never wore her hat after dusk when it would have been valuable protection for her and I couldn't help wondering if some unfortunate bat had not already met just such a fate and was being forced into permanent residence in her hair. Fortunately, I didn't voice my fears aloud.

Every day was wonderful in my eyes. Every day a magic, picnicking, sun-and-seaside day – every day, that is, except Sunday. Never on a Sunday, these delights. We might go into Sidmouth – oh yes, but we didn't even see the sea on a Sunday. Dressed in our best, hatted and gloved, we would drive to morning service and again to evening service at the Methodist Chapel in the main street there. Sometimes, we went to the Mint in Exeter where Uncle Robert sang in the choir. In between the two services came a roast chicken lunch, prepared by Mrs Mitchell in our absence and followed by afternoon tea in the garden. At least at Dovaston I was allowed to play in the garden on a Sunday – even in my best dress, and Aunty Kate went so far as to invite a little boy called Tony Jelly who was holidaying with his family in the big house on the other side of the lane, to come over to play with me. I liked Tony Jelly. I was glad he was a boy. I always preferred to have boys to play with rather than girls. I must have developed quite a penchant for him. I still have the photograph which Uncle Robert took of us both on one of those sunny Sunday afternoons. It shows us sitting side by side, cross-legged on the lawn and I have thrown a highly proprietorial arm around his shoulders. He looks resigned!

So passed the Augusts of 1924, 1925, 26 and 27 – in a haze of sunshine and enjoyment, but then something happened, which, combined with another unforeseen event, made the August of 1928 the last summer holiday we ever spent as a family together with Aunty Kate and Uncle Robert. This unfortunate happening occurred at the end of our holiday, which was a blessing, for otherwise, the atmosphere at Dovaston, becoming as unhappy as it did, would have prevented us from remaining there for the rest of the month.

It was a beautiful evening and we had come back from a happy day at Sidmouth. Clara had been standing on the carport in front of Uncle Robert's garage all day long whilst we had been out. When we arrived home, Uncle left his car on the drive and went immediately to feed his chickens. When he came back into the house, Father offered to shift his car out of the way.

"Fine," said Robert. "You move it and I'll come out in a minute and put mine away in the garage for the night." I was on the drive when it happened and saw it all. Father backed his car out of the carport and placed it to one side so that Uncle Robert could drive the Austin into his garage. Father then stepped out, closed the door after himself and started to walk away. At this moment, Uncle Robert was coming from the back door of the bungalow and walking towards his car. Suddenly, I saw that our car was beginning to roll slowly backwards down the slope of the drive towards Uncle's Austin.

"Daddy, Daddy," I shouted. "Clara's moving!" Father turned to look and Uncle Robert started to run towards his own vehicle. He reached it just in the nick of time, for Clara was gathering speed. Uncle Robert hadn't time to leap into the driving seat of his car, but he wrenched its door open, leaned in, released the handbrake and turned the steering-wheel through forty-five degrees, so that it rolled out of Clara's path, off the drive and onto his beautifully manicured lawn! By this time, Father had come to life. Realising either that he had left the handbrake off our car, or that its brakes had failed. He sprang into action, dashed back to the Singer, but had no time to run round the car and get to the driver's door where the handbrake was situated. Instead he flung open the nearside door and reached in to the steering-wheel. What happened next, I shall never understand. I couldn't believe my eyes. Father deliberately steered his car towards Uncle Robert's car – wherever it went, he followed. Backwards over the lawn careered both cars, one apparently chasing the other and both gathering speed as they approached the far bank which bordered the lane. Whichever way Uncle Robert tried to turn out of Clara's path, so Father changed her direction, making his car follow the big brown Austin. There was so much angry shouting from Uncle Robert that Father must have panicked. He seemed determined to bash into Uncle's car. I stood on the drive, rooted to the spot and watched the inevitable happen. Uncle Robert's car hit the bank at the end of the lawn and stopped dead, but almost immediately, following it up, Clara banged its front bumper with her rear bumper and drove it some distance up the bank. There was the sound of shattering glass as headlamps were dislodged and scattered. Both cars locked together then the Austin, being the heavier of the two and higher up the bank, slowly descended, pushing Clara along in front of it until at last both came to rest on the edge of the lawn – a lawn now churned up and scarred with four sets of tyre marks weaving sinuous patterns over its once glass-like surface.

Uncle Robert's face was purple with rage. I thought he would hit Father. Instead, as Father was trying to apologise and explain, he pushed him out of the way and rushed off in the direction of Mitchell's cottage. Father stood quite still for a long time, then, slowly he got into our car and started the engine. He drove it off the front of the Austin, up the lawn and back onto the drive where he left it, putting on the handbrake very firmly this time. Meanwhile, Uncle Robert had come back with Mitchell. He ignored Father and me, and with Mitchell's help, he managed to push the Austin clear of the bank. Between them, they got the engine going and drove the car straight into the garage. Neither vehicle was seriously injured, but there was more damage to Uncle's Austin than to our Singer and Mitchell was sent off on his bicycle to alert the local garage. Before Mitchell left, I remember Father asking Uncle Robert whether he could, whilst he was there, enquire about repairs to Clara also.

"Do what you like – I wash my hands of you!" shouted Uncle Robert, turning his back and stalking off into the house. Father did ask Mitchell to take the message, however, and the upshot was that the garage promised to work on both vehicles if they could be driven there first thing the next morning.

Uncle Robert's rage continued – cold and terrible. His beautiful car had been despoiled despite all his attempts to save it. Its headlamps were smashed, its front bumper torn off. He spoke to no one, ate no supper and sat at his desk in the lounge furiously writing all the evening. The atmosphere was painfully embarrassing. I hated it when the grown-ups were angry with each other, it gave me a frightened, excited feeling in the pit of my stomach. I was bewildered and couldn't understand why my father hadn't just steered his car into the bank straight away instead of following Uncle's car wherever it went. When I tried to say as much, I was told to be quiet; so I ate my supper and went to bed.

The next day was the last one of our holidays. We were to have had a final picnic and bathing party at Jacob's Ladder, but both cars were in the garage at Ottery St. Mary all day long. After a distinctly chilly breakfast, Uncle Robert disappeared, Aunty Kate set about the house-cleaning so vigorously, that she had no time to talk to anyone, Father walked into Ottery to see about the car, Mother started our packing and I kept out of the way in the farthest part of the garden, miserably saying 'good-bye' to the cats, to the flowers, to Mitchell's dog and to the horses. The following morning, all seemed to be well again. Aunty Kate and Uncle Robert were their old, talkative selves. I think what I felt was relief that we all seemed to be out of the dog-house, but I'm sure my parents must have felt quite bewildered. Since nothing further had been said about the accident they obviously didn't want to bring up the subject and promote another row before they left, so they just accepted this sudden change of attitude, and everybody was nice to each other again. Aunty Kate produced picnic goodies for the journey and Uncle Robert helped Father to carry out our cases and strap them on to the luggage grid at the back. We said loving good-byes, and were seen off by both of them who stood together on the dusty lane, smiling and waving until they disappeared from view as our car rounded the corner at the crossroads where Uncle Robert's fields ended. Dainty, Matt and Stella had galloped along with us on the other side of the hedge, in their own way, whinnying their good-byes also.

But of course, we hadn't heard the end of the incident, for one morning, about three weeks after we arrived home, a letter came from Uncle Robert's solicitor demanding that Father pay for the damage he had done to Uncle Robert's car. At the time I didn't understand what it was all about, but years later my parents told me that it was quite a threatening letter. Of course my parents paid up immediately, as they had always intended to do once they knew the cost, but what seemed to upset them much more than the bill they received, was the fact that Uncle Robert had thought it necessary to bring a solicitor into the affair. They were now quite convinced that Uncle Robert's furious writing on the evening of the accident, had been a directive instructing his solicitor to threaten action against them, and yet the following day all had appeared to be forgiven and forgotten! However, all was eventually settled and when Christmas came round, my parents received a long letter from Dovaston and a calendar attached to an enlarged photograph of one of our beach parties taken by Uncle Robert the previous summer.

What about next year though? What about the summer holidays for 1929? In the Christmas letters, no mention had been made of them from either side. It was as if the subject were being carefully avoided by both parties. Fortunately, the problem resolved itself, for early in the New Year, Father's eldest brother, Uncle Bert, wrote to us from Cuba; he was coming on a trip to England to see Grandpa and Aunty Mill at Roose, but he wanted to spend some time with us all in August when Father would be on holiday. That settled it. Uncle Bert couldn't have stayed at Dovaston anyway, so my parents decided to look for 'Apartments' in Sidmouth where all four of us could be together and also be able to see quite a bit of Aunty Kate and Uncle Robert. 'Apartments' meant that you paid for your bedrooms and a sitting-room but bought your own food which the landlady cooked for you. Mother and Father were lucky. They found just the right place and now all was arranged. Uncle Bert would be able to travel with us in Clara. Not only would he be able to see something of Devon, but on the way there, we could stop at Draycott in Somerset to see many of the elderly Smith relatives who were still living there. So it was that 1928 proved to be the very last time I ever actually stayed at Dovaston with Uncle Robert and Aunty Kate, and 1929 was the very first time that I ever spent my summer holiday at Bon Cottage, Sidmouth.

Bon Cottage was different from, but in its own way just as delightful as, Dovaston. It stood, and still stands today, the centre cottage of five in Amyatts Row. Backing onto the churchyard, facing the tennis courts, and opening onto a little private road which separated it from the latter and was a cul de sac, it had the air of being surrounded by open lands. The whole terrace was uncluttered by other buildings, yet it was within a stone's throw of the shops and the sea front. These Georgian houses were probably built for the fishermen of the past. Today, Bon Cottage marks its central position amongst the five houses by bay windows, top and bottom, one on each side of the low, wide and almost square front door. They were not there in my early days, but the large triangular entablature was. It rises still above the roof line and remains decorated at apex and side angles with three important-looking stone balls! In spite of these pretensions to grandeur, from the first moment I saw it, I thought of it as a gently pleasing place – homely and inviting.

It seemed strange at first in 1929, not to be going to Dovaston for our holiday, but as soon as Clara pulled up in front of Bon Cottage, I felt its attraction and realised that I was going to be very happy in this little house. And the occupiers of the little house saw to it that we were all treated like royalty. They were a couple who might have stepped straight out of an old fashioned picture book. Frank and Ida Martin were Edwardians, both in appearance and behaviour. She wore high-buttoned boots – black; high buttoned blouses with stiff, starched collars; her skirts were ankle length and covered by snowy linen aprons, tied at the back in the neatest of bows with long white streamers trailing from them. She was a short, bustling little person with frizzy black hair done up in a bun and she laughed a great deal in a sing-songy kind of way. He was a sailor, retired from the Royal Navy. He wore long bell bottoms when he was working in the house in the mornings, and seamen's jerseys. His skin was brown and leathery, crinkling at the corners of his eyes when he laughed. To me, his hair was quite dramatic. It fascinated me and I couldn't take my eyes off it until Mother rebuked me for staring. It was silver and appeared wet due to the pomade with which he plastered it. Although it was cut very short at the back, long strands of it were combed forward from the crown, to end in two kiss-curls on each side of his forehead.

On that first arrival, these two were standing stiffly to attention, side by side, in the doorway, waiting to greet us. She bobbed and he bowed and then they both shook hands with each one of us and welcomed us to Bon Cottage. As we walked up the path, their garden shouted at me to be noticed. It was memorable and I have never forgotten my first glimpse of it. Here, outside amongst the flowers, Frank Martin had created a world of his own. Here, he had peopled it with garishly painted figureheads from old sailing ships, with small animals modelled in clay, with carved birds and glass butterflies. To a delicate wooden archway over the front door, he had nailed a whole Noah's Ark of cut-outs. Animals in bright eye-catching colours marched in procession, nose to tail, over the lintel of the door from one window to the next. The Martins liked children and my father thought Mr Martin had made these animals specially when he knew that a child would be amongst their visitors that summer. I don't know about that but the figures delighted me, as did the whole garden. Every morning before breakfast, I would run up and down the pebbled paths between the miniature box hedges, gazing and talking and singing tuneless songs to the immobile little creatures who sheltered beneath the leaves and flowers.

Frank Martin kept everything 'ship-shape and Bristol fashion'. Paintwork was always fresh and window-panes polished and gleaming. Every morning, he would roll up his trouser legs and long underpants to the knees, take a bucket of hot, soapy water and scrub the tiled corridor which led from front door to back kitchen. He had sailed all over the world and had wonderful hair-raising stories to tell. He had been in the Boxer Rebellion, cut off from his ship with a small group of fellow sailors and forced to rejoin it by marching bravely through a crowd of "Silent, hostile, slit-eyed Chinks who never took their eyes off us and who held carved knives between their teeth! If we had faltered, or made one false step, they would have skinned us alive!" I never took my eyes off him either when he was in a story-telling mood. He taught me how to splice a rope; how to recognise a reef-knot and how to distinguish it from a granny; how to make a running bowline and how to tie a sheep-shank when I wanted to shorten a rope. I thought it all very wonderful, and as we continued to visit Bon Cottage year after year, even after we went to live in Torquay, I developed a violent teenage crush on Frank Martin. It lasted for a couple of seasons until my fickle attention was attracted elsewhere.

Before she was married, Mrs Martin had been 'in service'. A veritable 'Mrs Bridges'. I can imagine her presiding efficiently over the 'Downstairs', whilst producing delicious repasts for the 'Upstairs' of some large country mansion, until one day, Mr Martin came along and 'took her away from all that'. When I first knew the pair of them, they must have been in their fifties, and still looking after the 'gentry', for upstairs in one of the two front bedrooms of the cottage, lived a mysterious old lady. She must have been a very rich old lady for she employed Frank and Ida to minister to her every need. She was reputedly bedridden and never appeared. All her meals were carried upstairs, many on special plates, which had a hollow compartment beneath, into which hot water was poured and then sealed in by a cork. The old lady was a slow eater apparently. Her bath water was always carried up the steep, narrow stairs in two white enamel pails by Mr Martin who was followed by Ida, laden with a pile of towels and a tray of assorted soaps and unguents. The bedroom door closed behind them; Mr Martin came out shortly afterwards, but Mrs Martin was always immured for at least an hour . . . All kinds of special foods and delicacies were bought and taken in to the old lady. Money seemed no object, in fact, now, in hindsight, I think that Bon Cottage probably belonged to her and she let Mr and Mrs Martin live there provided that they looked after her until she died, when the cottage would become theirs.

This is what must have happened, for the last time I ever saw the Martins was during the war years when I was at University in Exeter. We must have been given a day off from lectures, for I can remember visiting them with a college friend. The old lady had died, but the cottage and Frank and Ida were the same as ever. They gave us a great welcome and Ida produced large quantities of her home-made toffee which I remembered so well. She had always been a supreme cook, and although Mother, during our stays in Sidmouth, bought only the plainest of food for her to prepare, it was always beautifully presented and tasted delicious. She was the finest runner-bean shredder I have ever known – all done by hand –

no fancy gadgets in those days. One other thing about Mrs Martin which I specially remember was her high-pitched, sing-songy voice. She would bustle up the twisty stairs each morning carrying a steaming, enamel hot water jug in each hand. One of these she would deposit in front of my bedroom door and one in front of my parents' door, then, after rapping loudly on each, she would stand in the centre of the landing and intone in the strangest manner. The sound produced was almost that of a scream – but a very musical scream which seemed to have a tune to it.

"Water ple-eees," she would cry, sending forth such violent sound waves that the ornaments on my mantelshelf would visibly tremble when I opened the door to collect the jug and to watch the performance.

As a result of our first coming to stay at Bon Cottage, a wonderful thing happened. Aunty Kate and Uncle Robert invited Uncle Jim Giddings, my father's college friend, his wife Aunty Jessie and their youngest daughter Eileen, to stay with them at Dovaston during the same weeks that we were to be at Sidmouth. Eileen was the little girl who had so faithfully and so fruitlessly saved a seat for me at Newton Heath Sunday School week after week. She was my age and we were both delighted to have the chance to be together on holiday. Now August afternoons on Jacob's ladder beach saw quite a party of Lancastrians. To start with there were eight of us, as the years went on, right up to 1937, the numbers of our friends and relatives coming to holiday with us at Sidmouth, grew until often there would be over twenty of us bathing and picnicking together. Muriel, Eileen's older sister, brought her fiancé, Gordon along; Margaret, Eileen's cousin, was introduced to Arthur, Aunty Kate's nephew, on Sidmouth beach, and had a holiday romance there which ended in marriage; the Hamblins, the Hartleys, the Berrys, all originally Manchester folk, joined us from time to time.

My first summer holiday at Sidmouth with Eileen was unbelievably happy. I can see her now – an over-excited, bubbly little girl – thin, almost skinny, bouncing down the steps of Jacob's Ladder well ahead of the rest of them, to where I was waiting on the beach. Under her arm, a vivid orange bath towel rolled into a fat sausage and containing as I later discovered, the latest in cotton bathing costumes – a zig-zag patterned top with navy blue attached bottoms, a white belt and a white rubber helmet made in two flat pieces.

"Bee-Bee," she cried, jumping off the bottom step, dropping the sausage and flinging both arms around me – "Hello, hello, hello." Locked together, we girated like a spiralling whirlwind over the pebbles towards the sea, laughing and shouting our joy. Sidmouth, Bon Cottage and now Eileen! It was almost too good to be true – but it was true, and what was more, I hadn't lost Dovaston either.

We were still invited there – after morning chapel, for Sunday lunch, or for an evening's musical entertainment during the week. Now Eileen and I could run round the garden, talk to the horses and play with the cats together. Together now, we could sit on the floor in the dining-room and read Aunty Kate's books or study the photographs on the back of the cupboard door. One day Eileen discovered Joan Lowell's *Child of the Deep* on the bookcase shelves in the lounge. She shared it with me; quite a prize find. Together we devoured it – surreptitiously, almost guiltily, curled up on the loggia settee, keeping a low profile in case our parents discovered us reading it and removed it, declaring it not suitable reading matter for little girls.

The idea of a baby girl being taken to sea by her father when she was only a few months old, being raised on his sailing ship in a rough seamens' world until she was eighteen years of age, appealed to us both tremendously. We developed a passion for the sea, we longed to be sailors, all things nautical held fascination for us.

All that summer holiday of 1929 and for the next two summer holidays Eileen and I roamed the rock pools at Jacob's ladder beach for hours on end. We were explorers. Each pool was a different land where we rested awhile. Each shallow, water-filled, sandy-bottomed basin became a world of our creating. We peopled it, wove our fantasies around it and voiced our imaginings to each other – discovering, enjoying, inventing until we were ready to wade on to the next pool and the next and the next, working our way to the open sea. The thrill of arriving safely at our goal after so many adventures never palled, but sometimes we never reached it. We would be called away to join in the communal bathe. We could both of us swim by this time and the fun was fast and furious. Eight of us there were, splashing and dipping, performing backward somersaults off each other's shoulders and taking turns to dive head first through the centre of Uncle Robert's inner tube.

Afterwards, when the bathe was over, Eileen and I would try to smash open the pebbles at the foot of the cliffs to see if any crystallised jewels were embedded in their centres, or we would walk along the water's edge into the heat-shimmering haze. On and on past the mysterious redness of the cliffs which rose in great heights towards Peak Hill. We knew that Ladram Bay lay just round the corner, but we never made that goal. The further we walked from our family base, the more isolated we began to feel. People thinned out until there was no one around and I became afraid; afraid of the red, high-towering cliffs which were alive with noise. Tiny bits of sandstone were falling in showers from them all of the time and blood-coloured streams were trickling down their gashed flanks. I would see in my imagination a huge landslip crashing down to bury us both in a soggy red grave. I was afraid of the tide suddenly coming in and cutting us off from safety, from our parents and from all that was familiar to us. Then I would be seized with a great panicking loneliness and, much to Eileen's disgust, I would turn back. She always wanted to go on. She was braver than I and she, it was, who led our expedition over the high pebbled wall and into the grounds of a big house high above Jacob's Ladder beach where the Connaught Gardens are today. Once over the top, we tried to find our way into the Clock Tower, but it was locked. To me the garden suddenly seemed dark, overgrown and mysterious. Again I got cold feet and beat a hasty retreat.

In 1933, when we were thirteen, Jacob's Ladder beach saw us no more. It seemed that the Ladder itself had finally 'done for' Mother and Aunty Kate. Instead, we all now met on Sidmouth's main beach. At first Eileen and I didn't take kindly to this desertion, but we soon adapted to the change of venue, and anyway, it did have its compensations. Walls'-

Beryl on the beach at Jacob's Ladder, 1931.

A party of Lancastrians at Fire Beacon Tea Gardens, nr. Sidmouth in the 1930s. Taken on the occasion of Uncle Robert's 60th birthday. He took everyone out to tea on that day and he took the photograph. Eileen and Beryl on right in 2nd row. Mother, Father, Aunty Kate on left near back. Uncle Jim and Aunty Jessie in the middle row.

Bon Cottage – Sidmouth, 1929.
Mrs Martin, Mother, Mr Martin and Beryl.

Eileen and Beryl at Sidmouth in the late ’30s.

Father, Mother and Beryl, Gatley, 1929.

21 Belmont Road, Gatley. Taken at 6.00 am, when the family were about to set out for Devon. 'Clara' is loaded and Father waits at the gate.

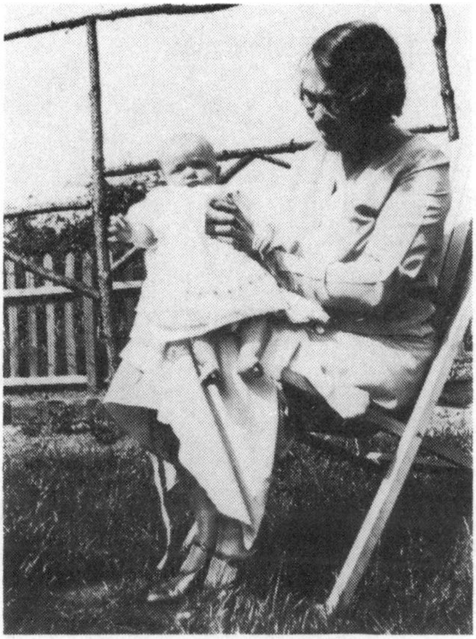

Mrs Harrison and Lillian at
Belgrave Road, Gatley, 1930.

The Harrison children in their garden
at Belmont Road Gatley. Ruth, George,
Lillian and Joyce, 1930.

Grandma, Aunty Gertie and Mother.

A stop on a Shropshire road on the way to Devon.
Mother, Uncle Bert and Beryl, with 'Clara', 1929.

Summer 1930 – Visit to Leashaw House, Holloway, Derbyshire. Back row: Father, Mother, Uncle Charlie. Front row: Tommy, Grandpa Haydock, Baby John, Beryl, Grandma Haydock and Charlie.

Beryl's father making his inaugural speech at the opening of the South Devon Technical College, Torquay in September 1931.

stop-me-and-buy-one ice cream vendor would park his trolley on the prom just above the spot where our beach party would gather. Here also, the pony girl would hire out her horse for 3d rides along the front and back, or 6d rides in a big circle along Manor Road past the Manor Pavilion, down Glen Road past the house where Queen Victoria had spent some of her babyhood and where her father had died, and on back again onto the prom – and, joy of joys, here moored offshore from the main beach was a raft! Many were the swimming races to see who could be first to reach it. Many were the sun-bathes lying flat on it with our feet dangling in the water, and many the dives from it as we raced back to the shore.

At low tide it was possible to wade out to the raft and Mother, Aunty Kate and Aunty Jessie would then sometimes venture there. None of them could swim and on one memorable occasion when all eight of us had reached the raft, it almost sank with the overloading. Aunties Kate and Jessie took fright, jumped off and waded back hand in hand to the shore. The rest of us, including Mother stayed. Gradually, one by one, we began to swim back until only Mother and Uncle Robert remained, talking together. Unnoticed, the tide came in. The raft lifted higher in the water and Uncle Robert said, "Come on Lily, it's time to get back." He jumped in and swam away shouting, "Hurry up or you'll soon be out of your depth!" That was enough. Mother froze and stayed where she was. Eileen and I were dressing in the red and white striped tent which our parents hired for £1 a week from Sidmouth Council, when we heard a commotion on the beach. We opened the flap and stuck our heads out. There in the distance we could see Mother, standing, legs astride all alone in the centre of the raft, waving frantically and calling.

"Sam, Sam!"

Uncle Robert was walking up the beach saying, "Lily's back there, somebody should do something."

Kate and Jessie were at the water's edge screaming, "Lily. Lily, take care or you'll overbalance." My father, already dressed, had momentarily disappeared, but Uncle Jim was waiting his turn to dress just outside our tent. Eileen and I, thinking the whole scene very funny, doubled up and became quite helpless with laughter. Uncle Jim was the only member of the party to come to Mother's rescue. He dashed down the beach, waded out, swam a few strokes and reached the raft. He managed to calm Mother down and finally persuaded her to trust him and to let herself be lowered into the water. He was a very good swimmer and life-saver. Supporting her head, he soon brought her to safety and delivered her into the waiting arms of Kate and Jessie. He was her hero forever afterwards. She never forgot how Uncle Jim had once rescued her from a watery grave.

On another occasion when Eileen and I were off together on our own affairs, and Uncle Jim and Father were watching the cricket, Mother and Aunty Jessie arrived on the beach before anyone else.

"The sea looked lovely," said Mother later. "White horses dancing and sparkling in the sunshine." They decided that it was too rough for them to get right in and bathe properly, but they thought it would be safe and quite all right for them to sit together in their costumes on the water's edge and just let the waves splash over them. They changed and walked down the beach. One tall thin lady and one short plump lady, hand in hand, helping each other over the pebbles. Seeing no danger, they reached the point where the pebbles ended and the sand began. Here they squatted and chatted, waiting for the tide to come in. It came quite rapidly, one big wave after another, and they were thoroughly drenched and enjoying themselves. Suddenly, without warning an extra large wave thundered inland. It knocked them over and carried them well up the beach! Before they had time to recover, it rolled them back into deeper water. Over and over they went like two big pebbles in company with all the others which were being combed down the slope – and before they had time to wonder what had hit them, another incoming wave carried them again, high up the beach! Fortunately, Uncle Jim and Father arrived on the scene at this juncture. Each husband was quick to take in the situation and to react to it. Each rushed to the water's edge, grabbed the nearest part of his wife's anatomy available to him and hauled her to safety.

All through the late twenties and early thirties, Eileen and I longed to be boys. I in particular, wanted to be a sailor.

In those days boys had a far better time than girls and we thought it most unfair. It was easier for Eileen to ape a boy than it was for me. She was less in awe of her parents. She did things which I would never have dared to do. One year she came on holiday looking exactly like a boy. I was so envious. Back in Manchester, she had saved up her pocket money, taken herself to the hairdresser and without her mother's knowledge had her hair cut into an Eton Crop. A really 'short back and sides' to go with the green shorts and green jacket which she had persuaded her parents to buy for her. When we were together I was often asked 'and who is your boyfriend?" She had succeeded, so she told me, following the best traditions of *Child of the Deep*, in spitting a curve in the wind, of such proportions that Joan Lowell herself would not have been ashamed! This was something which I had never managed to do and even Eileen admitted that her achievement had been somewhat marred by the fact that just as she spat, the wind must have changed direction and her 'curve' flew in through the open kitchen window and landed in her mother's washing-up water! Then again, her attempt to use the toilet 'just as boys do', had proved disastrous. She had been made to clear up the mess and to promise never again to attempt such a thing!

I was not allowed to be masculine. I begged for a pair of beach pyjamas with bell-bottomed legs which I thought would make me look like a sailor. My wish was never granted and eventually I ceased to request them in my prayers. Instead, I changed my tactics and asked God to help me to save up enough money to be able to buy a pair of them for myself. By the time I had the required amount put by, beach pyjamas were out of fashion and anyway, I had grown out of the boyish phase, so I used the money to buy myself a pair of slinky french cami-knickers with lace insets. My mother promptly returned them to the shop and demanded the money back.

One of our favourite pastimes when we were not on the beach and could escape from our parents for a short while, was to cross the bridge over the River Syd at the eastern end of the promenade, and mount the path through the gardens to the cliff top where we came out into the fields. We always had to say where we were going and were always given the latest time to report back. It was never long enough for all the exploring we wished to do and on one never-to-be-forgotten occasion we stole away early one afternoon without telling anyone of our intentions – Eileen, myself, and my cousin Phil Haydock whom we had brought from Manchester to holiday with us and who was a couple of years younger than Eileen and myself. We were determined to reach Branscombe via the cliff path. The sight of those great slopes rising and dipping almost vertically into the distance had tantalised us all the holiday and the fact that we had now realised that they could be climbed and descended by following a path all the way to Branscombe, had proved too much for us. We simply *had* to follow that path. We knew that none of the adults in our party would be inclined to accompany us, and that if we asked permission to go alone, it would be refused – so, we just went. It was a cruel and thoughtless thing to do, but of course, we didn't think.

It took us much longer than we had anticipated – but we made it – and all the way back, following the same route, up and down, up and down at least four times with a big detour at Weston Beach where the path bent inland and then out again. It must have been at least five miles there and five miles back. Ten strenuous miles out in the country, right on the edge of some of the highest cliffs in the South West with not a building in sight and very few people either. It was after six o'clock when we finally crossed the Syd bridge again, tired but triumphant. We knew we were late and we had run on the way back wherever it had been possible, but even so, we had been missing for over four hours. By this time Mother was almost hysterical with worry and when we ran into our parents on the promenade, they were on their way to alert the police. Phil and I were in big trouble. Eileen not so much so. Her parents were far more relaxed than mine and quite used to her escapades. I was made to kneel down and ask God's forgiveness for my sins!

After that we never roamed too far from base. If we felt the need to leave the family circle for a while we would potter round the local churchyard, peering at the inscriptions on the tombstones. They held a kind of macabre fascination for us. Eileen discovered one of a young girl who died aged seventeen years. She brought her sister Muriel to look at it. Muriel was seventeen. I was intrigued with R.I.P. which appeared on many of the headstones.

"Why does it keep saying 'rip'?" I wondered aloud.

"It's not 'rip'," remarked Eileen, "it's R.I.P. and it stands for 'Rise if Possible'."

"You don't think it is possible, do you?" I asked, half scared and completely taken in.

If we had any pocket money to spare, we would have a ride on the pony, or a round of putting on the Green opposite the public lavatories, but mostly we contented ourselves with playing on the shore, in and out of the wreck of the old paddle steamer, *The Duchess of Devonshire*. It had recently gone aground there and remained high up on the pebbles, becoming rustier and rustier as the years went by. It wasn't at all the same as playing in the rock pools off Jacob's Ladder. The ship's dark and dankly-smelling interior, dripping as it was with red rust, was a poor substitute for sunlight glinting through clear water; for shifting sand patterns and waving sea-weed forests.

One day our fathers took us out in a rowing boat and showed us how to row. We learnt quickly and wanted more, but trips were limited, so we saved up until we could afford to take ourselves out. An old sailor hired us a boat for half an hour and provided us with two fishing lines. Out we went, again telling no one. Eileen took one oar, I another. For some time we rowed in circles, then in a zig-zag pattern, until finally, we managed to keep the boat on an even keel. We enjoyed ourselves hugely. At last we were sailors in charge of our own craft. We called out orders to each other using all the nautical terms we could remember – we were discoverers, explorers, on the high seas, venturing into the unknown. We rested our oars – some way from the shore now, and put out the fishing lines. Oh the thrill of that first tug on the line! I shall never forget it. We were hoping to catch mackerel, but between us we hauled out, no mackerel, but six orangey-red fish with big heads which neither of us could remember ever having seen before. We were convinced that we had caught something quite unique. As we caught them, we placed them carefully on the bottom of the boat. It wasn't long before the sight of the poor things gasping their lives away began to get to me. I wanted to throw them back into the water, but Eileen protested so much that I decided to put them out of their misery by bashing them over the head with one of the rowlocks. Have you ever tried to chase a slippery fish with a rowlock all over the bottom of a rowing boat? It's downright dangerous. However, we didn't lose the oars, the boat didn't capsize and I succeeded in killing the fish.

Back on the shore, the old sailor helped us to pull the boat up the beach. He looked disparagingly at our catch and deflated our pride with his remarks that, "They be Gurnard, they be, and some commo' they be too!" Refusing to be put down by his scorn, we divided the fish between us and threaded them through their gills and open mouths onto the fingers of our right hands. We ran along the prom, triumphantly swinging our catch and hoping that the passers-by would recognise us as experienced in the art of fishing. We spotted our parents on the beach and waltzed up to them, proudly presenting to each of our mothers, three Gurnards with squashed heads. They wouldn't believe us and we couldn't convince them that we had actually caught the fish ourselves. They thought we had bought them in Sidmouth Market. Our fathers did believe us, however, and they made us promise never to go out in a rowing boat again unless we had an adult with us! Nobody had a word of praise for our prowess. We were disgusted.

The years passed by and almost imperceptibly, they took our childhood with them. Gradually, we ceased to be attracted to rock pools and rusty old wrecks. We started to spend long hours on our lilos, lying on our stomachs, trying to bronze our bodies by oiling each other's backs with sun-tan oil. We read our library books and our conversation was all of film stars; Clark Gable and Gary Cooper, Fred Astaire and Ginger Rogers and a host of others who were at their zenith then. We would stroll together through the town as far as the Radway Cinema to study the stills displayed outside and to decide whether or not our parents could be persuaded to take us to see a matinee of the latest attraction should the weather turn cloudy. It rarely did, the sun still shone brilliantly for us most of the time, or so it seemed to us in those days.

The summer holiday arrived when Eileen appeared no longer Eton cropped and short trousered, but with flowing shoulder length hair tastefully permed. She was growing up fast. She was far more worldly-wise than I. She had boyfriends back home. She had been kissed! She had actually received attentions from the RHB (Roving Hand Brigade) she told me. She had an elder sister who passed on tips and helpful information about sexual matters. I was envious and curious, for I was woefully ignorant – kept so deliberately by my parents. I suppose they wanted to preserve my innocence for as long as possible – especially so, my father.

"You don't want to have anything to do with boys," he would say. "You'll never know what a young girl's life should be if you become involved with boys."

Chance would have been a fine thing, I thought. I attended an all girls' school where sex was never discussed, at least, not amongst my friends. I had no brothers and my friends seemed to have none either. Now that we had moved to Torquay to live, Charlie and Tommy had been left far away and we never wrote to each other, so that Eileen became my only source of information on a matter which had come to me quite uninvited and was assuming an almost obsessional rôle in my life. My feelings were strange, strong and confused and made more so by the repressive attitude of my parents. I felt constantly guilty about asking for information or trying to obtain it from snatched secretive glances at the diagrams and involved language of medical text books in the Reference Library. Sex indeed had raised its ugly head. The carefree days had gone and the fact that I saw Eileen only once a year, meant that the months which passed between our meetings, when I was able to glean further enlightenment, were not always happy ones.

1937 was the last time that our families were all together on holiday at Sidmouth. By that time Eileen had left school and throughout the year had been training in Manchester for secretarial work. She had become very feminine looking and her figure was beautifully slim. Her interest in the opposite sex had increased and she already had a number of boyfriends about whom she talked at great length. I, on the other hand, was still at school working for A-levels which we called Higher School Certificate in those days. I was straight haired, plain featured and quite fat and no boy of my own age had ever shown the slightest interest in me. In spite of the differences in our appearance and development, we remained great friends – Eileen and I, and we still managed to have a good holiday together. Nevertheless, I knew I was being left behind in her world. Quite different horizons – immediate and challenging were opening before her, and the next year she broke away completely from the family circle. She had been working for some months and had saved up enough money to holiday abroad. Taking a week of her annual fortnight's leave, she had sailed away to foreign parts. We were never again to be on holiday together in Sidmouth. In 1938, although all the adults were present, I was lonely there. I missed her very much.

It was the end of an era, for in 1939 Father took Mother and myself to Switzerland in August to celebrate their Silver Wedding Anniversary. After ten days there we were advised by some very pleasant Germans who were staying in the same Gasthaus, to go home as quickly as possible, and when our courier came specially to the little hotel to urge us to do the same thing, we cut our holiday short, packed our bags and travelled home to England. The journey was long and tedious. In company with hundreds of others, all doing the same thing, we were squashed in to the overcrowded, overnight train at Basle. We were locked into our compartments and armed guards patrolled the corridors outside. It was Mother's first and only experience of holidaying abroad! We reached the Channel port hours late. There were so many people on board the waiting ship that it seemed to me to be very low in the water. There were no seats to be had and we sat on our cases all the way over. When we finally reached London, we found our car waiting where we had left it ten days previously in the open car park at Chiswick Station, alone, unattended and unharmed. We piled our luggage on to the back seat, I squashed in beside it and we drove home to Torquay. It was three o'clock in the morning when we arrived. Dead beat, we went straight to bed and didn't surface until eleven the next morning. As soon as we turned on the wireless, we knew. It was September 3rd 1939. The War had started!

I often visit Sidmouth nowadays. I live not far away. Sometimes I walk along Amyatt's Terrace which is still so named; as is Bon Cottage. All the buildings in this Georgian Terrace are now protected and have been saved from so-called 'development'. Mr Martin's little animals have all disappeared from the central cottage as, of course, long ago he and Mrs Martin also left the scene, but the delicately arched beam to which he fixed them now runs between bow windows and the front garden looks as ship-shape as ever, if not so interesting as it was in his day. All is neat and tidy, however, the window-panes still sparkle and the paintwork is as fresh as he would have wished.

Dovaston is another story! Some years ago, when first I came from London to retire in Devon, I went in search of Uncle Robert's house. When I found it, I felt as my Uncle Ed must have felt when he came back to Roose village in the sixties and discovered it so different. All around was change if not decay. Perhaps it was as well that I never saw the interior of the house itself. I stood in the road and gazed long and sadly at the developers' handiwork. Here, they had been busy indeed. Dovaston was no longer Dovaston. The old gate which used to take the skin from my heels was off its hinges and lying against the hedge in the newly macadamised lane. A completely new gate with another name had been erected across the entrance. The drive had been bifurcated, the garden chopped in half, and a new bungalow, extra to Dovaston, had been erected where once the prize sweet peas were grown and where Clara had chased Uncle Robert's car over the lawn. As for the fields where Dainty, Matt and Stella used to gallop – here were houses, houses, houses, all the way to the crossroads at the end of what had once been Uncle Robert's land. Mitchell's cottage was still there on the road which leads to Tipton Cross, but of course it had had a 'face lift' and I hardly recognised it.

I came away sadly, sick with nostalgia, and as I drove homewards, through the scented lanes, I conceived a gift for them as some small return for so much that Kate and Robert had once gifted to me. A gift I fear too late!

UGLY DUCKLING

(Written in memory of Aunty Kate and Uncle Robert at whose beautiful home near Ottery St. Mary I spent many happy holidays over sixty years ago!)

Are you still there?
You, in your chip-straw hat
That shades your eyes
And hides your hair,
You, with the wistful,
Hungry air – you with your
'Orphan-Annie' stare?

Are you still there?
Lonely young lass
On holiday lawns
Where sweet-peas mass
And foxgloves bloom
Down the sunken lane
Of a Devon Combe.

Are you still there?
Where warm brown hens
In pecking order
Play 'follow-the-leader'
Along the border
And out through a hole
In the hedge.

Are you still there?
In white canvas shoes
With the one-button strap
And the bright-blood stain,
Freeing a rabbit from its trap
And crying for its pain.

And do you hide still?
Dreaming for hours
Beneath the pungent pines
And do you rest your head?
Where ivy intertwines
With grass and columbines
Along a needled bed.

Plain little daughter of Eve
In your world of make-believe
Do you dream yet?
Through long drowsy days
Beneath murmuring trees,
Through warm, scented haze
Of pollen bees
That cloud the mignonette?

And are you there still,
Fifty years on?
Ugly duckling,
Still aping the swan?
I have come to find you again –
But the lawns have gone,
And the gate is stone,
And why is it that the lane
Is a shopping street
In pouring rain?
Where I wait
And I wait alone!

6

21 BELMONT ROAD, GATLEY, CHESHIRE

It was 1928; I was eight years old and we were moving into the country, for in those days, Gatley was sufficiently on the edge of Manchester to be counted as country. Although it was developing fast, it still had woods and fields and little streams. I don't know why we left New Moston, but I do remember how relieved I felt to be saying 'good-bye' once and for all to my hated school. Perhaps my parents had realised that it was doing me no good or perhaps they had just grown tired of living in rather gloomy Edwardian houses and when the chance came of a move into a small modern house situated at a decent distance from coal mines and chemical works, they seized it. The railway line from Gatley to central Manchester ran along an embankment at the back of the houses on one side of Belmont Road, and Gatley Station itself was at the far end of the road. This meant Father could reach the city quite quickly each day without too much hassle and Mother could still conveniently make her Saturday morning pilgrimage to Lewises each week.

We had returned early from our summer holiday in Devon that year so that we should have time to settle into our new house before term started in September. I have no memory of the move. I must have spent it at Primrose Bank with Grandma and Grandpa Haydock, but I do remember, after all the furniture had been moved into the house, sitting on the bare earth in our new back garden. My parents were busy inside, so there I sat in bright summer weather, surveying my new surroundings and experiencing a deep-down joy to know that in no way could I now be sent back to New Moston School on the first Monday in September.

This was a brand new house on a brand new estate, the first of its kind I had ever experienced. Everything was rather raw-looking, but fresh and exciting, smelling of paint and sawn wood. The roads were not yet paved and in some of them, houses were still being built. Many gardens were still undug, but here and there were newly sown lawns with sparse and tender grass, and the fences between the houses were bare wire-netting affairs. Everything was very open at first, neighbours could see right through into each other's gardens – no high brick walls and backyards here. Eventually, rustic fences, thick with climbing roses, would take over and give a measure of privacy to each oblong patch.

Inside, the houses were all the same – simple, unimaginative and well-built. Typical of the estates of the time, three up, two down, kitchen and bathroom, they were semi-detached with a drive-in but no garage. Few people on the estate possessed cars. One of Father's first jobs was to build a garage. "Clara must have shelter and somewhere to sleep," he explained. At a cost of about £400 to £500 each, they were quite ordinary houses, occupied by quite ordinary people. Most of the latter were young couples like Mother and Father and many were bringing up small families. Gone were the lavish days of Edwardian England, so well remembered by my parents' generation, when five or more children was the norm. Many of my Gatley friends were, like me, only children – the Harrisons who lived across the road had three and eventually four children, but theirs was looked upon as a really large family.

Before ever I arrived at Gatley, Mother had found a friend for me. "Such a nice little girl – your age. She lives three doors away and she is looking forward to playing with you. Her mother is a very pleasant lady." On my first day, I was duly taken along and introduced. The 'nice little girl' was called Betty Waites – we got along well together. She had many more toys than I had, in fact I had never before seen such a plethora of dolls. We played happily for half an hour, when suddenly I grew tired of washing dolls and putting them to bed. I looked at the sunshine in the road outside.

"Let's be horses and canter round the houses. You can be Black Beauty," I offered magnanimously. "I don't mind being Ginger."

Betty looked at me sadly. "I'm not allowed out, Mummy won't let me."

Full of confidence I approached Mrs Waites in her kitchen. "Can Betty and I go out?"

"Of course you can. Shall I spread a rug for you on the lawn and then you can carry the dolls out and have a tea-party with Betty's own little tea-set?"

"Not in the garden," I replied somewhat impatiently. "I mean outside in the road – we'll stay on the pavements."

"Certainly not, Betty is never allowed out on her own. Of course not." Mrs Waites was adamant. "Now run along and play, I'm busy." I went back to Betty. She didn't even ask the outcome of my request – she knew. Suddenly I felt trapped, imprisoned. I wasn't used to being confined to home and garden. The freedom of the streets and the right to play with whomsoever I wished, had never been denied me. Panic seized me. I must get away now, or I may never be able to escape. I would become a prisoner like Betty. It was a struggle. Betty clung physically, her mother clung psychologically; harsh words were exchanged, but I broke free, ran home 'hell for leather' and never played with Betty again.

Many times after this incident when I was running up and down the road with the gang of neighbours' children into which I was quickly welcomed, I would see her standing and looking longingly over the low garden wall which fronted all the houses, at the collection of fairy bikes, scooters, pedal cars, hoops and roped-together 'horses' as it went bowling past on its noisy way. Sometimes I would break ranks and go over to urge her to open the gate and come to join us. But her mother would tap on the window-pane and call her indoors.

I soon made many friends in Belmont Road. Manchester people are companionable and so are their children. On the other side of the street, in the last house, lived the Harrisons: Mr and Mrs, George, Ruth, Joyce and Lillian. Twelve-year-old George was the eldest child, Ruth was about my age, Joyce was a toddler and Lillian arrived on the scene about a year after we first came to live in Gatley. At the far end of the road near the station lived Alfred Cook and his sister and in between were several young families with children.

We would all play out together in the long summer evenings. Down the side of the Harrison's house ran a dirt lane. It wound its way towards the railway line which backed on to the houses opposite ours. It went under a bridge – tall, echoing and dripping with water, and it ended in a field on the other side. Here, the lane turned into a pathway which was reached through a little white swing 'kissing gate' and on it went along the edge of the field bordering the railway line until it turned away at right angles to follow another hedge, cross another lane and on and on until it came to Cheadle, a mile away.

I couldn't believe my luck when I first saw that path, for it bordered real hedges which were full of clean leaves and branches and which were not cluttered at their bases with discarded household debris. It bordered real fields which in spring and summer were high and bright with sweet-smelling grasses – wonderful for making 'dens' and for hiding from the world deep down inside their waving walls. Here, wild roses climbed the hedgerows between the hawthorn blossoms, and buttercups, daisies, campions, field poppies and even bluebells grew in season.

This was the country – and I was living in it at last. Here we would play, seven or eight of us together, riding our 'horses' through the long grass, gathering flowers to sell to our mothers and neighbours at a half-penny a bunch, sitting astride the big five-barred black gate which was alongside the little white swing gate which led into the field. The former was 'Black Beauty'. It would accommodate half a dozen of us at a time sitting one behind the other astride the top bar. The swing gate was 'Silver King', Tom Mix's horse, and whoever rode Silver King was able to swing violently from side to side in the saddle. From this spot near the railway arch, we set out to cross the world. We had a leader, elected by 'Eenie Meenie Minie Mo', who rode at the head of our group and was expected to keep up a running commentary as to what sort of scenery we were passing through, where we were to dismount to water our horses, where to pitch tents for the night, etc.

One evening in late spring, when the grass in the field had grown up almost above our heads and waved enticingly, sweet smelling and full of buttercups and clover, five of us plunged in and crawled on our stomachs Red Indian fashion to the very middle of the meadow, leaving a gorge-like trail behind us. Here in the centre, we flattened the grass even further and made ourselves a den. Here we rolled about in ecstasy on the soft bed of broken stalks, lost in the exciting depths of our green world. Suddenly we heard angry shouts and the noise of a motor-bike revving up. The shouts continued and grew nearer. Intrigued and a little frightened, we stood up and grew even more frightened. Two furious-looking men were standing in the lane at a gap in the hedge on the far side of the field. They were shaking their fists at us and threatening to 'skin us alive' if they caught us. We didn't wait to be caught. We ran. As we ran we could hear the motor-bike roaring down the lane and back towards the main road. We knew instinctively where the men were going and what they would do. We scattered and each fled to the safety of home. Two of us rushed through the swing gate, but I and the two others who were left, rather than wait in a queue to get through the kissing gate, climbed 'Black Beauty' with shaking legs and staggered on, under the railway arch, up the lane and back into Belmont Road. The first house we reached was the Harrisons' where Ruth and George lived. They ran indoors and took the other two with them. I had just time enough to reach home. Our garage door was open – Clara was inside. I flung myself into the back of the car, shut the door behind me and lay hidden on the floor. For a long time I lay there. I could hear the motor-bike going up and down Belmont Road. Sometimes its engine stopped, and petrified, I imagined the two men questioning passers-by, or making house-to-house searches. They didn't manage to find any of us, but it taught us a lesson. We never again flattened down the farmer's grass.

Houses were being built in the unfinished roads all round the estate. There were a couple going up round the corner at the end of Belmont Road, opposite the Harrisons'.

Sometimes, during the light evenings, our gang would play in them after the workmen had gone home. The houses were left quite open and unguarded with plenty of ladders lying around. One thing which delighted our hearts was the appearance, in the back garden of one of the houses, of a great hollow triangle formed out of smooth roofing and flooring planks, stored one on top of the other, all ready for use. We found that if we were careful, we could insert our toes between one plank and another, and in this way we could climb up to the top of the triangle and down its inner side to the bottom. There hidden in a grassy-floored well of planks towering many feet above us, open to the sky, but not to the eyes of passers-by, we would stay, plotting and planning our next game until the light began to fade and the bottom of the 'well' became dark and creepy and somebody's mother could be heard calling that supper was ready.

We had no fear and no imagination as to what might have resulted from our games. We played in those houses from the time they were just brick foundations to the time they were ready for occupancy and the doors and windows were in place and locked against us. We watched them grow. We thought nothing of climbing ladders to the first floor long before the floorboards had been put in and only the joists ran across from wall to wall. Laughing and sure-footed, we would race each other across the front bedroom 'floor', jumping the gaps from joist to joist and looking down through the spaces between, to the drawing-room below!

Apart from playing in the field and in the new houses, we often congregated for games in the road. Nearly every child owned some kind of toy vehicle. For some reason I was never allowed to have a bike or a scooter of my own. I was told it was too dangerous, but there must have been another reason, for my parents knew about and never objected to my borrowing friends' bikes and fairy cycles. After school, the gang would congregate by the Harrisons' gate and set off 'en masse' for the first ride of the evening. I never took part in this. No one was willing to surrender the enjoyment of 'first ride', so I had to wait until the party returned, skidding to a halt after a race round the houses. then, if I were lucky, I would be able to persuade one of them to let me 'have a lend' of a bike for second ride.

Gatley Church had well organised groups of Cubs and Brownies. One evening during the week, all of my friends seemed to disappear. The road would be empty. Joan, Ruth, Donald, Alfred, Gerald, Peter and George, were off to the Cubs or the Brownies. I begged to be allowed to join the Brownies. I heard all about it from the others and imagined myself part of that highly desirable group. I saw myself standing before a benevolent Brown Owl, making the Brownie Promise and subsequently becoming a 'Sixer'. But it was not to be, for anything organised by the church was a forbidden activity as far as I was concerned. Also, my father seemed to think that there was something vaguely military about Guiding and Scouting. He spoke darkly of them as 'trying to put a gun in every baby's cradle!'

Just at the back of our estate, facing Old Hall Road, there was a Congregational Chapel and here I was sent to Sunday School. I quite enjoyed this. Ruth Harrison came along also and we always walked there together. There was a big, old and dilapidated house at the top of Old Hall Road which faced an open grassy triangle which may once have been the original village green. Nearby were a brook and woods which we called Gatley Carrs and through which Ruth and I would sometimes make a detour en route for Sunday School, until we were forbidden to go there following the rumoured sighting of an unpleasant character lurking amongst the trees in wait for little girls. Just what he was waiting for, I didn't know and no one would tell me, so I imagined he was after our collection money.

I was always given a whole penny to put into the box. Ruth was also given a penny, but it always seemed to be in the form of two halfpennies so that she could put one in the box and was able to keep the other! Occasionally, we took Joan Peters along with us. She lived at the back of my house, our gardens abutted. She was even craftier than Ruth – she played dumb! The collection was a noisy, lively affair which I greatly enjoyed. A big box was placed on a table at the far end of the hall and all the classes from the babies to the seniors formed a big circle of about thirty children. Round and round the hall we marched, skipped or danced according to our mood, singing as we went:

> "Hear the pennies dropping,
> Hear them as they fall,
> Every one for Jesus,
> He shall have them all.
> Dropping, dropping
> Dropping, dropping
> Hear them as they fall,
> Every one for Jesus
> He shall have them all."

It went on and on until all of us had been past the box on the table at least three times. On one of these times, we were expected to drop our penny into the box. The thumping of the piano, the clinking of the coins, the waving of arms and legs and the shrill sound of young voices made a lively scene whose purpose was quite obvious to me. When we came out of Sunday School, however, Joan Peters was still clutching her penny.

"You didn't put your penny in the box," I accused.

"No one asked me," she replied defensively.

At first I thought her stupid, but of course I was the stupid one, I continued naively to put my penny regularly into the box, so regularly that at the end of my Gatley days I won a prize for 'very good attendance during 1930'. I still have the school story-book which they gave me – labelled, inscribed and treasured.

Although the Congregational Church never came up with a Brownie Pack, it did occasionally have a Club Evening for its youngsters. I was allowed to participate in these when they took place and also in the Christmas shows which the Sunday School teachers produced. I was given the lead in two plays. I remember having to scream loudly off-stage the whole time that I was being made up for my next appearance. It was ear-splitting but effective I was told. The following year my part involved singing alone in the centre of the stage! That nearly finished me. I was in tears. I thought I should have to give up the part – I was sure that I couldn't sing, but I did so want to act. My parents were supportive. Mother comforted and Father rehearsed the song with me every evening at the piano, over and over and over again until I actually managed to keep in tune from beginning to end – and it was all right on the night – just. I remember that song to this day and can still sing it in tune. Even the dancing part which I was given in my final year at Gatley, was condoned by my father. I suppose the fact that the entertainment was being organised by the Congregationalists, the next best thing to Methodists, made it permissible. I danced and loved every minute of it – delighted to take the part of a boy, delighted with my black sateen knee britches and delighted to partner a pretty little girl to the tune of an old-fashioned minuet.

Only two weeks after we first arrived at Belmont Road I was sent to school. Having escaped the tortures of Moston Board School, I was now dismayed to learn that I was to attend another council school. The nearest one was in Cheadle – a mile away and quite a big school. I was apprehensive.

"Couldn't I go to a private school?" I asked.

It seemed there was nothing suitable and in any case, my father was not in favour of private education.

"There must be a village school in Gatley that I could go to?" I begged.

There was – a Church School! Out of the question as far as I was concerned, so off I went and became a pupil at Cheadle Council School in Cheshire for the next three years.

There was a tram which ran past Gatley Station, along the Cheadle Road passing through Cheadle High Street on its way to Stockport. The journey cost a halfpenny. I had to make it four times a day since I came home for dinner at twelve-thirty and had to be back for afternoon school at two o'clock. I was allowed a penny a day for tram fares which meant that I had to walk two miles a day at least and when I was told that I could keep any tram fare which I didn't use, I would often walk four miles a day back and forth to Cheadle. I soon became quite used to this and never thought of it as a hardship even in bad weather. Most of the neighbouring children went to school in Cheadle and by the time

Ruth Harrison and I had reached the far end of Belmont Road at half past eight in the morning. we had collected quite a band of boys and girls who had come out of their gates to join us as we passed by.

All that winter of 1928 six or seven of us, mackintoshed and wellington-booted against the weather, would short-cut under the railway embankment, through Gatley Station Yard, across the lane used by the motor-bike farmers, along a narrow path, open to fields on one side and the back gardens of houses on the other, until we came out through a gap in the hedge onto the main road leading into Cheadle. There was a pavement all the way with fields and open spaces on our side of the road and houses on the other. We would run and jump and play follow-the-leader pretty well all the way to school, but before we could actually reach the building and the relative safety of the playground, we had a busy main road to cross. It seems fantastic in these days to think that four times a day we were expected to cross alone. The only help we received were parental instructions.

"Be sure you all cross together. Be sure you stand and look right and left before you cross. Once you set foot on the road, be sure you run very fast to the other side!"

We used to join hands and skip across in twos and threes. No one to my knowledge was ever run over. I must have had a great deal of energy for I can remember on fine days, half running, half walking the mile home at dinner-time, swallowing down the hot meal which Mother always had ready for me, taking my big wooden hoop which hung on a nail against the wall under the kitchen window and bowling it at a fast run all the way round the block, returning it to its place, kissing Mother good-bye and half-running, half-walking, back again to school.

My first day at Cheadle Council School stands out clearly in my mind. I shall never forget it. I was in great discomfort all day long. Father delivered me into the playground and abandoned me to my own devices. Unfortunately, as we had left home, a piece of grit had blown into my eye and it refused to come out again. Father tried to dislodge it with no success but was quite sure that it would come out of its own accord. By the time we reached school my eye was watering non-stop.

"Try not to rub it, but if you must, rub towards your nose and tell the teacher as soon as you get the chance." Was Father's advice as he left me. The chance was a long time in coming. I was lined up with all the other new children, marched here, marched there, questioned, labelled and docketed and I finally came to rest in an oversized double desk alongside an unknown girl of about my own age. I, with forty-nine others occupied a makeshift classroom at one end of a large draughty hall where enormous stuffed birds in glass cases looked menacingly down on our dutifully bowed heads. Suddenly the stranger beside me put up her hand.

"Please Miss, there's a girl 'ere wot's crying."

Only then was I able to say what was wrong with me, but it wasn't until playtime that the overworked teacher could take me out into the cold stone cloakroom to bathe my eye. But it was all to no avail and by this time my eye was very red and quite swollen. I ran the mile home at lunch-time with one hand covering the left side of my face. Mother did her best for me and wanted to keep me at home but felt sure that Father would not have liked me to miss my first day at a new school. So back I ran and sat through afternoon lessons in a miserable, half-hearted sort of way. At afternoon playtime another teacher tried to look into my eye, but by this time it was quite puffed up and almost impossible to open.

Again, at four o'clock, I ran home, all on my own, and as fast as I could go. Mother was lovely when you were ill. She was so comforting and had the softest bosom in the world on which to lay an aching head. We sat quietly together until Father arrived back from work. He took one look at me and announced that as soon as the doctor's surgery was open, he would take me there. We set out again, he and I, after tea – hand-in-hand along the road to Cheadle. The doctor was kind, reassuring and very clever. He took a matchstick and rolled my eyelid onto it.

"There's the little blighter that's been causing all the trouble," he said, as he and Father peered at the red-raw surface where the grit had embedded itself. He took a piece of white bandage and deftly removed the speck, rolling my eyelid back into place at the same time. The relief was immediate and wonderful and cost one and sixpence. I skipped back home at Father's side and felt so happy that I was almost looking forward to going to school again the next day.

After my somewhat traumatic start, I tolerated Cheadle Council School quite well. During the three years that I was a pupil there, I was joined by my cousins Charlie and Tommy. When Grandpa's shop closed down and Uncle Charlie was out of a job, their big house on Moston Lane became too expensive to run, so the family moved to a smaller house in Cheadle Hulme, not far from Gatley, and suddenly there were my cousins again, with me at my new school. I didn't see much of them. Tommy was in a class below mine and Charlie was in the next class up, and at playtime boys and girls were strictly segregated into separate playgrounds, although on occasion, we were able to pass notes to each other through the railings.

None of the teachers at this school ever hit me – in fact one of them actually kissed me! It was Christmas time and my parents thought that I should give Miss Kettle, my class teacher, a small present before we broke up for the holidays. Much against my will, for no one else seemed to be giving the teachers presents, I knocked on the Staff Room door and handed in my offering, a box of notepaper and envelopes. Before I had time to make my escape, the door opened again, out came Miss Kettle, flung her arms round me and bestowed a big kiss on my cheek. I was horrified. It was so 'sissy' to be kissed by a teacher and I just prayed that none of my friends had witnessed the shameful event.

Although Miss Kettle showed me the softer side of her nature, she could be tough if occasion demanded. In our class, there was a boy called Charlie Machin. If there was ever any trouble, he was in it. He made trouble, he was trouble. The whole school knew about Charlie Machin – a poor-looking boy in a dirty jersey full of holes. He wore big boots but no socks, and he had dark, wicked-looking eyes. He it was who persuaded my cousin Tommy to pinch six Woodbines from an open box in the tobacconists' shop! They were both caught and reported to our headmaster – both received a caning and Tommy, to this day, has never forgotten Charlie Machin.

I remember one playtime particularly, when, authorised by a note from home, I had to stay in with one of my frequent colds. Charlie Machin had to stay in also, but for a very different reason. He had been up to no good again and Miss Kettle, exasperated beyond endurance, had decided, once and for all, to get the better of him. She took a ruler, and she put Charlie Machin over every desk in that classroom and whacked his bottom hard fifty times in all; twenty-five times one way round and twenty-five times on the way back, for the desks were double ones! When they reached the place where I was sitting, I was required to move out temporarily so that my desk could also be used for Charlie's chastisement. It seemed to subdue Charlie for the rest of the day, but in the long run I don't think it did any good – Charlie's reputation as bad boy of the school seemed only to be enhanced at the hands of Miss Kettle.

She was my class teacher for two out of the three years I attended this school. I met her in Standard II and again in Standard IV and I grew used to her ways. My parents thought highly of her as a teacher and she must have been good for she managed to control fifty lively boys and girls admirably well considering that she was short of stature and very young. In addition, she had that essential quality for a teacher, a sense of humour.

One morning, when Ruth Harrison had called for me to walk to school with her, Father came out with us as far as the front gate.

"Give my love to Miss Kettle," he called after us as we walked down Belmont Road. I thought nothing more of it. I knew Father's ways and realised that he was joking.

In the middle of an arithmetic lesson, Ruth's hand shot up, "Please Miss, Mr Smith sends his love to you." I gasped, the class tittered and Miss Kettle solemnly replied.

"Well, that is very kind of Mr Smith, when you next see him Ruth, please tell him that I am most gratified and I send mine back to him." Ruth didn't deliver the message, but I did and Father thought it a huge joke.

Miss Kettle divided her class into 'rows' according to

ability. 'Top Row' pupils were seated one behind the other in a line of double desks nearest to the windows. 'Bottom Row', was at the other side of the room all down the wall which bordered the corridor and 'Middle Rows' came in between. I was near the top of Miss Kettle's 'Top Row'. Charlie Machin was at the very end of her 'Bottom Row'. One morning, when we were reading aloud, sentence by sentence round the class, a whispering could be heard to be going on somewhere in the middle rows. It didn't escape Miss Kettle's attention.

"Stop," she said, putting down her book. "Just tell me Katherine Howarth, what you are whispering to your neighbour."

"Please Miss, it's a pass-on message."

"From whom? From Whom?" – "Well, I'm waiting, we are all waiting." The class held its breath, curious, intrigued. We all looked at Katherine Howarth – a white little girl, turned pink and pop-eyed with embarrassment. Eventually, unable to stand the silence any longer:

"From Charlie Machin," she giggled nervously.

"I might have known it." Miss Kettle sounded resigned. "And to whom is this message to be passed?"

Katherine Howarth swallowed visibly, you could see her pink throat expanding and contracting above her Peter-Pan collar.

"To Beryl Smith."

"Well stand up then Katherine Howarth and tell Beryl Smith directly what it is that Charlie Machin wants her to know."

"Ooh Miss, I couldn't . . . "

"Nonsense, of course you can – if you can whisper it, you can speak it out aloud. Hurry up, the sooner you deliver this message, the sooner we can all get back to our reading."

Katherine Howarth didn't stand up; she told me later that her legs had gone to jelly, but she looked straight at me and in a high pitched, hysterical tone, announced, " 'Ee luvs yer – 'ee just wanted yer to know."

My mouth fell open with astonishment. I couldn't control it. I must have looked very silly, for everyone, including Miss Kettle, started to laugh.

"And is this true Charlie Machin?" she asked.

"Aye, it is an' all," came the answer loud and clear, from the opposite corner of the room.

"And what do you say to that Beryl Smith?" asked our teacher when the laughter had finally subsided.

I tried to say that I didn't believe it, but no sounds came from my mouth.

"Well," she said, taking pity on me, "you know now how Charlie Machin feels about you. We all know, so let us get on with our reading – shall we?"

Under cover of the ensuing drone which moved reluctantly round the classroom, I stole a glance in Charlie Machin's direction, but he was far away amongst the shadows in the gloomiest, most unenlightened part of our prison cell. He didn't look up but I could see that his eyes were closed and that his nose was actually touching the page of his book. He had never spoken to me before the episode and we never spoke afterwards. Pointedly and poignantly now, we continued to ignore each other.

The one year which I didn't spend under Miss Kettle's guidance I endured at the hand of another teacher who trimmed hats and crocheted collars whilst 'teaching' her flock. I had done so well in Miss Kettle's 'Top Row' that I was removed from her care to be 'put up' into Standard III a term before my 'due date'. The uprooting wasn't much to my liking and moreover, Father afterwards always attributed my inability to multiply correctly to the fact that I had missed a whole term's chanting of my eight times' tables at Miss Kettle's hands. I started off in a middle row in Standard III where, far from being notorious as Charlie Machin's 'girl' I was now regarded as so respectable that I was expected to befriend my new teacher's daughter who was a pupil in her mother's class at this time, and alongside whom I was chosen to sit. In this privileged position, I experienced not only a constant whispering chatter from the daughter, but also the entire blame for it from her mother! Mary, as the daughter was called, was a giggler and a tickler, I was her victim and she got away with murder because of who she was.

About this time two new schools opened in Gatley. Half

way along the road to Cheadle two big old houses, standing next to each other, each in its own grounds, put up boards advertising the fact that in the coming September they would be taking pupils. Parents of prospective scholars were invited to contact the respective heads of each school. One of the two was to be called Gatley High School, but I cannot remember the name of the other. Both, however, were to be private schools.

The first time I saw these notice-boards I stopped and stared and from the other side of the road, read and memorised every word on them. As soon as I arrived home I enlightened my parents of my discovery and begged to be removed from Cheadle Council School into what I imagined would be a far more favourable environment inside the walls of one of these establishments. All through the summer term I plagued them both with my entreaties, but of course it was hopeless. I think Mother would have relished the snob value of my removal to a private school but Father just laughed at the very idea. I watched those schools take shape. On my way to Cheadle and on my way back, I would linger, gazing at the two old houses from the other side of the road. I saw the windows cleaned and curtained, the gardens tidied, the hedges cut and steps swept. One day as I passed, a big furniture van stood in front of the main entrance to Gatley High School and in great excitement I watched the pupils' desks being carried in. Little single ones they were, with a box-like space beneath for the owner's personal books and property to be carefully stored. Oh how I longed and longed and longed!

Two children from Belmont Road were entered as pupils in these new schools for the following September. They were friends of mine, Joyce and Peter. Joyce was to go to Gatley High School and Peter to the adjoining school. I questioned Joyce interminably until I knew every detail of the uniform which her mother had bought her from a special shop. I was obsessed, I almost devoured every article, from the brown reefer coat and leather gloves, brown velour hat with brown and gold hat-band, brown pleated gymslip, cream silk blouse and brown and gold tie right down to the brown shoes and socks and the brown fleecy-lined knickers. Joyce was very patient and told me all she knew about her new school but she didn't seem over-interested in it. Peter's uniform was blue and silver, but he wasn't at all interested and one day, when I pestered him too much for details, he lost his temper and rushed at me with a poker! I didn't bother him after that. I concentrated on Joyce.

Eventually, I was forced to accept the fact that I would never become a pupil in either of these schools and in order to alleviate my frustration, I invented a school of my own, full of wealthy, fee-paying pupils. Rosy-cheeked girls with bobbed hair and lacrosse sticks arrived, tumbling out of school charabancs which had brought them to the old ivy-covered, cliff top manor house which was to be their 'alma mater' for the next term at least. I drew plans of the whole building, I wrote out a prospectus which centred round the school's gymnasium and the nearby beaches and sandy coves where dancing and swimming lessons and learning to dive from the rocks occupied a large part of the curriculum. I appointed a staff and wrote a character study, of each, from the sour, embittered maths teacher, to the 'Jolly-Hockey-Sticks' games' mistress and the much-ragged 'Mademoiselle'. I made myself Headmistress and settled back to dream. It was the best I could do in the circumstances.

Some months later, on the way to 'real' school, Ruth informed me that she was to have ballet lessons on Saturday mornings. Immediately, I was smitten with a desire to learn to dance. Instead of plaguing them about private school education, I now subjected Mother and Father to a non-stop barrage of entreaty on behalf of dancing lessons. I knew that I would never be able to sing, but dance I could, and did, at every possible opportunity. I was supple and I had rhythm even if I couldn't distinguish one note from another. Mother, Grandma Haydock and Aunty Gertie were on my side, but Father was deaf to all pleading. Aunty Gertie said it was wicked that I should be denied the chance to develop what seemed to be a natural talent, I high-kicked, I pirouetted, I stuffed all my shoes with cotton wool and wore out their caps by constantly rising on to my toes – all to no avail. Once again, I lived my dream through the experience of others. Ruth introduced me to bar exercises which I would put into practice whenever possible by holding on to the kitchen sink, and then it was that I discovered Ena Ashworth.

Ena was rich and she went to Cheadle Council School – just why, I could never fathom. Perhaps she also had a father who was as much opposed to private education as was mine, but he certainly wasn't opposed to dancing lessons and saw to it that his daughter had plenty of them. She and her family lived in a big detached house on the way to school and she would often join our gang en route and walk along with Ruth and myself. She was a plump, pretty little girl with corkscrew ringlets and a nurse who washed her knees for her each bedtime and put her hair into curling-rags! I was impressed, but, best of all, she attended special ballet classes and lavishly bestowed on me a discarded tutu and six pairs of toe shoes which had become too small for her. It's a wonder that I was allowed to keep them, but having learnt a little sense after my experience with glass marbles, with Mother's co-operation, I managed to keep them well out of Father's sight and put on shows only when Grandma and Aunty Gertie came to visit.

About this time Grandpa's business was folding up. He and Grandma were struggling to find enough money to pay off creditors. Grandpa was too proud to declare himself bankrupt and so the struggle went on for some time. Eventually, about a year before we left Gatley for good, Mother and Father managed to 'lend' my grandparents £100. My parents must have known that there was no chance of the loan ever being repaid, so they sold our old piano and took, as security, the lovely Rudi Ibach piano from the drawing-room at Primrose Bank, together with many pieces of Grandma's valuable jewellery. There was an understanding that these items were to be returned once the money was paid back. Father was especially delighted with the piano.

"Now that we have a really good instrument," he said, "Beryl must learn to play. She must have music lessons!"

My heart sank. "Couldn't I have dancing lessons instead?" I asked. The question was ignored. A teacher was quickly found, an all-leather music case purchased from Lewises and 6.00 pm to 7.00 pm on Fridays set aside for the initial stages of my musical education. My progress was slow to say the least. I tried, I really tried, but soon, from merely tolerating the sounds which came from those black and white keys, I began to loathe them and when I was introduced to a small fiendishly devised contraption which whirred and ticked above my head and with which I was expected to keep in time, I almost became a nervous wreck. The most farcical thing of all was when I was sent to stand in the far corner of the room, my back turned to the piano. I had to cover first one ear and then the other whilst my teacher played certain notes which I was then expected to recognise and name. I might just as well have stuffed both ears full of sealing wax! I made wild guesses at the sounds, but I couldn't even tell whether one note was higher or lower than its predecessor. My instructor was very patient, and times being hard, she probably didn't want to lose a pupil. We managed to survive the experience and each other for two terms, but when it finally came to an end, I don't know which of us breathed the greater sigh of relief. Release came for us both at the end of March 1931, for in April Father took up his new appointment and we moved to Torquay. The music lessons ceased, never to be recommenced!

It was in the summer of 1929 that I first met my father's eldest brother, my Uncle Bert. He came alone from Cuba, to see before he died, he said, what was left of his family in England. In those days everyone travelled by ship between continents. Great ports like Liverpool and Southampton fairly hummed with trade. It was to Liverpool that we went in Clara to meet Uncle Bert and to see him onto the train for Barrow and Roose. We arrived before his boat had docked and were told that it was delayed and would be two hours late in docking, so we all took a trip on the ferry to the Birkenhead side of the estuary. It was quite an adventure. I don't think any of us had been on the ferry before. We had no sooner landed and were walking away to have a look at Birkenhead, when we saw a huge liner slowly coming upstream to dock on the Liverpool side. It came so close that we could read the name on its starboard bow . . . it was Uncle Bert's ship! So much for Birkenhead. We dashed back to the ferry and managed to leap aboard just before it started off again on its return trip and we reached the

Liverpool shore just as Uncle Bert was coming down the gangplank.

The two brothers had not seen each other for thirty years and their reunion was a very emotional one. I took an immediate liking to Uncle Bert in spite of his rather forbidding appearance. He was tall and thin with a prominent, hooked nose and a very pronounced limp. Dressed completely in black except for his white clerical collar, to me he looked like the male counterpart of a witch, but when he removed his big black Homburg, gave a brilliant smile and opened his arms wide to enfold Mother and me both together in an enthusiastic embrace, I knew there was nothing to be scared of. That was the thing about Uncle Bert – he was enthusiastic in all he did. We wanted him to come back to Gatley with us for the night, but no, he must go immediately to see Grandpa in Roose, no matter what time of night he arrived there. It was getting dark when we finally waved him off on the train which went only as far as Barrow. Later, he reported to us that when he arrived there, it was so late that all the buses had stopped running so he found a taxi to take him to Roose. The village was in darkness and No. 73 was well locked up for the night. Uncle Bert hammered on the front door and the taxi driver threw pebbles against the bedroom panes and finally an upstairs window opened, Grandpa's head, nightcap crowned, emerged and Grandpa's voice demanded: "Who's that howling and prowling about in the night?"

Uncle Bert stayed with Grandpa, Aunty Mill and Uncle Sam for a month and then came back to us in Gatley. The holidays had started by this time and we had arranged to take him with us to Sidmouth. En route for Devon we were to visit Draycott in Somerset where many of the older generation of Smith relatives were still living. Father and Uncle Bert were quite excited at the prospect of reliving the memories of boyhood visits to Somerset. In fact they laughed and larked about so much in each others' company, that Mother said they were behaving like a pair of schoolboys themselves. Uncle Bert was fun. We had a wonderful holiday in Sidmouth. Mr and Mrs Martin took to him immediately as did Aunty Kate and Uncle Robert and we were all of us during that holiday, often invited to Dovaston for a meal. On these occasions Uncle Bert was always asked to say grace. He did this well and dramatically, but once, when my mouth must have been watering at the sight of the roast chicken steaming away on its dish before our eyes, I was reported to have remarked, as Uncle finished our devotions with a particularly flowery phrase:

"Ooh, that was a long one."

Uncle Bert liked Sidmouth. He said it was the first time that he had felt really warm since arriving in England. Nevertheless, that didn't stop him from wrapping his long black coat firmly around his legs and wearing his big Homburg pulled well down on his head when he sat all afternoon in a deck-chair on the beach. There was another thing about him – he loved bananas. He would buy whole bunches of them at a time, but before he ate them, he would insist they be put into the oven in their skins and heated until they turned mushy and brown. He complained that you couldn't buy a really ripe banana in England. Where he came from it seemed they had to turn to pulp before they could be enjoyed! And then there were the 'sour saps'. He introduced me to these. I hadn't known of their existence before Uncle Bert came on the scene, but he made me promise never to eat these leaves unless he had inspected them himself first. I remember finding a clump of them on the edge of the field beyond the railway bridge in Gatley and dragging him out to inspect them. When he pronounced them safe to eat, the gang and I devoured the whole lot. He was, like my father, a great raconteur. He would tell me 'Brer Rabbit' stories by the hour, his voice richly toned and full of the accents of the deep South. I would listen entranced as he created a world for me of which hitherto I had known little. Of course I had heard of the one-time slaves and the rich plantation owners in the Southern States, but with Uncle Bert they came alive. He could produce the southern drawl to perfection. For a short while, Brer Rabbit filled the gap which had been left in my life by the deliberate murder of Betty and William.

When he finally went home to Cuba, I felt sad. I missed him for quite a long time afterwards, for not only had he enlivened our Sidmouth holiday, but we had also spent some time with him at Roose before school started again, and when my father, Aunty Mill, Grandpa and Uncle Bert got together, there was never a dull moment. I couldn't go to see him off at Liverpool since he left long after term had started at school. Father took a day off work and met him there while Mother stayed at home to look after me. We none of us ever saw him again. He wrote often and when the war started a letter arrived from Cuba saying, 'If you have anything precious which you would like to entrust to our keeping, Agnes and I will cherish it for you if you would like to send it to us now.' My father always thought that by 'anything precious' he meant me. I was very touched but I was nineteen by that time and my roots had gone deep into my own soil. Before he left, Uncle Bert gave me two presents – I have them still. One is a little silver box lined with North American cedarwood, a decoration of pressed flowers from the Cuban countryside inserted beneath its glass lid and the other is a copy of the *Adventures of Brer Rabbit*.

My greatest friends in Gatley were the Harrisons – particularly Ruth. Her little sister Joyce was too young to participate in our games and George the eldest often took such a high-handed attitude, being a boy and older than Ruth and myself, that we often avoided playing with him. There was one big advantage, however, in keeping in with George. He knew how to make a kind of 'go-cart' out of two sets of dolls'-pram wheels, two planks of wood, a few nails and a length of old rope. When completed, these odd bits and pieces were transformed into a wonderful vehicle – especially wonderful to me who had no form of transport except my own two legs. Two of us could ride astride the planks while a third person pulled. Down any slight slope the go-kart would career on its own and the front rider could guide it by means of the rope attached to the front two wheels. Unfortunately there were few slopes round Belmont Road, so Ruth and I used to take it in turns to pull George round the streets until he grew bored. He would then leap off and stride away with a curt injunction to Ruth to 'take it back our kid'. We would then seize our opportunity and play with it for the rest of the evening, overloading it with other members of the gang, until one night we broke it and the next day Ruth showed me a bruise on her arm which George, in his fury, had meted out to his sister!

We all had our weekly comics delivered in those days. The Harrisons took *Tiger Tims* and I had *Bubbles*. We loved our comics. Once a week, on a Tuesday, I would be up specially early to catch the current highly coloured edition as it dropped through the letter-box. By the evening I had devoured it from cover to cover. The next day I would take it over to the Harrisons and we would swop copies. I enjoyed their *Tiger Tims*, but I still preferred *Bubbles* even though George said it was 'sissy', but I noticed that he was not above reading it when Ruth had finished with it. Of course we returned each other's comics and during our first year at Gatley, my pile of back numbers of *Bubbles* grew so big that one day, Mother, who maintained proprietorial rights over my toy cupboard, had a clear out and gave them all to the dustbin man! I returned from school to find them gone. I made such a fuss and was so rude that Mother slapped me and I sulked for a week. Gradually, over the next few months, the pile built up again – and then, suddenly, something awful happened.

Just before seven thirty, as was usual on a Tuesday morning, I came galloping, half dressed, down the stairs and caught *Bubbles* before it could drop onto the mat. I rushed back upstairs with it to finish dressing whilst reading the adventure of the Jumbo Boys on its front page. I opened it out on the bed and caught my breath in horror. It wasn't *Bubbles* at all. It was something called *The Children's Newspaper*. Quick as lightning, I seized it, flew back downstairs again and whilst I was struggling to open the front door, Mother's hand closed over mine.

"Whatever do you think you are doing, trying to open the front door in your knickers!" Mother was horrified.

"It's *Bubbles*, it's *Bubbles* – look what the paper boy's left instead of *Bubbles!* I must catch him, he's got my *Bubbles*." And in much agitation, I waved the offending *Children's Newspaper* under Mother's nose. At this juncture Father came downstairs and took the tabloid from me.

"Ah yes," he said, in his quiet way. "Mother and I both think that now you are beginning to grow up, you should be reading something a little more serious than *Bubbles. The Children's Newspaper* is interesting and you will find some very good articles in it."

I felt shattered and asked if I could have *Bubbles* back again the following week, but apparently I could not. *The Children's Newspaper* seemed to have come to stay. It had the same effect on me as the music lessons; I tried to like it, I tried to enjoy it, but I just didn't. After a while indifference set in and then downright dislike. I resented it. I missed *Bubbles* tremendously and to make matters worse, the Harrisons wouldn't even look at *The Children's Newspaper*, let alone swap it for *Tiger Tims*. Nowadays, I sometimes wonder whether my unfortunate aversion to newspapers in general could have been caused at the age of eight by this sudden deprivation of *Bubbles* and the inadequate and unacceptable substitution of *The Children's Newspaper*.

The only way I could then get even a sniff of a comic, was to go over to the Harrisons and snatch hasty glances at their current copy of *Tiger Tims*, in between times whilst playing games with Ruth and George. This is what I was doing the afternoon before Lillian Harrison was born, I remember clearly, Ruth, George and I were sprawled on the floor in front of the fire. We were playing Snakes and Ladders and when it wasn't my turn to throw the dice, I had a quick read of the latest copy of their comic. I had no idea that Mrs Harrison was about to have a baby. I don't know if George and Ruth had any idea of it. They certainly hadn't said anything to me. Mrs Harrison just sat there all through the late afternoon, nursing Joyce on her knee and watching our game proceed. Everything was as it always had been. When I got up the following morning, most unusual things seemed to be happening in our house. There was no sign of Mother. Father was making the breakfast; the grate in the dining-room which normally during the winter had a bright coal fire burning in it, was black and empty and cold-looking. Outside, snow had fallen during the night and a thick mantle of it had obliterated our lawn and flower beds and made a great quiet come down on everything. It was chilly in the dining-room and Father had lit the Valor Perfection Oil

Stove.

"I'm cold," I complained. "Where's Mother and why isn't the fire going?"

"Eat your breakfast and you'll soon warm up," said Father. "Mother is with Mrs Harrison and there isn't a fire because the sweep's coming this morning."

I was more interested in the sweep's visit than in Mother's absence. With my mind on the festive season, I was sure that any interference with the chimney might impede Father Christmas's descent. Thoughtfully, as I made a big treacly letter 'B' drop from my spoon into the middle of my dish of steaming porridge, I voiced my doubts as to the wisdom of ever having the sweep at all. Father looked at me across his plate of egg and bacon and suddenly said, "It's really time you knew – you're old enough now. Father Christmas doesn't really come down the chimney, in fact there is no such person!" I laughed, I knew he was joking. He was a great tease my Dad. But he persisted and eventually, I began to realise that I was facing the truth. It was very difficult to believe in view of the many times I had watched my letters float up the chimney, never to return. Had not Father Christmas's voice actually floated down to thrill me to the marrow with the assurance that he had received my requests safely?

"Well, I am a bit of a ventriloquist, you know," said Father in answer to my disappointed accusations. I felt so sad and let down, that I didn't even ask what a ventriloquist was.

The sweep arrived; in he came, stamping the snow off his boots, he covered all our dining-room furniture with dust sheets; he stuck his great rod-like contraptions far into the darkness of the flues; he sent firing rockets roaring upwards from the grate so that passers-by kept knocking on our front door to say that flames were coming from our chimney and did we know? – all this took my mind off my loss. That same morning, Father told me stories of Victorian orphans who had been sold to sweeps and made to clean the inside of chimneys by climbing up them. He told me of the adventures of 'Tom' and promised to buy me a copy of Charles Kingsley's *The Water Babies*. I think he must have been feeling guilty about Father Christmas!

The sweep had been and gone when Mother returned from seeing Mrs Harrison. "George, Ruth and Joyce have a new little sister," she announced. Utter amazement relaxed my muscles and my mouth fell open. The same feeling that I had experienced in Grandma's kitchen just a few months previously when I heard that my cousin John had been born, now swept over me again. How on earth could this have happened? Just as I was beginning to forget my bewilderment over babies, here was another which had arrived over the road – plop! Without warning, unannounced – it wasn't fair.

"She wasn't there yesterday afternoon," I said in an aggrieved tone of voice, "and Mrs Harrison didn't tell us she was coming either!"

My parents laughed, went into the kitchen and shut the door behind them. I could hear them talking together but was too stunned and full of unanswerable wondering, to follow them. What a morning! Father Christmas had been exploded for all time, the sweep had almost set our chimney on fire and a new baby had arrived at the Harrisons'.

Many years later, Mother told me of how Mr Harrison had come knocking at our front door early that morning, just as my parents were about to get up. He was very agitated. The baby was obviously on its way and he didn't know what to do. He had tried to telephone the midwife, but in the night, the snow had brought down the wires and he couldn't get through, so he was on his way to Gatley on foot, to fetch her. Their next-door neighbour had taken in the three children and was giving them their breakfast; in his desperation, and not wanting to leave his wife alone, he had turned to Mother. Would she please, please go over the road for a little while. He shouldn't be long, it wasn't far. Mother dressed and went straight away. She didn't think twice about being on her own in the house with a woman about to give birth. She was very plucky. Of course, she had had some experience when my cousin John had been born, for then, so Aunty Gertie told me years afterwards, she, Gertie, had held on to Mother's hand so tightly during the birth and in her pain had dug her nails into Mother's flesh so deeply, that when it was all over, Mother's palm had bled so much that the nurse had to bandage it for her. At that time there had been a doctor and a mid-wife present, but now, Mother was on her own and the baby was actually appearing! Calmly, Mother rolled up her sleeves, scrubbed her hands, and delivered the baby. It was one thing to deliver it, but quite another to separate it from the afterbirth. Poor Mother, she didn't dare cut the cord in case she injured the child in some way. She was just wondering what on earth to do, when in walked the midwife, all bustle and bag, and took over. Mrs Harrison, the baby and Mother, soon recovered from the ordeal and Mr and Mrs Harrison were so grateful for her help in their emergency, that they named their new baby, Lillian, after Mother, but to differentiate, they gave their new daughter two 'l's.

The snow persisted for a long time after Lillian was born. We Gatley children revelled in it. One of the most exciting things which we did was to go 'exploring'. Ruth and I had been taken with our class from school to see a film at the Cheadle Picture House called *With Byrd to the South Pole*. The memory of the movie, together with the vast expanses of snow lying on the fields on the other side of the now frozen little brook at our end of Belmont Road, fired my imagination so much, that one Saturday morning, I organised our gang and we set out to find 'The South Pole'. The snow was deep and virgin and stretched in a great blurry whiteness as far as the eye could see. I suspect that nowadays, those fields over which we trudged on that freezing day, are covered with buildings. I can tell from the map, that where we eventually planted our 'flag', a piece of stick with Peter Murgatroyd's old vest tied to it, there is now, a motorway approach road. Actually, we must have been heading towards a railway line, but we could see nothing except a great expanse of snow. On and on we trudged enduring terrible hardships; icicles hung from our beards, our toes and fingers had dropped off, our eyelids had frozen and wouldn't move up or down, all our huskies had perished, all our supplies were lost and we were becoming sleepy, so sleepy! We had actually crossed two fields before we began to realise our extreme isolation. When we looked back we could hardly see Belmont Road, in fact, we could hardly see anything at all except our trails in the snow. Ahead of us and to the right and left, as far as the eye could see was a great white quietness, empty of all life. Suddenly we realised that the snow was coming in over the tops of our wellingtons, that our fingers and toes really were turning numb and that it was probably dinner-time. In fact, we all knew without a doubt that our mothers would be waiting for us with platefuls of steaming Saturday hot pot at the ready!

"This is the South Pole," I announced with hasty determination. "Plant the flag for England." Peter Murgatroyd stuck his old vest into the snow whilst we stood in a circle and sang a tuneless version of *God Save the King*. When the last screeching note had frozen into the greyness of the air around us, we turned and ran 'hell for leather' back along our tracks until we reached the warmth and safety of our own kitchens. Everyone said afterwards that it had been a wonderful adventure in spite of complaints from our mothers about wet feet and lumps of snow being brought into the house. Frozen fingers and the painful thawing out process which followed were a small price to pay for having beaten the elements as far as the South Pole!

I was due to take the Scholarship in the summer of 1931. I started to worry about it in the summer of 1929! It meant so much to me to get through this Scholarship exam. It would free me forever from Council School education; it would give me a passport to the type of education I longed for; a school where the pupils were all girls who wore deep pleated tunics and had a gymnasium at their disposal. On and off for two years, I worried and was fearful. Even through our delightful holidays at Sidmouth, I worried. I can distinctly remember running across the lawn one hot Sunday afternoon at Dovaston. Suddenly I came to an abrupt standstill. My heart was in my mouth and my stomach had started to turn somersaults. I knew what was frightening me and I knew that the fear would not go away until I had lived through the ordeal that was to come. The trouble was that I kept living through it in my imagination. I was continually picturing myself entering a dark room full of dark desks on which startlingly white sheets of paper were waiting for my pen.

My hand was trembling so much that I could hardly write my name on the top sheet.

"You may now look at your question papers." A sepulchral voice reached me over the sea of heads stretching away into the distance before me. I turned the paper over and looked – and looked – and looked! Not one question could I understand. How could I answer anything if I couldn't understand the questions? It was always the same problem and I was constantly voicing it to my parents.

All Father said was, "Do your best when the time comes and no one can expect more of you than that."

Mother was more ambitious, and ignoring the question altogether, remarked, "It would be nice if you could pass well enough to get into Withington High School. The girls all wear gloves and are taught to be ladies." Neither answer comforted me nor alleviated my anxieties.

In September 1930, I went up into Standard IV – the Scholarship Class. Everyday we had tests; we worked on past papers and we were given extra work to bring home. My spelling was atrocious and in mental arithmetic tests, I rarely managed more than four out of the twenty questions, merely because I was expected to produce an answer in a very limited time. I worked myself into such a state of excitement wondering when that time would be up, that I became quite incapable of concentration. Father invariably helped me out with the arithmetic problems which I brought home each evening. The very sound of them was quite daunting. I slaved over ladies buying six and a half yards of dress materials at 1/11¾d a yard, or builders' labourers inadvisedly filling a seventeen-gallon tank out of two taps which ran at unequal speeds. In the latter case, it was apparently up to me to get the labourers to turn the taps off when the tank was three quarters full! In spite of all my calculations, the tank invariably overflowed!

Scholarship worries may have been the cause of some very strange and inexplicable feelings which I began to experience during my Gatley days – or rather, nights. Sometimes, long after my parents had gone to bed in the next room, I would lie wide-eyed and watch the moonlight bathing the walls and striking against the furniture. It seemed to bring the latter to life! Suddenly, it, the furniture, would start to vibrate. The dressing-table, the wardrobe, the chair – they were frighteningly still because they were moving within themselves very fast – vibrating with stillness. It was a really strange sensation. All the pieces of furniture in the room stared at me with a vibrating intensity which was then and remains today almost indescribable. The nearest comparison I can make is to think of my arm and hand being fully extended and held out so tautly that I am conscious of all the cells within the limb vibrating with life-force at a tremendous rate. Right down to my finger-tips I can feel the intensity of movement and yet my arm and hand seem locked in an almost deathly stillness. When this happens with inanimate objects, the sensation can become alarming. I was eight years old when I first experienced it and it persisted on and off until I was well into middle-age. When I was a child, it would frighten me so much that I would cry out in terror and my father would come in to comfort me.

"It's the furniture," I would sob. "It keeps looking at me!"

Then again at times I suffered badly from 'noises in the head'. Often after a party or a trip out to a Manchester pantomime, I would wake suddenly to hear all sorts of people talking to me; loud voices persistently calling my name. I would sit up in bed, open my eyes and say firmly, "Go away." The voices would stop but the moment I again laid my head on the pillow and closed my eyes, they would start up more persistently than ever, until once more, I was forced to call for help. Fortunately, it wasn't until much later when we were living in Torquay that my sleep-walking period began, but in the meantime, I had another weird experience which started in the Gatley days and continued sporadically for many years afterwards. This was a daytime experience. Perhaps it was an odd kind of punishment for my addiction to mirrors and my continued observation of myself therein. Perhaps this was at last my mother's 'devil' – 'Old Nick' – of whom she had warned me when I was very young, come finally to 'look over my shoulder' . . . I found that if I gazed at my image over-long, gradually a change would take place within myself. I would become so totally aware of myself that there was a stranger staring back at me and almost shouting at me – 'This is you, You, You!' yet all the time, I was losing identity, losing oneness, losing belief that this image which was now so intrinsic, so stripped bare of all pretence and trappings, was really me. Yet it was me – this stranger was me – so utterly me that I felt I dare not come closer to myself or something terrible might happen. I would turn away abruptly, look out of the window, pick up a book, and immediately the dreadful sense of losing myself inside myself, would leave me. The normality of everyday objects would fall about my shoulders like a cloak, to protect me from myself.

During the three years that we lived in Gatley, the economic situation in the country became steadily worse. Grandpa's business failed and he was forced to go out on the road as a commercial traveller. He must have been approaching sixty then, but I always thought of him as very old and I didn't like to see him packing a heavy case of samples which he would have to carry with him each day. He had no car and had to travel round Manchester on trams and in trains. This job finally folded up and then Grandpa became a kind of clerk, working in the back room of someone else's shop. Although this was more restful for him, I remember him saying sadly that it was not what he had been used to. In spite of all their troubles, however, Grandma and Grandpa still managed to make Christmas a wonderful time for their grandchildren. We all pooled resources and continued to meet at Primrose Bank on Christmas Eve – Aunts and Uncles, Charlie, Tommy, John and I; full of excitement and determined to enjoy ourselves in spite of the situation.

My father didn't escape the depression either. His pay packet was reduced. I remember him coming home to Gatley early one evening with the *Manchester Evening News* under his arm.

"Well, he announced, as he walked into the kitchen where I was toe dancing and Mother was preparing the tea. "They've cut teachers' salaries!"

I immediately imagined the worst – by next week we would all be starving!

"Will you lose your job?" I asked fearfully.

Father laughed. "There's one thing about being a teacher,"

he said, "you'll never be rich, but you'll never be out of a job."

Mother was a most wonderful manager. Although we didn't live lavishly, we never went hungry. She was a great saver in spite of reduced housekeeping money and would often remark that no matter how bad times became, if she were given only a penny, she would save a halfpenny! Aunty Gertie was just the opposite. She could never keep any money in her purse. As soon as it came her way, she had to spend it. She would say that it was burning a hole in her pocket. She loved to spend it on others as well as herself, and whenever she came to see us, she always brought little presents for everyone. Of course, with Uncle Charlie out of work and Aunty Gertie 'spending her money like water', to quote my mother, eventually her whole family had again to move, this time into the real country where property and living were much cheaper than in the suburbs of Manchester. There must have been some money still remaining from Gertie's parents' estate, for they found a lovely old house near Matlock in Derbyshire – Leashaw House where Florence Nightingale had once lived. Once they were established there in the summer of 1930, we took Grandma and Grandpa in Clara, to visit them. I fell in love with their new house where there were low ceilings, low dark beams, uneven floors, and windows which reached almost to the ground. Outside, the green fields of Derbyshire seemed to be almost coming in at the back door. So much so, that Charlie, proudly displaying to me the merits of their new property, picked a grass snake off the bank behind the kitchen window and attempted to put it down the back of my dress in order to make his point.

Gertie made us a wonderful meal. She was a great cook and her sherry trifles were second only to Grandma's. A good time was had by all until we came to leave. Our departure was traumatic! When it dawned on Baby John that we were about to go, he set up a terrible howling and would not be comforted so that we were forced to drive away leaving him screaming in Gertie's arms. As we moved off, Charlie and Tommy jumped on to the running board and could not be dislodged until my father increased speed so much that they were forced to leap into the hedge when they realised that he had no intention of stopping. On the other side of the car, Nobby, their black and white terrier, not to be outdone, galloped alongside, barking in frenzy until he finally dropped exhausted by the roadside, his four little legs still continuing to tread the air as he lay prone on his back!

"Of course, we could have given that dog a heart attack," remarked my father on the way home. I worried about this until Gertie's next letter arrived, telling us that Nobby had had to be collected and carried back into the house where his legs had continued to jerk spasmodically, but that he was now quite recovered.

In spite of hard times, Father seemed to be getting on really well in the educational world. He had now been the Headmaster at The Building Trades' School in Ancoats for some years and had made many contacts with Master Builders who sent their apprentices to him for a limited period each week. As a result, he and Mother were often invited out to functions and dinners in Manchester. At these times, Grandma would come over from Primrose Bank to look after me and to stay the night. Mother loved these affairs. Her years at the finishing school in Buxton had not been wasted. She had developed a social awareness and could behave with great dignity and charm to fit the occasion. The next morning, she would describe the event to Grandma and me in detail; the decor and the ladies' dresses. Backs had been bare, skirts very short and necklines plunging, it seemed. Mother recounted it all and Grandma assumed a semi-scandalised expression, but was really enjoying it immensely. Father would often add to Mother's descriptions by telling some of the jokes in the after-dinner speeches. Most of them went over my head, but Grandma laughed, so I laughed. One I do remember, probably because I understood it. It went as follows: A Master Builder, whose job it had been to propose a toast to the ladies, had risen to his feet and after complimenting them on their elegant gowns, he congratulated all the wives present for the loyalty and support they were so obviously giving to their husbands when the building trade, like the rest of the country, was experiencing such depressing times.

"You can see, gentlemen," he said, "how economical these ladies are, how practised in making a little go a long way. If you doubt me, just look at the dresses around you!"

On one occasion Mother and Father were invited to a particularly splendid dinner at a big hotel in Manchester. It was to be an important 'do' and Father gave Mother £5 to buy herself a really suitable evening dress. £5 was quite a respectable sum to spend on a dress in those days – at least it was in the circles in which we moved and Mother could easily have bought a suitable frock from a superior shop in the city. However, not Mother – not my economically minded mother. Instead, she bought what I called a 'skeleton dress'. It was just a plain, midnight-blue georgette shift over a plain block-bodice silk underslip of the same colour. It cost only a fraction of the £5. At this stage, Mother enlisted Gertie's help. Gertie needed little persuasion. She was very artistic and had great plans for Mother's dress. Together they travelled to Lewises and studied the creations on the models in the dress department. Then they bought thousands of tiny multi-coloured beads and several yards of blue silk fringing. They came home and sat for hours sewing the beads onto the 'skeleton' bodice in wonderful flower patterns which Gertie designed, and the silk fringing they attached to the skirt in layers, frill upon frill. Mother didn't fancy a feather boa which was all the rage at the time, instead, they added a dark blue chiffon scarf and the creation was complete. The effect was stunning.

"Aunty Lily looks a million dollars," said my cousin Tommy when Mother paraded before us in all her finery. She had added some long swinging beads and a pair of dazzlingly white kid gloves which covered her arms to well above her elbows and which must have been very hot to wear, but the things which intrigued me most of all, the real pièce de résistance of her outfit, were her shoes. I had never seen their like before. I thought them quite wonderful. They were of course the in fashion, one-button, strap-over affairs, with pointed toes and high heels, but here were none of your black patent-leather party pumps – what made these shoes so unusual in my eyes was that they were covered all over with tiny metal sequins in every colour of the rainbow. They sparkled and flashed with every movement of Mother's feet and I couldn't take my eyes off them. I was dazzled and mesmerised at the same time.

It must have been early summer when the big event took place. I remember that it was light and I was still out playing in the road when Mother and Father left the house. Father came out first. He reversed Clara out of the garage and parked her right outside our front gate. I had been babbling for days all round the district about my mother's marvellous shoes, so that now, not only 'our gang' but children from several streets away had gathered round to inspect this footwear and to witness the departure. There we all stood; there must have been a dozen of us – bicycles, tricycles, scooters and skipping ropes abandoned whilst we clustered round our front door. It opened and out came Mother. She looked so pretty in a little white fur jacket with a flashing slide in her hair and coloured stockings on her legs. But all eyes were focused on her shoes. All eyes were down. Neither were my friends disappointed. We had formed a rough guard of honour as Mother walked between us down the path to the car. There were sharp intakes of breath – appreciative grunts from the boys and ecstatic exclamations of " 'Ee by gum, but they're luvely!" from the girls. Mother dimpled with pleasure. She bent to kiss me good-bye.

"Be a good girl for Grandma and don't stay up past your bed-time." She swept round to the other side of the car, Father opened the door for her, then he got in himself and away they drove. Mother was waving and smiling and kissing her hand to me – just like royalty – just like Princess Elizabeth's mother, the Duchess of York, whom she resembled so closely.

All through 1930 the Haydock family finances declined. Grandma and Grandpa's affairs had gone from bad to worse. After the shop on the Oldham Road had closed down and Grandpa had found work as a travelling salesman, things became better for a while, but eventually, that job also folded up and Grandma's vegetable dish at the top of the kitchen cupboard was again empty of pound notes. My grandparents struggled on trying to keep Primrose Bank as their family home, but when the landlord, who was also trying to make ends meet, demanded a higher rent, everyone reluctantly agreed that the time had come to start looking around for a much smaller, cheaper home. Uncle Jimmy, unmarried and unemployed, was still living at home with Grandma and Grandpa. Edith Turner had finally abandoned him and he was bad tempered and depressed. Uncle Charlie couldn't work because of his asthma and his war wounds, so Aunty Gertie, far away in Matlock, had been forced to take a job. She moved Uncle Charlie and her family from Leashaw house to take over a shop and small sub-post office nearby. This business failed rapidly and Gertie didn't know what to do for the best. Uncle Tom's chicken farm at Brize Norton had also failed. Eventually during the following year, he was forced to sell up at a big loss and move back with his family to Manchester, where Grandma and Grandpa took them in to Primrose Bank.

All the Haydocks were in debt and all of them approached Mother and Father for monetary help. I think it was this constant worry of having to fend off the relatives which finally persuaded Mother and Father to make a move a long way away from Manchester. Father applied for two jobs, each would require him to build up and develop, virtually from scratch, a technical institution which would be able to cope with the growing demands of the surrounding areas. One job was in Torquay and one in Doncaster. Father was shortlisted for both. Torquay was the running favourite. All three of us loved Devon and the idea of living near the sea appealed to us greatly. Doncaster, on the other hand, was in the middle of a coalfield area and probably even dirtier than Manchester. Moreover, Grandpa Smith, who had once been cheated out of some money by a Church of England Doncaster butcher, wrote to Mother and Father saying that he wouldn't advise his son to move to a place where he may find himself subjected to 'thieving by the ungodly'! Father said we must wait to see which selection interview he would be summoned to attend first. When the first call came, it came from Torquay. Father travelled there one cold winter's day in 1930, was offered the post, accepted it and informed Doncaster of what he had done.

A great cloud disappeared from my horizon when, shortly

after this, I was told that there would now be no need for me to sit the Scholarship Examination. We would be moving to Torquay the following April and I was to be entered immediately for the local Grammar School, as – believe it or not – a fee-paying pupil. My joy knew no bounds. Between Christmas 1930 and April 1931, all was bustle and preparation for the great move. I was too excited to worry or even to think twice about leaving my Gatley friends and I was quite surprised when the Harrisons gave me as a leaving present a gilt photograph frame with a photograph of the four children in it.

In February, at half-term, I went to stay at Primrose Bank whilst Mother and Father travelled down to Torquay – house hunting. The weather was freezing, so they went by train and came back with tales of seeing the estuary of the Teign and the water's edge where the track ran alongside the river, actually frozen. They had a very limited time in Devon and they knew they must find somewhere to live before they returned to Manchester. Apparently they were whizzed all over the district by house agents and prospective builders. Finally they settled on a house in Kingskerswell about three miles from Torquay. It was to be a brand new house. In fact, it was not yet built but promised for the following July. It would back on to fields and woodlands and to me sounded everything I could wish for. As my excitement grew, so Grandma's sorrow at parting with us increased. She never seemed to stop crying in those days and the slightest thing would set her off.

Finally, moving day arrived. Since we had no immediate home to go to in Torquay, all our furniture was to go into store in Manchester. 'Pickford's Depositories', it was called, and once when we drove past it on our way through the city, Mother said, "That's where our furniture will be living for the next six months." It was a great black building with sightless windows, barred and begrimed. I imagined our couch and easy chairs on the bare boards of some upper storey, grouped in sad array around our dining-room table – alone, deserted and slowly gathering dust in the ghostly semi-darkness. It was silly to feel sorry for furniture, but I did. Fortunately, I didn't see it go. I was taken very early in the morning to Primrose Bank where Grandma burst into tears as Father handed me over for the day and then returned to Gatley to help Mother and to oversee the loading. Once operations were all over and our house was echoing-empty, they came to join me at Grandma's and we all spent the night there. Early next morning we set out for Devon in Clara.

I was bundled into the back of the car with boxes and bags piled up all around me. I knelt up on the back seat and looked out of the little celluloid window in the back of the canvas hood which Father had raised as it was such a chilly morning. We moved slowly down the drive, rounding the end of Grandpa's oval-shaped lawn, and drove out into Dean Avenue. I waved and waved at the two figures standing on the broad stone steps. (Uncle Jimmy had said good-bye to us the previous night – it was too early for him to get up. He was still in bed grieving over Edith Turner.) Only Grandpa was waving back at me. He had one arm round Grandma's waist, but she had thrown her apron over her head and I knew she was sobbing her heart out beneath it.

As we moved slowly down Dean Lane past Mrs Varley's house and out into the Oldham Road, my heart soared. The excitement of anticipation lifted away my sadness and with typical childlike disregard for sentiment I was soon forgetting the ties of family and friends which so often imprison the minds of older people. Mother, for instance, was having a quiet weep in the front seat. I knew this by the way she kept blowing her nose. Father said nothing which was a sign that he was thinking deeply and mustn't be disturbed, but I had too little of life behind me to be nostalgic about it. I was too young and too inexperienced for the qualms of apprehension that my parents must have been feeling as we drove southwards through Cheshire. We had all been born and bred in the North Country, but their roots had gone more deeply than mine into its soil. Moreover, I had all the optimism of a child to ease the uprooting, and as we travelled along, I gave myself over to the sheer joy of wishful thinking.

. . . I was off to a land of sea and sand, of sunken lanes and thatched cottages, to a land where the sun shone perpetually on a school where, hopefully I could be happy, and where, actually, although I didn't know it, I was to be very happy indeed and at last freed from the fears which had dogged my Council School days . . . As Manchester murk gave way to fresher air, sheer exhilaration possessed me. I couldn't keep still. I bounced up and down on the rear seat; I rocked backwards and forwards humming away and hugging myself. I couldn't have explained it. I could feel the page turning; I could feel the chapter ending and the first big stage of the book coming to conclusion.

"Manchester's gone," was all I could manage to say and Mother started to cry again.

SECOND CHILDHOOD

When I was young
And nearer to the ground
Than now I am,
Earth's sights, her scent,
Her very sound
Made impress
Vivid and profound
Upon the first excited
Stirrings of my mind.

And now, in the dotage
Of my later days,
They come again, I find
All the spectrum band,
Clear cut as crystal
Within my wrinkled hand.
Colours of the rainbow
To light my fading years
And the fragrant joys
Of childhood to dry
My age-old tears.

Kathleen Beryl Tyler